The Critique of Commodification

The Critique of Commodification

Contours of a Post-Capitalist Society

CHRISTOPH HERMANN

OXFORD
UNIVERSITY PRESS

OXFORD
UNIVERSITY PRESS

Oxford University Press is a department of the University of Oxford. It furthers
the University's objective of excellence in research, scholarship, and education
by publishing worldwide. Oxford is a registered trade mark of Oxford University
Press in the UK and certain other countries.

Published in the United States of America by Oxford University Press
198 Madison Avenue, New York, NY 10016, United States of America.

Library of Congress Cataloging-in-Publication Data
Names: Hermann, Christoph, author.
Title: The critique of commodification : contours of a post-capitalist society /
Christoph Hermann.
Description: New York, NY : Oxford University Press, [2021] |
Includes bibliographical references.
Identifiers: LCCN 2021011291 (print) | LCCN 2021011292 (ebook) |
ISBN 9780197576762 (paperback) | ISBN 9780197576755 (hardback) |
ISBN 9780197576786 (epub) | ISBN 9780197576779 | ISBN 9780197576793
Subjects: LCSH: Commodification. | Capitalism.
Classification: LCC HB501.H4697 2021 (print) | LCC HB501 (ebook) |
DDC 330.12/2—dc23
LC record available at https://lccn.loc.gov/2021011291
LC ebook record available at https://lccn.loc.gov/2021011292

DOI: 10.1093/oso/9780197576755.001.0001

3 5 7 9 8 6 4 2

Paperback printed by Marquis, Canada
Hardback printed by Bridgeport National Bindery, Inc., United States of America

Contents

Contents

Acknowledgments

As in most academic work, this book benefited greatly from previous research and publications and from the support of and exchange with colleagues and friends. Particularly inspiring was the work of Ursula Huws, who has been publishing on commodification since the mid-1980s. Her insights into the nature of commodification processes are among the most original and illuminating concepts ever published on the topic. Fortunately, Ursula agreed to read and comment on various draft chapters of the book. While her own book on commodification would likely look different from this one, our conversations were instrumental in shaping my understanding of commodification, and, subsequently, my argumentation as outlined in the following pages.

I am also indebted to Greg Albo, Stefan Kipfer, Colin Leys, Sarah Stoller, Sasha Lilley, and Michael Burawoy, who read and commented on parts of the manuscript and to three anonymous reviewers, who offered valuable feedback on the first draft. The book greatly benefited from their input. I also want to thank my editor, James Cook, who early on saw the potential of the book and superbly guided me through the review and production process.

While completing the manuscript, I received the sad news that Leo Panitch passed away. Leo was not only an intellectual giant, but also a terrific teacher and a gracious friend. I was looking forward to discussing the alternatives to commodification with him. He will be sorely missed.

The book would not have been possible without the emotional and intellectual support of my partner Sandra Eder. The book is dedicated to our son Noah Mpho. For the sake of the next generations, I hope that we will be able to create a less commodified and therefore more just, enjoyable, and ecologically sustainable world. And I hope that this book makes a small contribution toward this goal.

Berkeley, December 2020

Introduction

The argument

"Commodification" has become a widely used term in academic and occasionally even in political discourse. And most people who use it do so critically, i.e., in order to criticize certain aspects of our current economic system. But what is commodification? And what is the problem with commodification? After all, we consume commodities on a daily basis, and many of us enjoy buying goods and services and spend a considerable amount of time searching the internet for bargains. This book attempts to provide some answers to these questions. Its main argument is that commodification entails production for profit rather than social needs, and that production for profit has a number of undesirable and perhaps even harmful consequences—including, for example, the exclusion of those who cannot pay, the marginalization of those whose collective purchasing power is not large enough, and the focus on highly profitable forms of production at the cost of more socially beneficial and ecologically sustainable forms of provision.

As a result of commodification, people are obese while others go hungry. Healthy people in rich countries are bombarded with pharmaceuticals, which in some cases cause drug addiction, while millions of sick people in poor countries lack adequate drugs and treatments. Many are homeless, while at the same time luxury condominium apartments go vacant. Private partners in so-called public-private partnerships make record profits, while public hospitals have to cut beds and staff numbers, resulting in unnecessary deaths. Colleges spend more money for advertising and admissions than they do on teaching. Commodification, furthermore, has fueled the industrialization of agriculture with disastrous effects for the environment, including, for example, marine dead zones that are as big as the state of New Jersey. At the same time, commodification blocks the transition to more sustainable forms of production and consumption, such as public transportation. Last but not least, commodification undermines solidarity and fuels inequality as access to goods and services is solely decided by purchasing power. Given the negative effects of commodification, including the accelerating ecological crisis,

The Critique of Commodification. Christoph Hermann, Oxford University Press. © Oxford University Press 2021.
DOI: 10.1093/oso/9780197576755.001.0001

this book suggests that it is time to rethink commodification and to move to a social system that focuses on the satisfaction of social needs rather than the maximization of profits.

While the concept of commodification is widely used in academic discourse, few scholars are aware that it is a fairly new term. Many assume that it goes back to Marx, but Marx in fact never used the term. It was only in the 1970s that Marxist scholars started to talk about commodification in writing on art and culture, the emergence and spread of capitalism, as well as the de-commodifying effects of modern welfare states. For some of these scholars, the influence of Karl Polanyi was more important than Marx. In the 1980s and 1990s, non-Marxist scholars from philosophy, anthropology, and sociology also became increasingly interested in the term. And with the demise of academic Marxism (and the limited influence of Polanyi's work), these later accounts became dominant in academic discourse. As a result, the notion of commodification is not necessarily used as a wholesale critique of capitalism; some critics only object to the monetary exchange of certain services, such as paid surrogacy, and the marketization of specific goods such as healthcare. In these cases, the objection to commodification is based on moral and pragmatic considerations—paying for children is morally wrong, and markets for healthcare do not work. In contrast, the material critique of commodification insists that commodification is objectionable because it changes material relations, including forms of ownership and the way social needs are satisfied. This book largely follows the material critique but proposes a number of innovations to account for the variety of commodification processes and their distinctive consequences.

In order to understand the material impact of commodification, it is necessary to distinguish use value from exchange value. While largely ignored by contemporary economics, use value previously played an important role in the history of economic thought. Adam Smith, for example, noted that water has a large use value but a small exchange value, whereas diamonds have a small use value but a large exchange value. With the marginalist revolution in economics, these two aspects were merged into the concept of utility, and price became the sole indicator of the value of goods and services. Simply put, objects that have no price have no utility and no value. In this understanding, nature has no value as long as it has no price. Interestingly, the moral critics of commodification rarely acknowledge the existence of use value in spite of their critique of economic thinking and their concern for non-market-based values. For Marx, commodification is essentially the subjugation of use value to exchange value. It is this process that alters the substance of commodified goods and services.

This book builds on Marx's understanding of commodification but makes some important specifications. First, it takes market value, rather than exchange value, as the denominator of use value. While exchange value reflects the average labor time expended for the production of goods and services, market value describes the relationship between supply and demand. In an economy with highly competitive markets and with no shortage of supply, market value should more or less equal exchange value. However, today's markets are frequently subject to manipulation and speculation. To give one example: the production costs, including labor costs, of an Apple iPhone make up less than 50 percent of its price. Second, I argue that commodification is a process rather than a specific state of affairs, and the book subsequently distinguishes between three different forms of commodification: formal, real, and fictitious commodification. Formal commodification describes a situation in which goods and services receive a price but otherwise remain unchanged. Real commodification describes the profit-driven transformation of goods and services. Fictitious commodification refers to the introduction of markets and the invention of quantitative indicators in the provision of goods and services that have no price and are not sold for a profit. Precisely because commodification can be fictitious, commodification policies include not only privatization, liberalization, and deregulation, along with austerity-induced welfare cuts, but also the establishment of quasi-markets, the introduction of performance measurements, and the treatment of users as consumers even when they do not pay for a service.

While much of the existing critique of commodification focuses on moral decay as the main threat of commodification, this book argues that the main threat is the transformation of our livelihoods, including the destruction of the ecological base of human life and flourishing. The book identifies twelve tendencies associated with commodification that have problematic consequences, culminating in the drive for more commodification. For example, the commodification of agriculture has led to a shift from poly- to monoculture cultivation. However, monoculture farming comes with declining soil fertility and increasing susceptibility to infestation. Less fertility and more infestation create the need for artificial fertilizers, pesticides, and more recently genetically modified crops. These commodities are provided by highly profitable chemical and biotech companies. Monocultures, in turn, provide the input for an increasingly commodified food industry that no longer uses crops as a basis of food, but instead dissects them into their chemical components and then uses some of these components to create increasingly artificial products. Corn, for example, is turned into cornstarch, which is subsequently used for a large variety of food products. In fact, it is hard to find processed food in an American supermarket that does not contain cornstarch. The processing of food, in turn, creates even more incentives for monoculture cultivation. Among the consequences are increasingly obese children and depleted rivers, lakes, and coastal zones. Yet far from being the result of market failure or amoral behavior, industrialized agriculture and processed food are the logical outcome of commodification and the primacy of profits over needs. There may be a demand for organic crops and artisanal food, but with traditional production methods, producers can make only a fraction of the profits of modern agri-food businesses. Breakfast cereals, for example, have a profit-margin of more than 40 percent. Accordingly, this book argues that commodification may face social and political boundaries, but the most severe limits arise from the imperative to expand profits and the ecological damage this causes. Precisely because we do not know how much commodification the planet can take, there is a very real danger that depletion and pollution will reach a tipping point with dramatic consequences for the world ecosystem. The possible result is what the book describes as disastrous de-commodification.

However, the book also discusses alternatives to commodification. It argues that an alternative must shift the goal of production/provision from profits to needs, or from maximizing market value to maximizing use value. In order to do so, it must be recognized that the goods and services that we consume not only have an individual value, but also have social and ecological value. To take the example of transportation: automobility may be useful for an individual to get from point A to point B, but its social and ecological utility is rather disastrous—and it remains problematic even if we switch to electric cars. The favorable social and ecological alternative is public transportation. Yet the question of how to assess (social and ecological) use value remains. In contrast to exchange value and marginal utility, the nature of use value is precisely that it cannot be measured. The answer proposed in this book is democratic decision-making. People can democratically decide which goods and services, or ways of satisfying needs, are preferable. However, in order to make sure that decisions are not made at the cost of those who are not part of the decision-making process, or are part of a minority, use-value maximization must include a commitment to solidarity.

The same holds for the environment: insofar as decisions impact the environment, they also impact future generations that will live on this planet. And because future generations do not have a voice, use-value maximization must operate in the boundaries of ecological sustainability. The combination of democratization, solidarity, and sustainability would result in what the book calls a use-value society.

Plan of the book

Chapter 1 introduces the topic of the book. It traces the intellectual history of the term "commodification" and presents major arguments against commodification from different strands of literature. Commodification was introduced into academic discourse in the 1970s by Marxist scholars who analyzed the transformation of culture, the emergence and spread of capitalism, as well as the nature of the welfare state. The term was then picked up by non-Marxist academics in various disciplines, usually to criticize certain kinds of monetary exchange or specific markets rather than capitalism per se. The chapter identifies three major strands of literature with distinctive arguments against commodification: the moral, pragmatic, and materialist critiques. It argues that only the materialist critique is able to see that commodification threatens the livelihood of people and the environment. After discussing differences between the three approaches, the chapter points to an important commonality: all critics of commodification believe that commodification has gone too far in recent decades.

Chapter 2 follows the materialist critique but proposes a number of theoretical innovations. According to Marx, commodification is a process by which exchange value comes to dominate use value. Markets, money, and profit orientation are instruments that facilitate the subjugation of use value to exchange value. However, the book takes market value, rather than exchange value, as the denominator of use value. Market value depends on supply and demand and is open to manipulation and speculation. The chapter, furthermore, argues that commodification is a process and, subsequently, distinguishes between formal, real, and fictitious commodification. Typically, real commodification (the transformation of goods and services) follows formal commodification (the imposition of a price), but in some cases products first have to be standardized in order to become commodities that can be exchanged on a market. Fictitious commodification, i.e., the introduction of quasi-markets in public services and the transformation of service users into consumers, prepares the ground for formal and real commodification.

Even though commodification is a quasi-natural tendency of capitalist economies, the extent of commodification can vary over time, depending, among other things, on government intervention. With the dominance of neoliberalism in the past three decades, we have witnessed a reverse movement. Government policies have in various ways promoted (re-)commodification. Chapter 3 looks at six major policies: privatization, liberalization, deregulation, marketization, New Public Management, and austerity. Privatization promotes commodification by abolishing non-commodified alternatives to the sale of goods and services. Liberalization fuels commodification by exposing producers to competition and by forcing them to make profits. Deregulation eliminates restrictions that in one way or another limit commodification. Marketization creates markets in economic and social spheres where no markets have existed before, while New Public Management promotes metric output measurements that closely resemble what, in the private economy, are market values. Austerity and related cuts in welfare expenditure drive re-commodification by making citizens more dependent on markets and on private alternatives to the welfare state.

Chapter 4 explores the major consequences of commodification. It does so by focusing on five spheres that are crucial for social reproduction—healthcare, (higher) education, public utilities, housing, as well as food and agriculture. It then highlights twelve tendencies associated with commodification: the exclusion of potential users (e.g., homeless people who cannot afford rent); neglect of needs that are not backed by sufficient purchasing power or cannot be satisfied in a profitable manner (e.g., drugs for rare diseases); focus on those needs whose satisfaction promises high profits, frequently at the cost of needs that are less lucrative (e.g., universities opening overseas campuses and closing philosophy departments); focus on short-term profits at the cost of long-term sustainability (e.g., expansion of monocultures at the expense of crop rotation in agriculture); privatization of profits and collectivization of costs (e.g., various public-private partnerships); standardization and homogenization (e.g., fast food); bureaucratization and expansion of management/administration (e.g., hospitals); sacrificing quality for profitability (e.g., private for profit colleges); manipulation and speculation (e.g., California's electricity crisis); growing inequality; the marginalization of motivations not based on profit; and erosion of solidarity and more com-modification (as a cumulative effect of commodification).

Given the undesirable nature of these consequences, Chapter 5 asks if there are limits to commodification. The chapter identifies four kinds of limits: so-cial limits consisting of moral norms and standards endangered by com-modification; political limits arising from opposition to commodification and resulting political movements; systemic limits fueled by contradictions within capitalist accumulation and the need to increase profits; and ecolog-ical limits, which are a specific example of systemic limits that arise from the profit-driven destruction of the environment. This chapter argues that it is ecological limits that present the biggest threat to commodification. However, it suggests that the resulting ecological crisis presents a rather dis-astrous form of de-commodification.

The last two chapters look beyond commodification. Chapter 6 revisits the definition of commodification as subjugation of use value to exchange/market value. It shows that the distinction between use value and exchange value goes back to ancient Greek philosophy and that it played an impor-tant role in classical political economy. In fact, it was only in the late nine-teenth century that use value was replaced by the concept of marginal utility. Use value, subsequently, moved from the center to the fringes of economic thinking. However, even where it survived, such as in Marxist scholarship, scholars debated whether use value was a concern for political economy, or if the material quality of products was something better dealt with by the natural sciences. The chapter, furthermore, explores the value of nature and by doing so unveils the shortcomings of the concept of marginal utility. One problem is that marginal utility denies the existence of collective value. Following Polanyi, the chapter argues that products not only have individual value, but also have a social and ecological utility. And social and ecological utility can differ considerably from individual valuation.

Chapter 7 discusses alternatives to commodification. The opposite of com-modification is de-commodification. De-commodification imposes limits on the commodity character of goods and services traded on markets, but it does not provide for an alternative. Following an understanding of commod-ification as subjugation of use value to market/exchange value, the chapter argues that an alternative must seek to "free" use value and reinstate it as the prime goal of production. Or put differently, an alternative to commodifica-tion must focus on the satisfaction of human needs rather than the expansion of private profit. Three elements are crucial for the promotion of (collective and ecological) use value: democratization, sustainability, and solidarity. The chapter discusses each of these elements in a separate section. It then brings the three elements together into an alternative vision that is called use-value society.

1
The Critique of Commodification

Introduction

Commodification has become a commonplace in the social sciences. According to the *Oxford English Dictionary*, the term "commodification" captures "the action or process of treating a person or thing as property which can be traded or whose value is purely monetary."[1] I will provide a more useful definition of commodification in Chapter 2. Yet the *Oxford English Dictionary* also shows that commodification is a relatively new term. It was first included in the 1989 edition.[2] As shown in the following pages, commodification emerged in the 1970s as common expression in academic discourses.[3] And while initially being part of a fundamental critique of capitalism and the capitalist transformation of society and culture, it increasingly became a notion to question certain effects of market exchange and monetary valuation. However, in nearly all instances, commodification is used as a critical concept to describe unwelcomed effects of capitalist development.[4]

This chapter has two goals: On the one hand, it traces the intellectual history of the term "commodification"; and on the other, it identifies major intellectual contributions to the critique of commodification. Apart from a materialist critique based on Marxist theory, the latter also includes a moral and pragmatist use of commodification. Accordingly, the chapter proceeds as follows: it starts with an analysis of the emergence of commodification in 1970s English academic discourses. It then presents the main points of critique in the moral, pragmatist, and materialist debates. The chapter ends with a brief conclusion.

The intellectual roots of commodification

Perhaps surprisingly, the author that is most frequently associated with commodification processes, Karl Marx, never actually used the term "commodification" (or *Kommodifizierung* in German). Instead, he, on at least one

The Critique of Commodification. Christoph Hermann, Oxford University Press. © Oxford University Press 2021.
DOI: 10.1093/oso/9780197576755.003.0001

occasion, mentions the process of becoming a commodity, or more precisely of not becoming a commodity. In a passage in which he argues that commodity production depends on the division of labor, but that the division of labor does not necessarily depend on commodity production, he notes that in the ancient Indian community, labor is socially divided although the products do not thereby become commodities (Marx 1990, 132; Haug 2010). Karl Polanyi is another author who is frequently cited as an early critic of commodification processes. However, Polanyi in his major work *The Great Transformation* uses the term "commercialization" when referring to the commodification of land, and "proletarization" when describing the commodification of labor (Polanyi 1957, 82 and 179). It was not until the 1970s that the term "commodification" became popular in academic discourses.

There are at least three different sources of the term. First, commodification emerged as an expression in writing on art, literature, and culture.[5] A possible explanation is the influence of Lukács and Marcuse, as well as Horkheimer and Adorno, in cultural studies.[6] These authors did not actually use the term "commodification," but they criticized the intrusion of the commodity-form into culture, media, and other aspects of life under capitalism. Writing about cultural transformation, French author Guy Debord (1977, paragraph 42) noted in the late 1960s that "[t]he spectacle is the moment when the commodity has attained the total occupation of social life. Not only is the relation to the commodity visible but it is all one sees."[7] Clearly, Debord described a process that later became known as commodification. In fact, in the early 1980s, Kenn Knapp translated the latter part as "[c]ommodification is not only visible, we no longer see anything else" (Debord 1983, paragraph 42). By then, cultural theorists like Fredric Jameson had started to use "commodification" to describe similar processes. In a 1979 article, Jameson argued that following the prediction of the Frankfurt School, universal commodification had meant that mass culture had not become the liberating form as hoped for by some critics of (high) modernism (Jameson 1979).[8] Instead, art and especially aesthetics were increasingly integrated into consumer capitalism and had become an essential element of mass consumption rather than being a visionary, let alone revolutionary, force. Commodification, subsequently, became a common expression for the transformation of art, culture, and life in postmodernist cultural production (Jameson 1984; Harvey 1990; Featherstone 1991).

A second source is world system theory. In a 1977 article, Terence Hopkins and Immanuel Wallerstein described capitalist development as a process of commodification, including, most notably, the commodification of land and labor (Hopkins and Wallerstein 1977, 125). Even though the authors did not reference Polanyi in the article, the focus on the commodification of land and labor seems to follow Polanyi's analysis.[9] Both were familiar with his work. Hopkins attended one of Polanyi's seminars at Columbia University in the early 1950s and subsequently introduced him to Wallerstein (Dale 2016, 217). Wallerstein acknowledged the influence of Polanyi on his thinking in the introduction to a collection of essays published in 2000 (Wallerstein 2000, xxii).[10] Commodification, subsequently, became standard terminology in writings about the transition from feudalism to capitalism and the expansion of capitalism on a world scale (Wallerstein 1983; Giddens 1985; Meiksins-Wood 1986).

A third source is Marxist welfare state literature. Here the influence of Polanyi is even more apparent.[11] Polanyi had described the Speenhamland system, an eighteenth-century social safety net, as an obstacle to the emergence of labor markets and, hence, the proletarization of the poor in early industrializing Britain. Claus Offe (1972 and 1976) argued that modern welfare states have a similar effect by granting workers an existence independent from their ability to sell their labor power on the labor market, and he subsequently called the process "decommodification" (see Chapter 7). However, Offe also noted that in the light of growing fiscal problems in the 1970s, welfare protection had become too costly, causing governments to adopt a program of "administrative recommodification" (Offe and Ronge 1975; Offe 1984). While Offe has introduced the term, it was Gøsta Esping-Andersen (1990) who popularized de-commodification in his widely read book *Three Worlds of Welfare Capitalism*. Welfare state scholars have subsequently analyzed welfare state developments in terms of de- and re-commodification (Pierson 2001; Huber and Stephens 2000; Pierson and Castels 2006).

While the three sources seem to have developed independently, all three debates have in common that they emerged during a time of increased interest in Marxist and other radical thought. Europe and the United States had experienced a wave of student protests in the late 1960s in which students criticized racism, patriarchy, anti-communism, imperialism, and other forms of oppression, and subsequently questioned the legitimacy of capitalism, which was about to enter its first major economic crisis after the Second World War. At the same time, the developing world saw massive anti-imperialist movements and the subsequent transformation of

European colonies into independent states, with many governments critical of capitalism. These events did not remain unnoticed in academia and opened space for Marxist scholars to find employment in leading academic institutions and to force fellow academics to engage with Marxist theories, if only to reject them vehemently.[12] The growing interest in Marxist theory also spurred the foundation of a series of radical publishers and critical journals. Perry Anderson (1983, 24), consequently, noted in 1983 that "the sheer density of ongoing economic, political, sociological and cultural research on the Marxist Left in Britain or North America, with its undergrowth of journals and discussions, eclipses any equivalent in the older lands of the Western Marxist tradition proper." Anderson correctly observed the surge of Marxist thought in English-speaking academia, but he likely underestimated similar developments in France, Italy, and Germany (for the German experience, see Altvater 2007).

With the flourishing of (Western) Marxist thinking, the term "commodification" quickly spread outside the Marxist camp and was adopted by non-Marxist scholars in philosophy, legal, studies, anthropology, and sociology. According to Google Books' Ngram Viewer, the term "commodification" was used thirteen times more often in English academic publications in 1990 than it was in 1978.[13] However, non-Marxist scholars no longer used commodification as part of a fundamental critique of capitalism; instead, they used it to criticize certain aspects of capitalism, such as the sale of goods that are not suitable for exchange on markets.

The situation changed after the collapse of communism in Eastern Europe and the Soviet Union.[14] Western Marxism, even though mostly critical of the Soviet Union and its dogmatic reading of Marx, lost much of its appeal on college campuses and became increasingly marginalized in the 1990s and early 2000s. With Marxism in decline and the continuous disregard for Polanyi's work, the non-Marxist use of the term "commodification" became dominant in academic discourses (while the anti-capitalist use remained popular among activists outside academia, such as the proponents of the anti-globalization movement).[15] Hence a 2005 volume on *Rethinking Commodification* could largely ignore the vast body of Marxist literature that deals with commodification. Instead, the editors stated that "scholars across the ideological spectrum use the term 'commodification' only to discuss certain kinds of sales. They generally do not worry (let alone write) about the commodification of milk, garbage collection, or soybean futures" (Ertman and Williams 2005, 4).

Contrary to this statement, one of the objectives of this book is to demonstrate the continuous relevance of the Marxist critique of commodification. As shown in following chapters, there is plenty of reason to be concerned about the commodification of food, nature, healthcare, and other public services. For example, speculation with commodities such as soybeans contributed to a dramatic increase in world food prices in 2008, which meant that 40 million more people in the developing world suffered from hunger in that year (see Chapter 4). The following section will contrast the materialist critique of commodification, which sees capitalism as the problem, with the moralist and pragmatist ones, which oppose the existence of certain markets and the sale of certain goods.

The moral critique of commodification

Representatives of the moral critique of commodification do not reject commodification per se. They simply reject the commodification of certain goods, services, or human attributes and relations. Debra Satz is a good example of this approach. She states that "[m]any markets are rightly celebrated mechanisms of freedom and efficiency, yet some markets traffic in things that no decent society should allow its members to be without, some deepen objectionable hierarchies of class and privilege, and some undermine democratic values" (Satz 2012, 112). Hence for moralists the main question is which goods and services can properly be exchanged for money and which cannot, or, put differently, which markets are socially beneficial and which are not.

The moralist critique centers on four major objections to commodification. A first objection follows from the belief that human beings should not be bought and sold. The trade of human beings is called slavery. While slave-like relationships still exist in the contemporary world, slavery is widely considered as a violation of a basic human right and as such banned in most contemporary societies. Yet the moral critique does not stop with the objection of slavery. Moralists such as Margret Radin (1987, 1996) also criticize the sale of human attributes that make up a person's identity or that give a human being its individual personhood (which in Kantian philosophy makes a human being a person rather than a thing). Personal attributes, in Radin's words, are market inalienable (Radin 1987, 1853). Moralists, consequently, object to prostitution, paid surrogacy, and the selling of children (the latter even when the new parents raise them as independent human beings; Radin 1996, chapter 10).[16] This does not mean that personal attributes cannot be exchanged: people should have sex and mothers can give up their children for adoption. Yet the exchange should take the form of a gift; i.e., they should be given away for free. As gifts, so the assumption, they do not negatively affect the individual's personhood; as commodities they do.

A second objection of the moralist critique is based on the observation that not everything can be valued in terms of money. In order to be valued in units of money, goods must be commensurable—which means that they are comparable on a common scale such as monetary value. As a result, an observer must be able to tell if the value of a good is equal, higher, or smaller than another good (Anderson 1993, 55). Elizabeth Anderson (1993, 134) calls such goods "economic goods," and she argues that they can be properly bought and sold on markets. In contrast, goods that are incommensurable are non-economic goods. And non-economic goods should be provided outside the market. Anderson distinguishes three categories of goods that fall outside the market. The first are personal goods and relations (1993, 151). Here the assumption is that the value of friendship and affection cannot be expressed in dollars and cents (this critique partly overlaps with Radin's objection described earlier). A second category is what Anderson calls political goods and which are similar to what pragmatists call public goods (1993, 158–159). Essentially, they are shared goods or goods that no one should be excluded from using. Examples include streets, parks, and schools. The production and distribution of these goods should be based on democratic political norms rather than being left to market signals. A third category is professional services such as healthcare (1993, 147–148). Here the rationale is that doctors should care about the restoration of their patient's health, rather than thinking about how to make more money. The performance of professional services should therefore be judged according to the profession's internal standards rather than market norms.

A third critique is fueled by the assumption that commodification can corrupt the value of certain goods and services. A popular example is blood donating. In most countries, blood is donated for free by volunteers. In the United States, business(wo)men set up commercial blood banks in the 1950s, offering money in exchange for blood. Yet while the introduction of monetary incentives was supposed to increase the supply of blood, Richard Titmuss (1970, 65–66) found that blood supply actually decreased because fewer people were willing to donate blood. A similar effect was found when

Swiss researchers carried out an experiment in a small mountain village in the early 1990s. The village had been selected as possible location for a nuclear waste repository. The researchers found in an initial survey that a slim majority of respondents were prepared to accept the repository if the Swiss parliament were to decide that it was the most appropriate location. However, when the researchers asked the villagers about their stance when offered money as compensation for the repository, the acceptance rate dropped dramatically (Frey, Oberholzer-Gee, and Eichenberger 1996). In both cases, so the moralist explanation, money has corrupted what previously was perceived as collective responsibility or civic duty. According to Michael Sandel (2012, 9–10) markets embody values. And with commodification, market values crowd out non-market norms that are essential for the proper functioning of societies.[17]

A fourth critique derives its objection to commodification not from certain characteristics of goods and services that make them unsuitable for market exchange. Rather, it is the nature of specific markets that renders these exchanges objectionable. Debrah Satz (2012) calls such markets "noxious markets." They are noxious because they produce extremely harmful outcomes, either for some individuals or for society as a whole (2012, 91–99). Common reasons why they produce harmful outcomes include weak agency or high vulnerability on the part of some market participants. Weak agency is usually the result of incomplete information or of the fact that those affected are not directly involved in negotiating the terms of the exchange. Vulnerability is mostly the result of a lack of resources, especially compared to the other party involved in the exchange. Vulnerable individuals often have no choice but to accept whatever terms are offered on the market. The trade of kidneys is a prime example of a noxious market. The individuals in the developing world who sell kidneys are a classic case of a vulnerable group that has no other choice due to a lack of money. They usually also have weak agency, as many of them lack the ability to appropriately evaluate the risks involved in living a life with only one kidney under conditions that are not exactly supportive of good health. Yet because of the health risks, the selling of kidneys can cause considerable individual harm. Kidney markets may even be harmful for society at large when, as reported from India, individuals are pressured to sell their kidneys to settle their financial debt (Satz 2012, 195–202).

While moralists are right to point to the troubling effects of the intrusion of the commodity form into areas of social life that were previously not dominated by money concerns, a major weakness of the moralist critique is that moralists rarely if ever discuss the legitimacy of the moral standards that are threatened by commodification. They simply assume the superiority of non-market norms over market norms. By doing so, they overlook the fact that by dismantling oppressive non-market norms, commodification can be liberating. For example, many women experience the commodification of their labor as liberation from oppressive patriarchal norms and their confinement to household work. At the same time, moralists focus on the deterioration of common standards of behavior, the moral fabric of society, while ignoring the material consequences of commodification. Hence, moralists worry about prostitution and paid surrogacy, but they are less concerned about the millions of people who are hungry and/or lack a home, healthcare, and access to utilities (see Chapter 4). In the same way, they describe the trade in kidneys as a noxious market, but accept labor markets in which people are poorly paid, forced into self-employment, and are offered zero-hour contracts.

The pragmatic critique of commodification

There is some overlapping between the pragmatic and the moral critiques of commodification. Pragmatists such as Robert Kuttner (1996, 11) generally praise the merits of the market system—"[m]arkets accomplish much superbly"—while also pointing to possible negative effects for civility and morality. However, the main focus of this critique is not on the (im)moral consequences of certain market exchanges; the focus instead is on markets that do not function properly and therefore demand some sort of government intervention. In other words, the pragmatic critique focuses on market anomalies or imperfections. Yet because the focus is on market technicalities, most authors that adopt some version of the pragmatic critique do not use the term "commodification." Rather they criticize liberalization, privatization, deregulation, etc. Kuttner (1996) is an exception in this regard, although he uses the term "commercialization" rather than "commodification."

One form of market anomaly is what in economic literature is described as market failures. There can be different reasons for market failures. The classical case, as epitomized by Ronald Coase's (1974) lighthouse, is a situation in which potential consumers cannot be excluded from the use of a certain good or service (e.g., ships cannot be prevented from using the light signal). Because users cannot be forced to pay, the respective goods and services cannot be distributed through a market. This also means that potential investors are put off because the inability to charge a price makes it difficult to make a profit (as we will discuss in Chapter 3, public-private partnerships are a strategy to solve this problem). Adam Smith (1900, 666–667) therefore noticed that even in a market society, unprofitable but socially desirable goods and services, such as roads and canals, must be provided by the government as "public works."

While in the case of roads potential users cannot be excluded—except on some highly frequented toll roads—in other cases exclusion is possible but creates undesirable social effects. In economic parlance, these types of goods or services have positive externalities. This is why they are called public goods (Altvater 2004). As mentioned before, Anderson argues that the production and distribution of such goods should be politically determined rather than being left to the market. However, the reasoning of pragmatists is not that the exclusion is morally wrong; the reasoning is that exclusion can negatively affect those willing to pay. Prime examples of goods with positive externalities are healthcare and education. Limited access to healthcare can facilitate the spread of infectious diseases that may even affect those who pay for health insurance. In a similar way, lack of education and skills can undermine the economic growth of a country or region and thereby limit the earning prospects of those who have successfully attended college or university.[18]

In addition to externalities, some markets also produce excessive inefficiencies. For example, most observers would consider it wasteful to build two railway lines between two cities. The same holds for other kinds of infrastructure like electricity, gas, and water networks. Because these types of infrastructure demand enormous investments, they are sometimes called "natural monopolies." Not long ago, there was a broad consensus among economists that in these cases the relevant services should be provided by the government or that private provision should be heavily regulated. However, with growing concerns about state as opposed to market failure, this consensus has largely disappeared (see Chapter 3).

Kuttner (1996, 13–16) illustrates the pragmatic critique by comparing the retail and healthcare sectors. The distribution of retail goods such as food works pretty well through the market. Usually there are several supermarkets competing for customers. Competition forces them to provide high-quality goods at relatively low prices. Consumers can make informed decisions about what products they want to buy. In contrast, the market for healthcare exhibits all kinds of problems (Kuttner 1996, 17–18). On the supply side, provision is limited to individuals or organizations with special licenses. On the demand side, most patients lack the specific knowledge that would allow them to shop for doctors in the same way they can shop for cars. As a result, healthcare markets lack the degree of transparency and competition that is necessary for markets to work properly. And because healthcare "is a far cry from a perfect market" commodification produces all kinds of perverse incentives (Kuttner 1996, 18). In ordinary markets, providers increase profits by reducing costs. In the healthcare market, providers increase revenues by inflating costs. Health insurances respond to growing costs by reducing patients' ability to shop around and by requiring them to get treatments at selected providers, further limiting competition. If allowed, insurance providers also preselect costumers according to preexisting health conditions, excluding those who have the greatest needs. In sum, "health care violates all the premises of an efficient free market—perfect competition, perfect information, mobility of factors, and so on. Yet, unless we want people dying from preventable diseases for lack of private purchasing power, the cure does not lie in liberation of the health 'market' " (Kuttner 1996, 18).

Others use similar arguments to criticize the liberalization and privatization of public utilities. In electricity, for example, it can be more lucrative for private providers with considerable market power to limit supply in order to drive up prices than to invest in new power plants (Krugman 2001). As discussed in Chapter 4, this is considered one of the reasons for the 2000 California electricity crisis. California is an extreme case, but the lack of competition in network industries—five companies dominate the liberalized European electricity market—is widely regarded as a major reason why utility prices have not fallen to the extent promised by the advocates of liberalization and privatization.[19] In the United Kingdom, persistently high energy prices have caused a conservative government to contemplate the introduction of price controls (Asthana and Vaughan 2017).

The main weakness of the pragmatist critique of commodification is that it ignores the deeply political character of the definition of market failure. Market failure has never been only a technical matter; what is a public good and what isn't have always been highly politicized questions. Accordingly, it should not come as a surprise that the limits of commodification have shifted quite a bit in recent decades with the turn from postwar Keynesianism to neoliberalism and the correlated shift from market to government failure. In a neoliberal perspective, the market for healthcare may be imperfect, but it is still preferable to a wasteful government provision. Pragmatists also ignore that allegedly perfect markets can produce quite troubling outcomes—including, among others, unhealthy and dangerous food, a shortage of affordable housing, as well as an oversupply of pharmaceuticals for first-world diseases and an undersupply for third-world epidemics (see Chapter 4).

The materialist critique of commodification

The materialist critique of commodification is closely connected to the Marxist literature on commodification. However, despite frequent mention of the term "commodification," there are only a few cases where Marxists have discussed at length the wider implications of commodification and the reasons why commodification has problematic social consequences. The materialist critique of commodification differs from both the moralist and pragmatist critiques in that it tackles the general effects of commodification, rather than only focusing on some goods, markets, or market imperfections. This is why representatives of the materialist critique are sometimes called anti-commodifiers (Radin 1987, 1871).[20] The essential point of the materialist critique is that commodification is not only and, perhaps, not even objectionable for moral or technical reasons; it is objectionable because it alters material relations such as access to goods and services and the ways in which social needs are satisfied.

The materialist critique focuses on two main aspects of commodification: the dispossession of commonly held resources and negative consequences for the nature and substance of previously non-commodified goods and services. Critics of dispossession take their inspiration from Marx's concept of primitive or, more accurately, original accumulation (Marx 1990, chapters 26–33).[21] Marx argued that for capitalist accumulation to function properly at least two preconditions had to be in place. First, workers had to be separated from the means of production and have their access to land blocked so that they had no alternative but to sell their labor power to a capitalist for a wage. Second, capitalists had to acquire enough wealth to cover the initial expenses of capitalist accumulation. Original accumulation included processes of displacement, the privatization of common land, the plundering of colonies, etc. The fact that these processes took place before the emergence of capitalist accumulation made it possible that the latter appeared as the result of the voluntary cooperation of free individuals, including capitalists and workers.

David Harvey (2003, 145–152) has coined the term "accumulation by dispossession" to describe the private appropriation of common resources as well as collective attainments. Harvey's main argument is that far from being confined to the phase of original accumulation, accumulation by dispossession has continued to play a major role in capitalist development. And in addition to the initial features depicted by Marx, new forms of accumulation have emerged, such as the privatization of nationalized industries, the patenting of genetic material, and the depletion of global commons such as land, water, and air (Harvey 2003). Ursula Huws (2011) also mentions the commodification of public services through the outsourcing of government functions to large and often multinational corporations. She calls this process "secondary primitive accumulation." Rather than converting natural resources or activities that were previously conducted outside the monetary economy into commodities—the objective of primary primitive accumulation—secondary primitive accumulation focuses on the reappropriation of goods and services that had been de-commodified as a result of past class and social struggles (Huws 2011, 64).

Those worried about the negative consequences of commodification for the nature and substance of goods and services build on Marx's elaboration of capitalist accumulation (Marx 1990, chapters 23–25). Here the main point is that commodification is not only about exchanging goods and services for money; it is also about making money, or more precisely about maximizing profits. Capitalists use markets to advance profits, and this profit maximization leaves its mark on commodified goods and services.[22] Accordingly, commodification not only changes the social meaning of previously non-commodified goods and services, it also alters their materiality and manner of production and consumption.

The case where the material impact of commodification has been discussed most extensively is the commodification of labor. As mentioned before, the existence of a class of proletarians that is willing to sell its labor power is a precondition for capitalist accumulation. However, while the exchange of labor for money may be morally questionable, for materialists it is the capitalist application of labor power to increase surplus value that makes it most objectionable. Capitalists use two ways to increase surplus value: the extension of the workday and the intensification of work. Since the extension of the workday has natural limits, the intensification of work becomes the main method of increasing profits. As Harry Braverman (1974) has shown, in advanced capitalism, intensification is often coupled with a fragmentation of work and a deskilling of workers. While Braverman has focused on factory work, similar tendencies can be seen in the organization of service-sector work. Hence from the materialist perspective the problem is not that nannies or nurses are paid. The problem starts when care work becomes part of a profit-seeking operation and managers put pressure on care workers to spend less time with their clients in order to reduce costs (see Chapter 4).

However, the use of labor as an example to explain the workings of commodification is not without problems. Labor, after all, is a rather atypical commodity: The object of exchange cannot be separated from the seller, and the purchaser's ability to use the purchase depends on the consent and the initiative of the worker to perform the required tasks. This is precisely why Polanyi (1957, 72) calls labor a "fictitious commodity." Deskilling and fragmentation is a way to deal with this problem since it makes workers increasingly replaceable, including those who ignore or oppose the instructions from management. However, for the production process to be successful, some work has to be innovative in the sense that it can solve unforeseen problems and tackle new challenges. In these cases, deskilling, fragmentation, and intensification are not an option. This does not mean that highly skilled workers are not exploited. Yet exploitation of highly skilled workers usually takes place in less obvious forms and is typically coupled with a fair amount of autonomy, resulting in what some authors have described as self-exploitation (Hermann 2015a, 87–91).

Perhaps a more accurate example comes from the Frankfurt School's analysis of the culture industry. Horkheimer's and Adorno's (2002) main concern is not the fact that cultural products are sold for money—in fact, the new production model makes it possible to offer cultural goods for very low prices or even for free (2002, 126). Their main concern is how the content of cultural programs changes when they are produced by large profit-seeking corporations (whereas in previous eras capitalists would use profits from other businesses to fund artists and cultural events). In order to make sure that their investments are not lost, the proponents of the culture industry create products with a high probability of becoming a commercial success. Naturally, producers try to reduce risks by replicating previous successes or imitating the successes of competitors. As a result, the culture industry tends to promote conformity and uniformity (Horkheimer and Adorno 2002, 93–95). Novelties are reduced to minor differences, such as which actors have the lead roles in the newest Hollywood movie. At the same time, content is designed so that it can be instantly consumed without challenging the mind or imagination of the recipient (Horkheimer and Adorno 2002, 97–98). Everyone who turns on American TV these days can immediately see what Horkheimer and Adorno were hinting at: dozens of channels that air more or less the same uninspiring content day in and day out. However, Horkheimer and Adorno are also fierce moralists when they complain about the debasement of culture and the deception of the masses brought forth by the culture industry—including, in their view, popular jazz music.[23]

Industrialization affects not only culture and media, but also many other forms of production and consumption in advanced capitalism. And while industrialization does not depend on markets and profit-making—as shown by the Soviet experience before and after the Second World War—the existence of markets and the desire to increase profits creates a strong incentive for exploiting economies of scale (as both Marx and Schumpeter have noticed, the creation of cheap commodities is the secret weapon of capitalist production). In other words, commodification encourages industrialization. The most exclusive restaurant in the United States produces only a fraction of the profits of a fast-food chain such as McDonalds. The industrialization of food production and preparation is complemented by the industrialization of agriculture, including large-scale monoculture cultivation and factory farming (see Chapter 4). In spite of growing resistance to the use of fertilizers, pesticides, and genetically modified crops, as well as animal growth hormones and antibiotics, industrialized food and agriculture are not the result of a market anomaly. Quite to the contrary: they are the result of fierce competition and the search for more efficiency—the attributes that, according to many authors, make markets so admirable.

However, standardization and homogenization are only the first steps in an even more radical transformation of production and consumption: the substitution of manufactured goods for services. Huws (1985) found this tendency when analyzing the transformation of domestic work. In the first step, some domestic tasks became a service provided by mostly female workers for money outside the home. In the next step, the services were replaced by household appliances such as washing machines and dryers which can perform the same task for considerably less money. In this process, manufacturers also invented additional products such as detergent and dryer sheets. The household is only one example. According to Huws (2014, 71–72), capitalist development can be understood as a never-ending process in which non-commodified methods of production and consumption are first replaced by paid services, only to give way to manufactured or digitalized products, which, in turn, create the need for additional commodities. This process not only creates social ruptures as industries and jobs become obsolete; the process also alters the way in which society satisfies social needs. While some may welcome the many new products created by commodification—what is sometimes celebrated as the material abundance of market societies—the same process has also created all kinds of social deformities and ecological problems. As Huws (1985, 149) notes, "the pre-eminence of commodity production has meant that vast quantities of powdered cow's milk are available for babies, but there are no resources to educate their mothers to breast-feed them; . . . that it is easier to find a miniature Rolls-Royce for a child than a nursery place; that we can equip old people with colour televisions more readily than we can give them the warmth of friendship."[24] In the case of healthcare, the same development has resulted in a "de-emphasis on kindness toward patients, bias toward drugs and surgery, focus on treatment over prevention, and almost wholesale ignorance of nutrition and environmental hazards" (Sayer and Walker 1992, 95).

Like some of the moral critics, materialists also take issue with the inequality created by commodification. As the new owners of the privatized assets are mostly high-net-worth individuals or large corporations, accumulation by dispossession necessarily favors the rich at the expense of the less wealthy, and in many cases disproportionately the poor. However, standardization and industrialization can also disadvantage low-income households, who given their limited budgets have no choice but to consume the cheap industrially manufactured products, while the better-off can afford high-quality goods and even services.[25] Food is a case in point: It is not by accident that poor households mainly rely on fast- and ultra-processed food, while high-income households dine in exclusive restaurants and buy organic products. Here inequality doesn't just mean vastly different lifestyles. Because of the high amount of salt and sugar in fast- and ultra-processed food, it also means that the poor disproportionately suffer from affiliated health conditions such as obesity, heart disease, and diabetes (see Chapter 4).

The materialist critique of commodification clearly goes beyond the moralist and pragmatist one and challenges the very basis of capitalist societies. Rather than destroying morals or exacerbating market imperfections, commodification, in this view, is at the heart of many social and ecological problems—including, among others, lack of food, housing, and healthcare, as well the industrialization of agriculture and food production (major effects of commodification will be discussed in Chapter 4). From the materialist perspective, it also becomes clear that the solution to these problems is not moral or technical, but political. However, the materialist critique lacks a coherent theory of commodification that links different forms of commodification to different effects of commodification. Obviously, there are many commodities in capitalist societies that are of excellent quality. This is exactly what the next chapter tries to accomplish.

The age of commodification

In spite of all the differences, there is one theme that unites the three approaches discussed here in their critique of commodification: the perception that commodification has greatly expanded in recent decades and that in many cases it has gone too far. For example, Kuttner (1999, xiii–xiv) notes that "[t]oday commercialism is relentlessly encroaching on realms where it doesn't belong." In a similar way, Sandel (2012, 5) writes that we live in a time when almost everything can be bought and sold. "Over the past three decades, markets—and market values—have come to govern our lives as never before."

For Harvey (2003, 67) the recent upsurge of commodification is not an accident. Accumulation by dispossession always plays a role in capitalist development, but its significance changes over time. During the postwar period, accumulation was mainly based on the expansion of mass production and mass consumption, delivering increasing profits for capitalists (an advanced version of what Marx has described as extended reproduction). Yet by the 1970s, markets for highly standardized mass consumer goods in the United States and other advanced capitalist countries were increasingly saturated and the postwar expansion ended in what Harvey describes as a crisis of overaccumulation (2003, 139). The crisis was accompanied by major political upheavals and ultimately the triumph of neoliberalism as a new political and socioeconomic project (Harvey 2005; for more on neoliberalism, see Chapter 3). Confronted with stagnating profits, capitalists searched for new ways to generate revenues, and one way was to fall back on accumulation by dispossession.

Neoliberal politicians such as Margaret Thatcher handed them ample opportunities, with mass privatizations of public housing, national industries, and state-owned infrastructure (see Chapter 3). In addition, the potential for accumulation by dispossession has been pushed further through the conclusion of international trade agreements such as the GATS and TRIPS, opening resources and markets in developing countries and protecting the intellectual properties of private appropriators (Harvey 2003, 147–148).[26] Perhaps the greatest potential presented for further dispossession was the sale of state assets in Eastern Europe and the former Soviet Union which followed the fall of communism in these countries, and which subsequently made a small group of entrepreneurs and investors incredibly rich (see Chapter 3). The commodification of public services is also part of the neoliberal rollback of working-class gains achieved during the postwar period. Ironically, the greater the scope of de-commodification, the greater the potential for reappropriation (Huws 2011).

Focusing on the transformation of housing, David Madden and Peter Marcuse (2016, 26–27) argue that we have reached a stage of hyper-commodification: "Under hyper-commodification, all of the material and legal structures of housing—buildings, land, labor, property rights—are turned into commodities. In the process, the capacity of a building to function as a home becomes secondary. What matters is how a building functions in the circuits of economic accumulation." Madden and Marcuse see hyper-commodification as part of another trend: financialization. Financialization describes a process in which profit-making increasingly takes place on financial markets rather than in the goods- and services- generating parts of the economy (Krippner 2011). Financialization was fueled by the de- or re-regulation of financial markets, giving financial investors more leeway to maximize their gains. In the case of housing, the deregulation of mortgage markets and the invention of new financial products such as mortgage-backed securities made it possible to "turn solid structures into liquid assets" that can be bought and sold around the world (Madden and Marcuse 2016, 32). Financialization affects markets well beyond housing. The Private Finance Initiative (PFI), which until recently was very popular in England, has meant that schools, hospitals, and prisons, or at least the material aspects of them, become tradable commodities as investors who fund the construction and maintenance of the buildings sell PFI contracts on secondary PFI markets (Whitfield 2010, 192–193). Following from mortgage debt, student debt, which has increased dramatically in a number of countries as a result of fast-rising student fees, will soon be turned into securities to be sold on financial markets. While in the United States so far only private student loans are "securitized," the UK government has started to offload public student debt onto private investors. Securitization of student debt is another step in the ongoing financialization of higher education (Soederberg 2014; Eaton et al. 2016). Last but not least, nature has become a growing target of hyper-commodification: While nature for a long time has been the subject of capitalist commodification, the more recent creation of carbon markets and the conversion of natural habitats into carbon sinks has transformed nature into an object of financial investment and speculation (McAfee 2012; Brandt and Wissen 2014).

Conclusion

Though it is widely used today, "commodification" is a fairly new term in academic discourse. It was only in the 1970s that Marxist scholars started to use "commodification." Among the first who used it were critics of art and culture and proponents of world system theory, as well as welfare state theorists. During a time of notable interest in Marxist theory, the term was quickly adopted by non-Marxist scholars in the 1980s and 1990s. However, with the demise of Marxist academic thinking in the 1990s and early 2000s, commodification largely lost its anti-capitalist connotation and became a tool to criticize the intrusion of market norms and monetary valuation into spheres of social life where they do not belong.

Most authors who use the term "commodification" use it critically in that they associate it with problematic issues or processes in contemporary capitalism. However, the nature and scope of academic critiques of commodification within these parameters vary significantly. I suggest that the critique of commodification can be divided into three main approaches: the moral, pragmatic, and materialist critiques. In the case of the moral critique, representatives generally welcome market exchange, but object to the exchange of certain goods, services, and human attributes. Their main concern is that exchange for money affects the personhood of people, as well as the social meaning of the respective goods and services. Consequently, commodification can erode important social norms, with wider repercussions for social organization. Some moralists are not so much concerned about what is exchanged, as with how it is exchanged. Here the critique focuses on certain markets or frameworks of exchange that produce undesirable outcomes. Pragmatists also praise the beneficial effects of markets while arguing that in some cases the market is not an appropriate instrument for providing particular goods and services. However, pragmatists are not worried about moral consequences; rather, they argue that some markets do not work for technical reasons or because of what is sometimes described as market failure. In contrast to the other two approaches, the materialist critique analyzes the general effects of commodification rather than its effects on specific goods, services, or markets. The materialist critique subsequently focuses on two main consequences: the dispossession of commonly held assets or resources and the material transformation of previously non-commodified goods and services. For materialists, therefore, commodification has a profound impact on how individuals and societies reproduce themselves—including the relationship between humans and nature. Given the continuous deficiencies of capitalist economies (lack of healthy food, adequate housing, healthcare, education etc.) and the mounting challenges (e.g., climate change). I find the materialist critique particular promising for understanding the pitfalls of commodification. The following chapter will lay out my own understanding of commodification and proposes a scheme to cope with the variability of commodification processes.

2

A Theory of Commodification

Introduction

Although it is a relatively new term, "commodification" has become a widely used expression in academic discourse. In fact, it is now so common that some authors find it unnecessary to explain what it means.[1] Yet as the following pages show, commodification can have different meanings, and it is far from clear how to decide when a particular good or service is commodified and when it is not. For some, a good or service is already a commodity when it is provided for exchange; for others, it must be exchanged on a market for money at a competitive price and the producer has to make a profit for it to be considered a commodity. An alternative view focuses on exchange value and use value and argues that in order to become a commodity, a good must acquire exchange value in addition to its use value. In my view, commodification is a process in which market value comes to dominate use value.

The goal of this chapter is threefold. First, it shows the shortcoming of existing definitions of commodification based on exchange, market, money, competition, and the profit motive. Second, it presents a more useful understanding of commodification based on the relationship between use value and market value and proposes the distinction between formal, real, and fictitious commodification to capture the variety of commodification processes. And third, it argues that commodity production is not the best method for satisfying social needs. Accordingly, the chapter starts with a series of definitions related to exchange, markets, money competition, and profits and then proceeds to present an alternative account that is based on the relationship between use and market value. The next section introduces the concepts of formal, real, and fictitious commodification, followed by a final section that argues that markets and competition do not necessarily lead to better and more innovative goods and services. The chapter ends with a brief conclusion.

The Critique of Commodification. Christoph Hermann, Oxford University Press. © Oxford University Press 2021.
DOI: 10.1093/oso/9780197576755.003.0002

Exchange, money, and profits

Despite the popularity of the term "commodification," there is little consensus what commodification actually means. Arjun Appadurai (1986) has argued that anything intended for exchange can be a commodity. From his perspective, there is no fundamental difference between ancient forms of barter and modern trading systems. His conclusion is that there have been few if any human societies in which commodity exchange was irrelevant. Appudarai's conclusion stands in stark contrast to Marx's assumption that systematic commodity exchange is a specific feature of (Western) capitalism. While Marx may have been right in characterizing modern industrial capitalism as the most commodified society, Appudarai argues, commodification is a more universal phenomenon that exists and has existed for a long time outside the capitalist world. I will return to Marx's understanding of commodification and to the specific nature of capitalist commodity production below. Based on Appadurai's (1986) definition, commodification can be understood as the provision of goods, services, or human attributes for exchange.[2] In this definition, many processes count as commodification—including, for example, an exchange of homegrown garden products at a community bazar.

While provision for exchange is not an incorrect definition, it is very general and therefore of little use for grasping the specific nature of commodification processes. Some authors go further and define commodification as provision for exchange on markets. Kieran Healy (2006, 4), for example, notes that "to commodify something is simply to create a market for its exchange where none has existed before." Markets typically imply repeated transactions between a group of sellers and changing buyers, and as such constitute a specific form of exchange. Typically, market transactions also involve money, but in theory markets can also work without money, e.g., when a tomato is exchanged for two carrots. The result is what is commonly known as barter. Other scholars therefore emphasize the role of money in their definitions of commodification. Noel Castree (2003, 278), for example, describes commodification as "a process where qualitatively distinct things are rendered equivalent and saleable through the medium of money."

According to this understanding, any good, service, or human interaction for which recipients have to pay is a commodity, and the charging of money constitutes the process of commodification. Only goods, services, or resources that are freely available, i.e., that are accessible without any form of payment, are not commodities. This means that health, education, water, and other goods have in many countries been commodities for a long time, because users had to pay some sort of fee or price, even though these services were provided by the government, fees/prices covered only parts of the actual costs, and some of the expenses were later reimbursed. Eric Swyngedow (2006, 206) shares this view when he notes that "[i]rrespective of the public or private nature of service delivery, large-scale water distribution . . . is fully commodified and has been for a long time."

In a further specification, some authors argue that it is not enough that goods/services are sold for a price; the price must be determined by the market (rather than being determined by the supplier or imposed by the government). This implies that there has to be some form of competition, i.e., that there are at least two providers offering the respective good or service with an intent to extend their share of the market. This is what Karen Bakker (2007, 103) seems to suggest when she defines commodification as a process that "entails the creation of an economic good, through the application of mechanisms to appropriate and standardize a class of goods and services, enabling them to be sold at a price determined through market exchange." Based on her research on water privatization, Bakker notes that commodification may not be as easy as is often assumed. Water, for example, is an "uncooperative commodity" because, in contrast to electricity or gas, which is the same regardless of the source, its chemical composition differs. Water can therefore not be mixed without affecting its overall quality (Bakker 2004, 19). Competing providers are therefore reluctant to use the same pipes, with the effect that even in privatized water systems, households have no choice but to connect to the only available supplier (this is why, even in a privatized system, prices are often subject to government approval). And as long as there is no competition and hence no market price, water provision in Bakker's definition is not commodified. In this view, the privatization of English water suppliers which created private water monopolies does not count as commodification.

Alternatively, some scholars emphasize the profit motive rather than competition. Colin Leys (2001, 87), for example, argues that production for sale not only means "producing it in such a way to make it saleable," but also that the product "has to be given a price that someone is willing to pay, and under capitalism the price must yield a surplus over the cost of production or it will not be produced." Commodification, in this view, entails the production/ provision of a good/service for sale and for a profit.

While the previously cited authors refer to important aspects of commodification—exchange, markets, money, competition, profit—they fail to acknowledge that commodification is a process rather than a specific state of affairs. By doing so, their definitions fail to account for the complexity of commodification and the variety of commodification processes that exist in capitalist societies. The following section will propose an alternative approach that understands commodification as a process in which use value is subjugated to market value.

Use, exchange, and market value

An alternative definition describes commodification as an "extension of the commodity form to goods and services that were not previously commodified" (Jackson 1999, 96). In order to understand this process, we have to look at the difference between commodified and un-commodified goods. For Marx, the difference is that all goods have use values, but only commodities have exchange values in addition to their use values. While use value represents the usefulness of the product, i.e., its ability to satisfy human needs, exchange value signals the amount of other goods (or money) a particular object achieves when being exchanged on a market (see Chapter 6). For a good to become commodified, therefore, it has to acquire exchange value. In Friedrich Engels's (1937, 44) words, exchange-value needs to be "impressed upon use-value." Goods and services usually acquire exchange value by being exchanged on a market for money. It is through market exchange that two qualitatively different goods or services are rendered equivalent and commensurable. This means that the previously mentioned definitions of commodification are correct in emphasizing the role of markets and money in the process of commodification. However, as will be discussed in the following, there are also alternative techniques for quantifying the value of qualitatively unique goods or services.

Acquiring exchange value is only the first step in the process of commodification. According to Marx, goods can be exchanged without being commodities, or more precisely without being the result of commodity production (this is what Appadurai misses in his account of Marx). In pre-capitalist societies, households or communities traded abundant goods for objects they needed. However, barter in largely self-sufficient economies presented a direct exchange of use values (Albritton 2007, 30). In Marx's (1970, 5) words, in subsistence economies "[e]xchange value does not acquire an independent form but is still directly tied to use value." As a result, "[u]se value, not exchange value is the whole purpose of production" (1970, 5). For Marx, things change when products are no longer created for self-use. Marx is mainly thinking of household production or subsistence farming, but production for self-use can also mean communal or even national production if the self is seen as a larger collective.[3] In commodity production, in contrast, producers not only produce for others; the products themselves must become "non-use value" for the producers (Marx 1970, 42).

This is where money comes in: Money is a precondition for a systematic production for the use of others, rather than for self-use. Money not only greatly facilitates market exchange (a producer only has to find a buyer with money rather than another producer who offers something the first producer needs). Especially in paper form, money is also a distinctive—or in Polanyi's words—"fictitious" commodity, because for most people money itself has no use value—except for being a means for exchange and storage of purchasing power.[4] In a money economy, producers not only produce for others rather than for themselves; they are also compensated by exchange values rather than use values. Buyers, on the other hand, need exchange values to acquire use values. Money, as a result, fuels a phenomenon that Marx (1990, 163–177) has described as commodity fetishism. People increasingly value goods, services, and even objects that are not made for exchange in terms of prices. Conversely, things which have no price have no value and become worthless.[5]

The profit motive is also important because the interest in maximizing profits renders producers indifferent to the use values of their products. Capitalists, as Marx (1991, 297) notes, have no interest in particular use values; they produce and sell whatever promises the greatest return on their outlays. As the president of General Motors once famously said, his job was not to make cars, but to make money (Kymlicka 1989, 107). However, the interest in profit maximization is not the immoral attitude of greedy capitalists; rather, it is the result of a systemic constraint in capitalism—competition (Weeks 1981, 164). Competition is crucial because it forces individual producers to increase profitability since the failure to do so makes them a failing investment and a target for takeover. Indifference has been pushed further with the recent financialization of the economy, i.e., the growing investment in financial assets rather than productive facilities (Krippner 2011). In financial capitalism it is no longer enough to make a decent profit—which is a profit rate equal to or higher than comparable producers. Instead, the new yardstick is the profits that can be made in the financial sector. As a result, companies such as General Motors (until the financial crisis) put their efforts into expanding their financial services rather than producing better and perhaps more environmentally friendly automobiles (Krippner 2011, 29).[6]

With the production for others, rather than for oneself or the collective, the whole purpose of economic activities changes. The creation of use value stops being the main goal of production; instead, production is now geared toward the maximization of exchange value—or the accumulation of money. In Marx's (1990, 250–257) formula, the goal is not C-M-C, but M-C-M'.[7] Use value still plays a role since commodities need use value to acquire exchange value (without being useful, products rarely find a purchaser). But use value is demoted from the main focus of production to the means for increasing exchange values. For a capitalist society, "what matters is exchange-value, not use-value" (Marx 1969, 270). Following Marx, Andrew Sayer (2003, 343) describes commodification as "a change from producing what previously or otherwise might have been simply use values to producing things for their exchange value."

According to Marx (1990, 128–130), exchange value depends on the amount of abstract labor embodied in commodities or, put differently, the average work time expended for the production of a particular set of goods and services to be exchanged on a market. The labor theory of value is crucial for Marx because it allows him to demonstrate that capitalist accumulation is based on the exploitation of the working class (and, related to this, the transformation of work processes in capitalist factories). Yet there are substantial doubts that average socially necessary labor time can explain the prices of commodities (e.g., Steedman 1977).[8] In numerous cases the price of a product has little to do with the labor costs. In the case of Apple's iPhone, for example, total production costs make up less than half of the retail price, and labor costs account for even less.[9] An alternative explanation (which can be found in most economic textbooks) insists that prices are the result of supply and demand.

For Marx, supply and demand play a role in the determination of what he calls market value (Itoh and Yokokawa 1979). Yet in highly competitive markets and markets in which supply is sufficiently great to satisfy social need (i.e., there is no scarcity), exchange value should more or less equal market value and subsequently market prices (Marx 1990, 278–282; see also Indart 1987).[10] The problem is that markets rarely comply with this assumption.[11] Many markets or market segments have oligopolistic structures, and supply and demand are frequently manipulated—how else can we explain Apple's 50 percent profit margin on iPhones? I therefore understand commodification as the process by which market value comes to dominate use value. The important difference is that market value is open to manipulation and speculation—strategies that play a pivotal role in commodification processes (see Chapter 4).[12] However, for understanding commodification processes, even more important is the fact that both exchange and market value are measured quantitatively, usually in units of money, whereas use value can only be assessed qualitatively (Marx 1990, 128).

The next question, then, is how production for market/exchange values, i.e., the production for profit, differs from production for use values, i.e., production for satisfaction of needs. Commodities, after all, continue to have use values. Marx (1993, 267) noted that with the focus on exchange (and we may add market) value rather than use value, use does not come to a halt, but "it obtains its direction thereby." On another occasion he points to the potentially negative consequences of this process when he notes that a commodity acquires market/exchange value through "the alienation of its use value" (Marx 1970, 51). Marx (1964, 106–119) uses the term "alienation" mainly in connection with the alienation of labor in the capitalist production process. There he describes alienation as a process whereby workers lose the control of the content and purpose of their labor. Work, subsequently, is no longer an expression of human faculty, i.e., a medium to practice skills and to develop new abilities.[13] Instead, workers are dehumanized, as they lose the possibility of shaping their environment according to their own imagination (Ollman 1971, 131–152). Because labor power is not only a commodity but also a use value, the degradation of work in capitalist factories is also an example of the alienation of use value. The capacity of workers to turn resources into useful products are reduced to carrying out simple tasks in a repetitive manner. As a result, not only do workers become frustrated, but the use value of their labor power is also severely restricted due to deskilling and disempowerment (see also Chapter 4). Accordingly, the alienation of use value implies some limitation or perversion of the usefulness of a good or service.[14]

An example of the limitation of the usefulness of commodities is planned obsolescence. This is when products are deliberately designed and manufactured to wear out sooner than needed given the state of design, technology, and the available materials (Slade 2006, 5). The reason for this is that a shorter life span allows producers to replace existing consumer goods more quickly and thereby maintain sales numbers in spite of increasingly saturated markets. One of the best-documented cases is an agreement between leading light bulb manufacturers who decided in the mid-1920s to reduce the life span of incandescent light bulbs from between 2,000 and 1,500 hours to 1,000 hours (Krajewski 2011).[15] Less well-documented cases are printers and washing machines. According to Christian Kreiss (2014, 32), the average lifetime of washing machines has almost been halved in the last 20 years (from 12 to 6.5 years). Producers argue that shorter life span is the result of the use of cheaper materials, which makes products more affordable. But higher prices do not necessarily guarantee longer durability. Other methods of limiting the life span of products are frequent model changes, updates in software that need more memory capacity, as well as the creation of obstacles to replace frequently worn-out parts such as batteries, and the excessive pricing of parts and repair services (Kreiss 2014, chapter 1).[16] Because such practices can ruin the reputation of a company, they are usually not disclosed to the public, and therefore there are no statistics on planned obsolescence.[17] But Kreiss estimates that 11 percent of consumer goods bought by an average German household are subject to severe forms of planned obsolescence (2014, 114). Other instances where the focus on market value leads to sacrifices in the quality of goods and services will be discussed in Chapter 4.

Yet production for market value rather than use value not only affects the product; even more importantly, it also affects the way that social needs are met. A telling example is transportation: People's need for transportation can be met on an individual basis through private cars, taxis, or car services. Alternatively, they can be met by collective forms of transport such as public buses, subways, trains, airplanes, etc. It is widely assumed that it is the convenience of individual forms of transport, especially the private car, that has caused the demise of public transportation in the postwar period.[18] However, growing traffic congestion in urban centers, which means that commuters spend several hours in their cars going to and from work, has severely restricted the convenience of cars. Yet the response to this problem has not been the expansion of public transportation—at least not in the United States. Instead of investing in overcrowded and crumbling public transport systems, such as BART in San Francisco or the New York City subway, investors throw money at companies that are developing self-driving cars, some of them electronically powered.[19]

Hence the superiority of the private car does not derive from its greater convenience—at least not in urban centers. Its superiority derives from its greater market value or the potential for making a profit. It is much more profitable to sell millions of cars each year—including, in the future, millions of self-driving cars—than to run a public transportation system. One reason is that most cars are more than simply a means of transport; they also have symbolic values and as such are examples of what Thorsten Veblen (2007, chapter 4) has called "conspicuous consumption." Hence it is not by accident that automobile manufactures, despite periodic slumps and occasional bankruptcies, have continued to produce solid profits over decades, whereas public transport providers in many countries struggle to break even.[20]

Understanding commodification as subjugation of use value to market value also means that commodification is a process rather than a specific state of affairs (Prudham 2009, 125). As Karl Polanyi (1957, chapter 7) shows, it took more than a hundred years to commodify labor in Britain's emerging capitalist economy. The initial commodification of labor is an extreme case, but more recent commodification processes, such as the liberalization of public services in Europe, also took time and were introduced in several stages (Hermann and Verhoest 2012). Yet understanding commodification as a process also means that there is no general formula—such as the existence of a price—according to which a good or service can be qualified as (non)commodified. Instead, each case needs to be analyzed separately. In my view, a critical point in the process is reached when market value comes to dominate use value. Some markets allow use value to be the dominant or at least equally important motive of production (see Chapter 7). Usually it is competition and the profit motive that makes sure that market value comes to dominate use value. In addition, use value can also be marginalized by the maximization of non-monetary metric standards such as performance indicators (see later discussion).

To come back to a previously mentioned example: The fact that residents pay for water provided by a municipal water company which has no intention of making a profit does not mean that water is fully commodified. In this case we can assume that the main purpose of production is still the provision of use value, even though the water has to be paid for. If the same water network is taken over by an international corporation whose main purpose is to maximize profit, there is a good chance that market value will come to dominate use value—if the new owners are not hindered from doing so by strong government regulation. As a result, private water companies in the United

Kingdom have no problem watching millions of liters of water disappear through pipe leaks while demanding higher prices in light of a growing water shortage.[21] Another example is the difference between a local doctor's office and the local branch of an international healthcare corporation. Even though the local doctor charges fees for services and makes a decent living, she or he is usually not accumulating money; rather, the main motive of his/her work is still to care for patients (many public healthcare systems therefore allow for private outpatient care). In contrast, the purpose of a medical office run by a healthcare multinational is to produce growing returns for its investors, who are, indeed, quite indifferent to the health of the patients (to the contrary: patients who are too healthy may even pose a threat to their profits). The doctors who work in these offices may still care about the patients, but if they care too much and that eats into profits (e.g., when they frequently discourage patients from pursuing treatment), they will sooner or later have a problem. In a similar way, small-scale (family) farming differs from industrial agriculture, even though in both cases agricultural products are sold for money and the growers intend to make a profit. In the first case, farmers still have a close relationship to their plants and livestock and treat them accordingly. In the case of industrial farming, growers become increasingly indifferent to what they produce and how they produce it as long as it guarantees them sufficiently high profits. As a result, they switch to monocultures and use pesticides and fertilizers, and they breed animals in overcrowded indoor spaces where they never see natural light or have a chance to stretch their feet (see Chapter 4).

Formal, real, and fictitious commodification

In order to grasp the scope of commodification processes, I suggest distinguishing between *formal* and *real commodification*. Marx distinguishes between the formal and real subsumption of labor under capital (Marx 1990, 1019–1038). In the first case, the worker sells her/his labor power to the capitalist—which means her/his labor power is formally commodified—but the worker still labors as if she/he is an independent producer in the production process. The fact, as Marx (1990, 1021) notes, that a peasant or journeyman becomes a wage laborer does not "imply a fundamental modification in the real nature of the labor process, the actual process of production." This should not surprise, as capital has not invented the labor process; it took it over from earlier, pre-capitalist societies. This does not mean that nothing changes. Capital's goal is to increase surplus value. But at the stage of formal subsumption, capital focuses on the expansion of absolute surplus, i.e., the extension of the workday. The fact that workers have to work longer hours has no immediate impact on the production process which "proceeds in its traditional fashion" (Marx 1990, 1023). Yet as soon as capital shifts its attention to the augmentation of relative surplus value, i.e., the increase of output per workday, the production process starts to change. "With the production of relative surplus value the entire real form of production is altered" (Marx 1990, 1024). However, formal and real subsumption of labor under capital are only the starting and endpoints of a lengthy transformation process. Capitalists occasionally introduced changes in work processes in the nineteenth century, but it was only with the spread of scientific management in the twentieth century that capital captured full control over labor processes (Braverman 1974). And some labor processes, including those involving knowledge work, can still be controlled only indirectly (Hermann 2009a, 283). In a similar way, formal and real commodification present starting and endpoints in the commodification process. Formal commodification means that a good or service is given market value—a good or service receives a price—while real commodification implies that market value dominates use value—form or content are adapted to maximize profits.[22]

William Boyd, Scott Prudham, and Rachel Schurman (2001) make a similar point when they distinguish between the formal and real subsumption of nature under capitalism. Formal subsumption has the same effect as formal commodification, and real subsumption resembles real commodification. In the case of formal subsumption/commodification, natural resources such as wood, coal, or oil are plundered with increasingly sophisticated techniques, but the material composition of the respective resources is usually not affected. In contrast, real subsumption/commodification implies a transformation of the material composition or use value of nature (Boyd, Prudham, and Schurman 2001, 560). Early forms of real subsumption/commodification include crossbreeding and the use of hormones, fertilizers, and pesticides. Yet real subsumption/commodification entered a new phase with recent advances in biotechnology and the manipulation of the DNA of plants and animals (see Chapter 3). The purpose of these manipulations is not to improve quality; in fact, those who appreciate quality and can afford to do so buy organic products. Instead, the purposes are higher yields, shorter turnover times, and improved disease resistance. "Nature, in short, is (re)made to work harder, faster, and better" (Boyd, Prudham, and Schurman 2001, 564).

To take another example: The introduction of fees for a college education can be classified as formal commodification. The fact that students have to pay does not necessarily affect the way students are taught (what can make a difference, though, is when students are seen as consumers, rather than as individuals who want to learn). However, when colleges become investor-owned businesses that are expected to produce a profit, the structure of education changes, with increasing class sizes and increasingly standardized forms of teaching (see Chapter 4). In a study on the commodification of care, Deborah Stone (2005, 282) comes to the conclusion that the fact that caregiving is paid for is not the "great transformer of caregiving." Yet the quality of care changes when the care organization starts to reduce costs to make a profit or to cope with funding cuts. This is also when caregivers start to look for other jobs because they become increasingly frustrated by the fact that they cannot provide the care their clients need.[23]

The distinction between formal and real commodification is not only helpful for understanding the scope of commodification processes; it is also useful for grasping the various impacts of commodification. The main effect of formal commodification is the exclusion of potential users, either because they cannot pay, or they happened to be part of a group of consumers with insufficient purchasing power. In contrast, the main effects of real commodification are homogenization, standardization, and the deterioration of quality (see Chapter 4). The reason is that companies typically increase profits by reducing production costs. Whereas increasing prices usually limit the number of potential buyers, reducing production costs allows producers to increase profits while at the same time expanding the market. A popular way to reduce costs is to standardize products so that more output can be produced with the same inputs, or what is commonly described as maximizing productivity. This is precisely what Ursula Huws (2014, 71) means when she notes that commodification is a tendency "to transform ever more activities into products or services that can be delivered in multiple standardized versions." And because tangible output can more easily be standardized than services— services usually involve human interaction and human responses are not entirely predictable—commodification in the past came with a tendency to substitute material products for immaterial services. Digitalization changed this tendency. Today it is often digital goods such as cell phone apps that replace digital services such as call centers.[24] Examples for standardization and its impact on the way social needs are met will be discussed in Chapter 4. Some authors call the same tendency "rationalization" or "industrialization" (Healy 2006, 124; Ritzer 2013, 29–31). However, the result is far from rational. To come back to the example of transport: Standardization and profit-maximization means that we will be stuck in traffic in our self-driving cars (which, perhaps, will be equipped to allow us to work on the way to and from the office) instead of having a more efficient, sustainable, and healthier public transportation system.

Typically, formal commodification and real commodification are associated with exchange on markets for money with competing providers and the intent to make a profit. However, as mentioned earlier, there are also alternative techniques for subordinate use value to a quantitative indicator. Such cases are examples of a process that I call *fictitious commodification*. They can primarily be found in the public sector, where organizations are not required to make a profit, there is no real competition, and in a number of cases users do not even pay for the product. To some extent, fictitious commodification is the result of the spread of what in the public administration literature is called New Public Management (NPM; see Chapter 3). NPM theorists have pushed for the introduction of quasi-markets to offer choice to service users. However, while markets are supposed to force competing parts of the same organization to become more efficient and more responsive to users' needs, failing providers rarely disappear. In the same spirit, public service users are called consumers, even though they do not pay for the services. In absence of a monetary value of public goods, NPM advocates have, furthermore, urged the invention of quantitative performance indicators, such as the average number of days patients stay in a hospital or the number of publications of academic staff. When used to pressure providers to increase output, the impact of these indicators can be quite similar to those caused by the introduction of prices and the obligation to make profits (see Chapter 4).

Marx (1990, 1019) notes that real subsumption of labor under capital requires formal subsumption. In a similar way, real commodification usually follows formal commodification. Only when a good or service has a price does it become possible to make a profit and subsequently increase profits by altering the product and the production process. However, an increase in prices, or what may be called an acceleration of formal commodification, can also be used to prevent real commodification (in Marx's terms, formal subsumption can exist without real subsumption, but real subsumption not without formal subsumption). This is the case, for example, when consumers are charged exceptionally high prices in order to receive a good or service that is not standardized, or in any other way affected by cost-cutting strategies. Hence commodification does not necessarily imply a deterioration of the quality of goods and services. People who can afford to pay higher prices can, for example, buy tailored clothes or organic food. Wealthy families can also pay for elite schools with smaller class sizes, the newest equipment, and better trained teachers. Perhaps ironically, it is mainly underprivileged students from low-income families who are targeted by private for-profit colleges in the United States, while students from privileged backgrounds go to expensive Ivy League schools that are run as nonprofit organizations (see Chapter 4).

While an acceleration of formal commodification can prevent real commodification, some of the changes that I have discussed under real commodification can be necessary for formal commodification. The reason is that some degree of standardization is necessary for the classification of a good or service that is sold on a market for a price.[25] Classification, in turn, helps to avoid lengthy negotiations about what exactly sellers are offering and what buyers are looking for—which, again, is essential for the development of a competitive market with multiple suppliers and changing consumers.

The need of classification and standardization can be seen when we look at the creation of a fairly new commodity, wetland credits. Developers in the United States can buy wetland credits to make up for a loss of wetlands caused by a new construction site. Wetlands are protected because they are special habitats, and no wetland is exactly the same as another (Robertson 2006). However, to create a commodity that developers can buy, scientists had to come up with a common standard to compare highly diverse ecosystems. The result is the invention of a norm that is called ecosystem function. Ecosystem function is based on a crude abstraction of the (use) value of a particular ecosystem and as such is highly problematic (Robertson 2006). Yet, regardless of the scientific flaws, it allows for the classification of wetlands and subsequently the transformation of wetlands into wetland credits that can be bought and sold on a market (Robertson 2006).

As mentioned previously, fictitious commodification does not depend on real markets, competition, and money. However, experience shows that fictitious commodification is often followed by formal and real commodification. Fictitious commodification becomes formal when users start to believe that they really are consumers and accept that they have to pay for what used to be free services. And it becomes real when quasi-competitors are replaced by private contractors who want to make a profit and who can go bankrupt, as well as when the use of performance indicators teaches workers to focus on quantity rather than quality. Both formal and real commodification become more likely when budget cuts that were supposed to be compensated by efficiency gains have deteriorated service quality to the point that users lose faith in the public option and long for a private alternative.

Quality and innovation

According to mainstream economics, competition not only forces producers to lower production costs. It also encourages them to improve product quality. Consumers, after all, are not looking for the cheapest deal, but for the best one. Hence commodification should actually lead to better rather than worse use values. There are several problems with this view. The mechanization and automation of production, as well as exceptionally high product-development costs, mean that cots per unit of output tend to decline the more of the product that is produced—what economists call economies of scale (Chandler 1990, 17). This gives large producers a strategic advantage over small producers and subsequently fuels a process of concentration. Hence in a number of sectors a few large producers dominate the market. Until the arrival of Japanese and German car manufacturers, for example, three automobile producers essentially shared the US automobile market. In civil aviation, two producers—an American and a European company—dominate the market for large commercial jetliners. Concentration does not necessarily mean that there is no competition. But there is the possibility for collusion (see, for example, the aforementioned consortium that limited the durability of light bulbs) and there is certainly less pressure to improve product quality.

Second, there are markets where competition is dysfunctional or undesirable.[26] Network industries, for example, demand massive infrastructure investments that only pay off over a long period of time (this is why such investments are often made by governments). In such cases it makes little sense for two competing companies to create similar infrastructure to compete for customers. The result can easily be that both fail to recover costs. This was precisely the experience of many investors in the nineteenth-century railway boom in the United States (Perelman 2006, 78–79). Apart from railways, additional examples include electricity and water networks. Until recently, such sectors were considered natural monopolies (Baumol 1977).

While in Europe they were typically run by public companies, in the United States they were subjected to detailed regulations—including the regulation of prices that could be charged to customers. Network industries have been subjected to far-reaching deregulation and privatization in recent years. However, the experience of liberalizing electricity and gas provision in the European Union has been that a few large corporations end up dominating the market (see Chapter 3).

Third, competition has different effects on the quality of material output than on the quality of labor-intensive services. While in manufacturing the invention of new technology or new materials makes it possible to improve product quality while at the same time holding costs down, in labor-intensive services the quality of the product largely depends on labor inputs. While there are some possibilities for increasing productivity through rationalization or organizational innovation, generally this means that the quality of the services cannot be improved without increasing costs. And increasing costs can easily result in a loss of market shares. As discussed earlier, there are cases in which rich customers pay extraordinary high prices to receive first-class services, but overall competition in labor-intensive services induces producers to cut labor costs. In health and social services in particular, this tends to result in a deterioration of service quality. This is one of the main findings of a European research project that investigated the impact of liberalization and privatization of public services in a range of different sectors and countries (Hermann and Flecker 2012b, 202).[27]

Fourth, competition does not guarantee that the best good or service is delivered; it only means that the product has to be better than the one offered by the competitor. In highly competitive markets, some products may come close to the best output that can be achieved with a reasonable deployment of resources, but, as argued earlier, not all markets are competitive. In addition, the variety of choice can be severely limited if the need is rather specific (Waldfogel 2007). Consumers may therefore find themselves in a position where they have to choose between two or more unsatisfying solutions to their needs. With the shift from production for one's own needs to production for the needs of others, users have little say about what exactly is produced to satisfy their needs. They can only decide whether to buy a specific product or to continue living without it. In addition, it may not be entirely clear which is actually the best product for their money. Producers rarely admit that their competitors offer a better product for a similar price. This is not such a problem for goods with a short turnover time—an unsatisfied consumer of a specific brand of coffee can simply buy another brand when he/she runs out of coffee—but the decision can be a real challenge in the case of long-term investments. One way to deal with insecurity is to buy a well-established product. The fact that it is still available on the market suggests that consumers are not entirely dissatisfied with it. However, the same behavior makes it difficult for new producers with superior products to challenge a market leader.

Fifth, competition does not prevent producers from creating and selling poor and dysfunctional products. One-dollar stores and their equivalents outside the United States are full of them. While usually these products do not do much harm, except for creating unnecessary waste, it is rather assuasive to know that in the case of more expensive and riskier products, producers have to adhere to certain quality and safety standards. The product type may even be subject to approval by a government agency before it can be sold on a market. Hence, even though competition is supposed to improve quality, most capitalist economies still rely on government regulations to make sure that consumers are not harmed by flawed products.

Competition is not only meant to improve product quality; in combination with private initiative, competition is also expected to drive innovation and fuel the invention of new products. Capitalism, no doubt, has a very impressive record of technological and organizational innovations and the creation of astonishing commodities which satisfy needs. Yet, as Marianna Mazucatto (2013) has argued, the state plays a crucial role in financing the research that has led to some of the most striking inventions in recent history. In fact, most governments in advanced capitalist countries provide some form of support for research and innovation, including publicly funded universities, and few countries leave it entirely to the market to find innovative products or processes. What is more: even companies do not fully trust markets and instead create needs for their products (see Chapter 4). John Kenneth Galbraith (1958, 128) calls this behavior "want creation" and notes that it is an essential feature of advanced capitalist economies. As a result, advertising has become increasingly important. Even in supposedly innovative businesses such as the pharmaceutical industry, the budget for product placement and advertising frequently exceeds that for research and innovation.[28]

In addition, companies sometimes need external pressure to innovate. One example is the car industry. Even though we have known for some time that fossil-fuel burning produces carbon-dioxide emissions which in turn increase average temperatures and induce climate change with dramatic consequences for nature and human beings, the car industry has been very reluctant to build cars with lower emissions and to develop electrically powered vehicles that can replace fuel-dependent automobiles. Because of this slow progress, the European Commission took the lead and imposed a plan that forces European car manufacturers to bring down emissions levels.[29] Yet while the car industry has been slow in developing alternatives to fuel-burning, (minor) innovations in other areas such as the cell-phone sector have meant that millions of phones are discarded every year and end up as e-waste in a garbage site (Slade 2006, chapter 9). Innovation not only solves environmental problems; it also creates them.

This is not to deny the achievements of capitalist commodity production in creating amazing goods and services that in many ways have improved the conditions of human reproduction. Capitalism, furthermore, is unique in cutting production costs and increasing productivity, which has dramatically widened access to standardized commodities, even though they come at a price. However, this success is not least the result of the continued relevance of use value and, hence, the limits of commodification. Contrary to the premise of profit maximization, workers, engineers, and sometimes even managers continue to worry about what they produce or how they treat their clients. In addition, commodification also has a number of disturbing effects including, for example, leaving millions without access to healthcare, a home, and food; bombarding consumers in affluent countries with pharmaceuticals for every imaginable and sometimes imagined medical condition, while ignoring diseases that affect less than 200,000 people or affect millions in poor countries; selling food that not only has little nutritional value, but also makes people obese and sick; and setting up colleges in which more money is spent for advertising and admissions than for teaching (for a comprehensive list of the negative effects of commodification, see Chapter 4).

In sum, commodity production may not be the best method of satisfying social needs, especially if these needs cannot or can no longer be satisfied by material objects and in an individualized manner. The looming social and ecological crises affecting many countries around the globe are a strong indication of this deficiency. In the 1970s, social scientists expected that the demand for public goods or services with a pronounced social character would increase substantially, as the demand for purely private goods seemed increasingly to have been satisfied (Hirsch 1977, 4). However, precisely because of the dominance of market value over use value, this prediction did not materialize, and even in the most advanced welfare systems public consumption accounts for little more than a quarter of GDP (Hermann 2016, 7–8). In other words, commodity production has become an obstacle to urgently needed social and ecological transformation—including, for example, a more sustainable transportation system. However, the question is what system should replace commodity production. Producing use values as in pre-capitalist economies or in the state-administered systems of the Soviet Union and Eastern Europe is not a very attractive alternative. What is needed instead is a system that is based on the maximization of use values rather than profit. This is the main theme of Chapter 7.

Conclusion

In this chapter I have proposed an understanding of commodification that is based on the relationship between use value and market value. In order to become a commodity, a good or service must acquire market value, i.e., it must receive a price and be sold on market. Market value differs from exchange value by being open to market manipulations. However, the acquisition of a price tag, or what I call formal commodification, is only the first step in a longer commodification process. In this process, a critical point is reached when market value comes to dominate use value. In this view, markets, money, competition, and the profit motive are not markers of commodification; they are instruments for subjugating use value to market value. However, there are also alternatives methods to quantify qualitatively unique use values such as performance measurements and ecosystem function units. In turn, the subjugation of use value to market value changes the form and content of the product. The result is what I call real commodification.

Formal and real commodification tend to have different consequences. The main effect of formal commodification is that potential users who cannot pay the price for the commodity are excluded. In the case of real commodification, output is standardized and, whenever possible, services are replaced by material or digital goods. In addition, I distinguish a third form of commodification: Fictitious commodification refers to a situation in which goods and services are commodified without the help of markets, money, and the profit motive. Instead, commodification is based on the introduction of quasi-markets, forcing different parts of the same organization to compete with each other, and the application of performance indicators and the subsequent focus on quantity rather than quality. Forms of fictitious commodification are mainly found in the public sector. They were greatly enhanced with the shift toward New Public Management. The chapter, furthermore, has argued that commodity production has led to the invention of a series of amazing products which have greatly facilitated human reproduction. However, the downside of commodity production includes, among other things, a disregard for needs that are not backed by money and a focus on products that yield high profits at the cost of those that are less profitable but more equitable and sustainable. As such, commodity production has become an obstacle to an urgently needed social and ecological transformation.

3

The Politics of Commodification

Introduction

Commodification is at once a precondition and consequence of capitalist development. Piero Sraffa (1975) described capitalism as an economic system that is based on the production of commodities by means of commodities. Given the mutually reinforcing relationship between capitalism and commodification, the prime question, perhaps, is not why more and more aspects of human existence have become commodified, but why some things have not—a question we will return to in Chapter 5. Even though capitalism contains a natural tendency to commodify everything that can be turned into a commodity, the scope and degree of commodification vary over time and space. Among other things, the degree of commodification depends upon government interventions in the economy and the regulation of markets, as well as the provision of public goods and services. As mentioned previously, most critics of commodification agree that commodification has intensified in recent decades. Materialists associate the surge in commodification with the formation of neoliberalism as a new economic and social system in the 1980s, replacing postwar Keynesianism which entered into a crisis in the 1970s. In very general terms, neoliberalism is an ideology that favors private ownership and unrestricted markets as the most promising instruments for stimulating wealth creation, while emphasizing individual gain, choice, and responsibility as the guiding principles of social organization.[1] The "neoliberal counter-revolution" is frequently associated with the election of right-wing governments such as Margaret Thatcher's in the United Kingdom and Ronald Reagan's in the United States, and it is a response to the ineffectiveness of Keynesian policies to curb the 1970s crisis (Duménil and Levy 2005).[2] Many of the economic and social policies adopted by these and other governments on federal and local levels in the 1980s and 1990s fueled (re-)commodification. In this chapter I focus on six major strategies: privatization, liberalization, deregulation, marketization, New Public Management,

The Critique of Commodification. Christoph Hermann, Oxford University Press. © Oxford University Press 2021.
DOI: 10.1093/oso/9780197576755.003.0003

and austerity. Each of the following sections deals with one of the policies. The chapter ends with a brief conclusion.

Privatization

Privatization has different meanings. It can mean the transfer of the right to use a commonly held resource to private individuals or corporations, as well as the sale of a public asset to a private investor. Yet it can also mean the withdrawal of public organizations from the provision of certain goods and services or related tasks (Starr 1998). Common arguments for privatization include the assumption that users of commonly held resources act irresponsibly because they do not see the resources as their own property. It follows that the state is a suboptimal manager of corporate entities because the government takes into account too many highly diverse interests; the private sector is believed to be more efficient, innovative, and responsive to consumer demands.

An early example of privatization was the enclosure of common land. While Marx emphasized the role of enclosures in sixteenth- and seventeenth-century England as a precondition for capitalist accumulation, the privatization of common land never stopped and instead accompanied capitalist expansion over the following centuries. Even in the twenty-first century, commonly held land continues to be privatized on almost a daily basis. Large international corporations and even financial investors have shown increasing interest in the purchase of large stretches of land (Fairbairn 2020, 3–7). The World Bank estimates that worldwide between 2010 and 2030 an additional 120 to 240 million hectares of uncultivated land, a substantial part of it commonly held, will be converted into private large-scale farmland (Deininger et al. 2011, 16). Most contemporary enclosures take place in the developing world, while many of the international corporations who end up owning the land have their headquarters in the Global North. Critics call this process *land grabbing* (Borras and Franco 2012). Writing about the dispossession of small-scale farmers in Rajasthan, India, Michael Levien (2018) has documented the role of government agencies in enabling land-grabbing processes. However, enclosures not only take place in the Global South. Pressure to cut off access to land, parks, beaches, and wildlife has also intensified in developed countries such as the United States (Robbins and Luginbuhl

2005). The Trump administration, in particular, leased millions of acres of public land to private companies for oil and gas drilling and other activities (Simmonds, Dickie, and Byers 2018).

Enclosures can also affect urban spaces when squatted areas are cleared for real estate development (Harvey 2008). The city of Mumbai is a site of constant struggles over dispossession. With the dramatic expansion of the Indian metropole in recent decades, what used to be abandoned land on the urban fringes that was used by the poor to create informal housing is now highly valuable property. Millions of residents have lost their homes in Mumbai due to slum clearing; 90,000 hutments alone were destroyed in a few months in late 2004 and early 2005, leaving as many as 400,000 individuals without a home (Weinstein 2013, 300). Ironically, some of these clearings are justified by a policy that aims to improve the living conditions of the poor. Similar developments take place in other cities in the developing world, while in the developed countries poor residents are mainly forced out by increasing rents and property prices (Walks and Maaranen 2008). As discussed in the following, the deregulation of housing markets and the subsequent property boom have fueled gentrification in many cities in North America and around the world.

Dispossession can also take the form of patenting of genetic information. Following a major breakthrough in the ability to isolate and transplant the genomes of living organisms in the early 1970s, genetical engineering, or the de- and reassembling of DNA, became the foundation of the emerging biotechnology industry (Kloppenburg 2004, chapter 8). In order to protect their inventions, biotech firms, often in alliance with university researchers, not only patented newly created organisms but also some of their component parts, which they harvested freely from existing plants, animals, and human beings (McAfee 2003).[3] The US biotechnology sector has applied for 4,980 patents in 2015 (OECD 2017, 85). The privatization of genetic information has major consequences that go beyond the ownership of certain products. It means, for example, that farmers who use genetically modified crops have forfeited the right to use some of their harvest to grow new plants the following season. In fact, they and their neighbors have to make sure that none of their plants has the genetic traits of the GM crops—which, given the unpredictable ways nature reproduces itself, is not easy (Prudham 2008, 16–17).[4]

Patenting depends on the establishment of an intellectual property regime and the subsequent enforcement of intellectual property rights. Governments

have adopted intellectual property legislation and have provided the legis-
lative apparatus that allows individuals and businesses to fight intellectual
property rights infringements. Furthermore, in order to enforce these rights
around the globe, the World Trade Organization adopted the Agreement on
Trade-Related Aspects of Intellectual Property Rights (TRIPS) in 1995. The
signing countries agreed to adopt effective and adequate intellectual property rights which, among other things, prevented African countries from
copying antiviral medication to treat AIDS patients (Moerman and van der
Laan 2006).

Another major form of privatization is the sale of public assets. This
policy is particular prominent in those countries which have developed
large public sectors during the postwar decades. After being elected in the
late 1970s, the Thatcher government wasted no time in initiating a massive
privatization program in the United Kingdom. Between 1981 and 2002,
2.9 million council flats became private property, cutting the number of
apartments rented from local authorities in half (Ginsburg 2005, 115–117).
Yet public housing was only the beginning of a wave of privatization that affected state-owned energy, transport, communication, and water suppliers
(Florio 2006; Meek 2015). Starting in the United Kingdom, privatization
swept to other European countries in the 1990s and early 2000s. Total privatization revenues incurred between 1977 and 2007 across the European
Union amounted to more than 803 billion US dollars. In terms of sectors,
privatization mainly affected public utilities, telecommunications, and banks
(Frangakis and Huffschmid 2009, 15–17). In Eastern Europe, the lack of private capital encouraged governments to use rather unconventional privatization methods, such as management buyouts and vouchers given out to
citizens. However, it did not take long for the valuable assets to end up in
the hands of a few large-scale investors (Lóránt 2009, 33–34; Ther 2016, 91–
93). In Russia a small group of oligarchs became incredibly rich through the
fire sale of state-owned enterprises at grossly undervalued prices (Ther 2016,
91–93).

In some cases, privatizations are enforced by international organizations.
The International Monetary Fund (IMF) and the World Bank, for example,
strongly advised debtor countries to divest public companies in exchange for
continuous financial support (Hermann 2017a). Consequently, privatization became a widely applied policy in Latin America from the mid-1980s
to the end of the 1990s. In Brazil alone, the value of public divestments over
this time period reached 61 billion US dollars. As in the European case,

governments mainly sold off public infrastructures and banks (Lora 2012, 14). Privatizations still continue: After the 2008–2009 crash, Euro area crisis countries were pressured by the troika (European Commission, European Central Bank, IMF) to privatize public infrastructures such as electricity, gas, water, postal services, and railways (Busch et al. 2013).

In addition to the sale of public assets, privatization can also result from the takeover of government functions by private corporations. A popular method for boosting the role of private capital in the provision of public services is public-private partnerships (PPPs). Many countries use public-private partnerships to build roads, tracks, and airports. The United Kingdom stands out, as PPPs are used for a wide range of UK public services such as hospitals, schools, and prisons. The majority of new hospitals created in England between 1997 and 2007 were built by a special PPP called Private Finance Initiative (PFI). In a PFI arrangement, the private partner, usually a consortium including a bank, a construction firm, and a facility management corporation, funds, builds, and maintains a public facility such as a hospital and then leases it back to the government on contracts that span thirty years or more. According to the National Audit Office (2018), there are over 700 PFI and PF2 (the updated version) projects running in the United Kingdom, amounting to a capital value of around 60 billion pounds. Annual charges for these deals reached 10.3 billion pounds in 2016–2017. Even if no new deals are concluded, the Audit Office estimates that future charges which continue until the 2040s amount to 199 billion pounds (National Audit Office 2018).

Another form of engaging the private sector is outsourcing. Many secondary services in public organizations, such as security, cleaning, and catering, as well as IT procurement and maintenance, have been outsourced to private firms. According to a government report, outsourced public services accounted for nearly 6 percent of the United Kingdom's GDP in 2008. The author estimates that what is described as Britain's public service industry (PSI) amounted to as much as 79.4 billion pounds. In absolute terms, the United Kingdom's PSI was second only to that of the United States, with the size of 393 billion pounds (Julius 2008, 18, 62).

A study that looked at outsourcing in local government in the United States found that 28 percent of the services delivered by the municipalities included in the sample were contracted out (Girth et al. 2012, 890). In addition, US federal and state governments have made increasing use of private contractors to operate prisons and to deliver military services in foreign countries. The number of inmates in privately run federal and state prisons in the United States has increased from 87,369 in 2000 to 128,300 in 2016. Private prisons now house 8.5 percent of the federal and state prison population (Bureau of Justice Statistics 2001, 2018). The US government has also signed contracts with private military corporations, including the infamous Blackwater Security Company, to provide support for US military forces in Iraq, Afghanistan, and other countries. Between 1999 and 2008 the budget spent by the US Department of Defense for private contractors increased from 165 billion to 414 billion US dollars. Given the dramatic increase of private security personnel in relation to the total size of US military forces—in 2010, the US deployed 175,000 troops and 207,000 contractors in war zones—a significant portion of the money spent went to private military corporations (McFate 2014, 19–20).[5]

While in the case of outsourcing the government continues to fund services or related activities even though they are carried out by private contractors, inadequate funding can also fuel privatization. India, for example, spent only 0.93 percent of its GDP on public healthcare in 2016, compared to an average of 2.74 percent for low- and middle-income countries.[6] The underfunding of the public system invited the creation of a large private healthcare sector, relying on private and mostly out-of-pocket payments (the latter accounts for more than 60 percent of the country's total healthcare spending). While for-profit hospitals played only a minor role in India before the 1990s, private hospitals now provide about 60% of inpatient and 80% of outpatient care (Gupta and Mrigesh, n.d.).

Privatization fuels commodification by eliminating public or communal alternatives to the private provision or usage of goods, services, and resources. Furthermore, private ownership typically means that the respective good can be sold on a market—which again implies that it receives a market value in addition to its use value. At the same time, private owners usually have an interest in maximizing the returns on their investments, affecting accessibility of public resources and/or the way the respective goods and services are produced.

Liberalization

Liberalization is a policy that aims at transforming monopolistic markets and boosting cross-border trade. It has a lot in common with the process of deregulation described in the following section. However, rather than eliminating existing regulation, liberalization processes typically involve the creation of a new set of regulations, governing the newly liberalized sectors or trade areas. While in the case of privatization the main argument of public divestment is the beneficial effects of ownership, liberalization is based on the assumption that it is competition that forces (public or private) providers to increase efficiency and to deliver better goods and services at lower prices.[7]

Liberalization has frequently been applied to those sectors which in the postwar period were considered to be natural monopolies. The dependence of certain services on costly infrastructure, as in the case of an electricity network, meant that it was economically unfeasible to have two competing companies offering electricity to the same household (Florio 2013, 3–4). While in Europe network monopolies were usually publicly owned, in the United States monopolies are often held by private enterprises. In the European Union many of these monopolies have been eliminated in the past three decades. While the methods have differed somewhat between sectors and countries, the key innovation has been unbundling, or the separation of infrastructure maintenance and improvement from the other activities involved in the provision of a public good or service. In the case of electricity, for example, electricity transmission is separated from the generation and sale of electricity (Hermann and Pond 2012, 33).[8] As a result, competing retailers can use the same network and households can choose between two or more providers. However, the creation of electricity markets is not the result of deregulation. Quite the contrary: The use of common resources by competing providers has required the establishment of an elaborate regime of regulation, including the creation of market regulators (Hermann and Verhoest 2012, 20–22).

In some sectors, unbundling is not possible. Water companies, for example, refuse to use the same pipes, as mixing water changes the chemical composition and quality of water delivered to households. The British government simply created private water monopolies. In France, in contrast, the pipes remain in public ownership, but the operation of the water networks is awarded to private companies in temporary contracts. About 70 percent of water in France is provided by private companies through concessions that usually last between ten and fifteen years.[9] Hence companies do not compete for customers; they compete for the exclusive but temporary right to provide a service. Temporary concessions or franchises exist not only in the water sector; they are also used to introduce competition into railways, local public transportation, and other municipal services. Like in the case of unbundling, competitive tendering does not reduce regulation. Instead, it depends on the creation of an apparatus that drafts and observes highly complex contracts which not seldom become the object of litigation.[10]

Liberalization can also be enforced through free trade. Traditionally, free-trade agreements lower tariffs and other trade barriers for the cross-border exchange of goods. However, since the 1990s the focus of international trade negotiations has shifted to the trade of services. An important step in this respect was the adoption of the General Agreement on Trade in Services (GATS) in 1995. Excluded from a potential liberalization were only services supplied in the exercise of governmental authority, such as the police or the military (Krajewski 2003, 349–350). However, the GATS agreement does not force countries to open up their public monopolies. For the time being, countries still have to commit to the liberalization of specific service sectors. Attempts to make these commitments mandatory in a new round of GATS negotiations in the early 2000s have failed. Following the breakdown of the negotiations, some countries have sought to promote cross-border trade of services through bilateral agreements such as the EU-Canada trade deal (Raza 2016). Here, too, liberalization is based on a complex set of rules and processes rather than an eradication of existing regulations.

Liberalization enhances commodification by exposing private and public providers to competition. Faced with competition, providers are forced to cut costs and increase revenues with subsequent consequences for the form and content of services, as well for their accessibility. Furthermore, there can be liberalization without privatization, but in many cases former monopoly enterprises end up being privatized after the opening of markets (Hermann and Verhoest 2012, 17–19).

Deregulation

Deregulation has many commonalities with liberalization. In both cases the objective is to enhance competition. However, while liberalization depends on the adoption of new and often complex regulatory regimes, deregulation centers on the elimination or weakening of norms, standards, or rules that in one way or the other limit the freedom of action of profit-seeking corporations. The main rationale for deregulation is that these external interventions into markets prevent them from achieving efficient equilibria and therefore burden market participants, as well as the wider economy, with unnecessary costs.

A prime target of deregulation has been financial markets. In the United States, a series of financial reforms introduced in the 1980s and 1990s dismantled the New Deal system of financial regulation that was introduced in the 1930s in response to the 1929 stock market crash (Krippner 2011, chapter 3; Sherman 2009). Among other things, the reforms repealed the Glass-Steagall Act, which had separated commercial from investment banking in order to shelter households and non-financial businesses from the risk of financial speculation. At the same time, the government was reluctant to regulate new financial instruments and practices such as the trading of derivates, including, most notably, credit default swaps. Deregulation, in turn, has made financial investment more lucrative and has fueled speculation, with the effect that an increasing share of profits in the United States is made in the financial sector (Krippner 2011, 4, 15). Several authors have called this process financialization (Krippner 2011; Epstein 2005; Stockhammer 2004).

The deregulation of the US financial sector has also affected the housing market. While in the aftermath of the Great Depression regulation was introduced to streamline mortgage lending, and the thirty-year low-interest mortgage became standard among American home buyers, the deregulation of the mortgage market opened the possibility for the provision of all kinds of mortgage contracts, including mortgages with variable or adjustable interest rates and with delayed payments.[11] The latter two were particular popular among subprime borrowers and, together with predatory mortgage selling practices, played an important role in the 2007 subprime mortgage crisis, which led to the 2008–2009 financial collapse (Madden and Marcuse 2016, 28–29). However, deregulation also changed the rental market. Deregulation in this context involves the weakening of tenants' rights and protections. To take one example, between 1981 and 2011 the number of rent-controlled apartments in New York City shrank from 285,000 to less than 39,000 (Madden and Marcuse 2016, 30). Similar developments took place in other cities in the United States, as well as in other parts of the world.

Another major target of deregulation has been labor markets. Governments around the world have introduced major reforms in employment legislation. The content of the reforms differs depending on the national employment system, but a comparison of measures introduced in Latin American countries during the period of structural adjustment in the 1980s and 1990s with the structural reforms imposed in the European crisis countries after 2008 reveals a number of similarities. Among these are the promotion of fixed-term contracts, the extension of probation periods, the shortening of notice periods, and the reduction of severance pay. The changes in employment contracts are complemented by a decentralization of collective bargaining, i.e., the shift of the bargaining arena from the national or sector level to the company level (where unions are more susceptible to the power of employers), a weakening of trade union rights, and the reduction or freezing of minimum wages (Hermann 2017a, 523–526).[12]

In some cases, deregulation has fueled precarization. Precarious jobs are forms of employment that provide very little, if any, security, incomes close to the poverty line, unpredictable work schedules, and little prospect of moving up the career ladder (Standing 2011, chapter 1). For example, the German government introduced a labor market and welfare reform in the early 2000s named after the former Volkswagen manager Peter Hartz. Part of the reform was the creation of so-called mini jobs. Mini jobs are positions that pay 450 euro or less per month. They are highly attractive from an employer perspective because they are largely exempted from the obligation to pay social security contributions. The number of mini job holders subsequently increased from 4.83 million in March 2003 to 7.1 million in December 2007 (Hermann 2015a, 144–145). Of course, 450 euro per month hardly covers living expenses in Germany. However, conditions elsewhere are far worse: British employers increasingly use so-called zero-hour contracts. These agreements hold workers on call without requiring employers to provide them with employment and, hence, a minimum income they can count on. Zero-hour contracts account only for 2.8 percent of all jobs in the United Kingdom, but their number has increased dramatically from 108,000 in 2004 to 905,000 in 2016 (Office for National Statistics 2017).

Because they come with few obligations, employers also like freelance contracts, or what in some countries are called self-employed workers. In contrast to regular employees, self-employed workers are not entitled to vacation, sick pay, overtime pay, and other employment rights. When the "contractor" is highly dependent on the "purchaser" and subject to management instructions and time constraints, critics call such practices bogus self-employment. Platform enterprises, i.e., companies whose businesses depend on internet platforms, have been particularly keen to avoid regular employment contracts (Sundararajan 2016, 162). Uber drivers, for example, are paid as independent contractors even though they are closely monitored and frequently instructed by the company.[13] Drivers not only suffer from a lack of

security—among other things, they receive no income when they are sick—
but their hourly wages hardly pay for a decent living (Zoepf et al. 2018).[14]
However, in these cases, precarization is not the result of the elimination of
existing regulations; rather, it is the result of the reluctance or unwillingness
of governments to regulate new businesses or newly emerging industries. Yet
the lack of regulation gives new businesses a decisive competitive advantage
and puts pressure on established companies which employ their staff on regular contracts (Plimmer 2018). The result is what Benjamin Edelman and
Damien Geradin (2016) have called "spontaneous deregulation."

Deregulation promotes commodification by eliminating regulations that
in one way or another limit the commodity character of goods and services exchanged on markets. Labor is a prime example: The deregulation of
labor markets has resulted in a recommodification of labor power. The deregulation of financial markets has fueled financialization with the effect
that profit-making has largely been detached from the production of (non-
financial) goods and services. By decoupling market value from use value,
financialization can be seen as the most advanced form of commodification.

Marketization

While liberalization and deregulation are aiming at "freeing" markets and
promoting competition, marketization refers to the creation of markets
where none has existed before. The rationale for marketization is the same as
for liberalization: market incentives are supposed to induce service providers
to increase efficiency, improve quality, and in the case of markets for environmental goods to adopt more environmentally friendly technology.

An example of a newly created market is the European Union Emissions
Trading Scheme. The roots of the European emissions market go back to
the Kyoto Protocol. The Kyoto Protocol is an international agreement that
was adopted in 1997 under the United Nations' Framework Convention
on Climate Change. While all signatories declared their intention to reduce greenhouse gas emissions, 37 industrialized countries and the then
15 member states of the European Union committed to binding targets. EU
member states promised a joint 8 percent reduction of greenhouse gas emissions by 2012 (compared to 1990 levels). To give signatories some flexibility,
the Kyoto Protocol allowed for countries to buy emissions rights from other
countries that are below their targets.[15] Emissions trading was included as a

concession to the United States and against the will of the EU member states. However, while the United States subsequently pulled out of the agreement, the European Union made emissions trading a cornerstone of its environmental policy (Ellermeran et al. 2010, chapter 2).

The basic idea behind an emissions trading scheme is that polluters initially are granted or sold a certain amount of emissions that they are allowed to release over a specific period of time. Governments, then, reduce emissions by cutting back allowances in subsequent periods (Nordhaus 2013, 223). The beauty of emissions trading is that companies are not forced to cut back emissions. Companies which have used up their allowances can buy additional emissions rights on the market (therefore the term "cap and trade"). However, the increasing price for emissions (caused by the reduction of allowances) should provide a strong incentive to adopt emissions-reducing technology. Not only that: polluters can even make a profit by cutting emissions below their allowances and selling the difference on the emissions market.

This is essentially how the European Union Emissions Trading Scheme works. After the adoption of the legal framework in 2003, major polluters such as power stations and industrial plants were identified across the European Union and emissions allowances assigned to them free of charge.[16] At the same time, polluters were permitted to trade emission allowances with the price per ton of carbon dioxide decided by demand and supply (Ellerman et al. 2010, chapter 2). From 2008 onward, allowances were reduced, and from 2013 onward, allowances were increasingly auctioned off rather than allocated for free. However, the price of a ton of carbon dioxide has not increased steadily as anticipated. Prices fell close to zero at the end of the first trading period, mainly as a result of very generous initial allocations. After recovering, prices again dropped by about 50 percent in 2009 as a result of the economic crisis. Prices fell even further in the post-crisis years and remained low until 2017 when they started to pick up again (Ellerman, Marcantonini, and Zaklan 2015). The price volatility has hampered investment decisions as companies have difficulties deciding if it is cheaper to introduce new technology or to buy allowances on the emissions market.

Markets have also been installed in areas of social provisioning that are traditionally based on planning and coordination. An example of this strategy is the British National Health Service (NHS). Rather than being broken up and privatized, as were other public services in Thatcher's Britain, the NHS was subjected to a series of reforms that were aimed at introducing market elements into a genuine public service. The NHS was created after the Second World War as a universal healthcare system, funded through taxes, administered by the government, and delivered free of charge by a nationwide organization (Lister 2008, chapter 1). It was widely admired as a modern, rational, and highly efficient healthcare system in the postwar decades. However, when growth in healthcare costs started to outpace growth in GDP, the NHS was increasingly seen as too costly, wasteful, and out of touch with patients' needs. The prevailing answer to all of these problems was marketization (Lister 2008, chapter 3).

After the introduction of mandatory tendering of secondary services such as cleaning and catering within the NHS, a decisive step was the establishment of the internal market in 1991 (Lister 2008, 81–82; Pollock 2004, 43–47). The reform established what in the literature is referred to as a purchaser-provider split, simulating the existence of buyers and sellers in regular markets. Essentially it meant that the NHS was broken up into two parts: one that is responsible for funding and the other for delivering health services (Hermann 2009b, 133). The regional Health Authorities that were established in the 1970s to increase local influence in NHS planning became the purchasing arm of the NHS. Occasionally, purchasing authority was transferred to general practitioners with large practices. Together, they became responsible for buying health services for local populations from NHS hospitals. Hospitals, in turn, became semi-autonomous organizations, so-called hospital trusts, which could no longer rely on payments from the Department of Health, but instead had to win contracts from fundholding organizations (Hermann 2009b).

Subsequent reforms attempted to improve the functioning of the internal market. While initially being hostile to the internal market, New Labour quickly went on to strengthen the autonomy of market participants after winning the 1997 elections. On the purchaser side, Regional Health Authorities were replaced by Primary Care Trusts, set up as business-like organizations with their own chief executives and with individual budgets to monitor (Talbot-Smith and Pollock 2006, 41–43). On the provider side, hospital trusts became foundation trusts, which meant that they received even more autonomy, including the autonomy to borrow money and carry over operation surpluses into the next yearly budget (Talbot-Smith and Pollock 2006, 63–66). More frequently, however, they accumulated debt (total debt accumulated by hospital trusts and foundations trusts in 2015–2016 was 2.5 billion pounds; Kings Fund 2018). A 2012 reform, introduced by a conservative government, abolished Primary Care Trusts and instead created Clinical Commissioning Groups made up of local general practitioners as new entities responsible for purchasing secondary health services (Nuffield Trust 2010). The hope was that assigning financial responsibility to general practitioners would make them more reluctant to refer patients to specialists or hospitals, thereby reducing costs. However, the government also instructed the new commissioning organizations to purchase services from selected private-sector providers and to give patients a choice between different specialists and hospitals (Leys 2017, 13).

Despite two decades of reform, the NHS internal market is still a far cry from a real market. Its main difference from a real market is that failing providers rarely disappear. The simple reason is that closing hospitals usually means leaving communities without access to care—and this contradicts the government's responsibility to provide adequate healthcare across the country (Leys 2017, 14). Typically, failing hospitals are integrated into more successful trusts, even though success is relative given that two-thirds of hospital trusts and foundation trusts in England run a deficit (Kings Fund 2018). This is what happened in the case of the South London Healthcare Trust: It was dissolved in 2012 after accumulating 250 million pounds in debt, and its three hospitals were reassigned to neighboring trusts. What's more, to avoid hospital closures, local healthcare commissioners tend to renew contracts with established providers, thereby limiting the effects of competition (Goddard, Manion, and Ferguson 1997, 12–13).

Marketization fuels commodification by creating markets where none has existed before. The market for emissions allowances has, subsequently, turned carbon-dioxide emissions into a tradable commodity. Some of the markets have been created in the public sector where users do not pay for services and failing providers rarely disappear. Such quasi markets, and other New Public Management strategies discussed in the following section, are part of a process of fictitious commodification.

New Public Management

New Public Management (NPM) is an additional reform policy that has had a major impact on the supply of public goods and services in recent decades. At a very general level, NPM attempts to introduce private business management tools and techniques into the public sector. As such, NPM embraces marketization and outsourcing, but in addition suggests a series of related reforms of activities that cannot be turned into market transactions and contracted out to private companies. NPM proponents argue that the proposed reforms increase administrative efficiency and make public organizations more flexible and accountable.

NPM captures a series of public management reforms that were initially introduced in the United Kingdom, the United States, and other Anglo-Saxon countries in the late 1970s and from there spread around the world. Even though the reforms differed somewhat between countries and sectors, public administration scholars identified a set of key strategies or NPM doctrines that the various proposals held in common (Hood 1991; Osborne and Gaebler 1993; Diefenbach 2009). Among them are a move toward decentralization and the creation of semi-autonomous units with individual budgets and executive managers. They also include the widespread use of contracts to formalize inter-institutional relationships and responsibilities. At the same time, services provided by different units of the same organization are billed as if they were provided by an external contractor. NPM also implies a focus on output measurement and the development of performance indicators. Finally, NPM entails a change in the perception of service users from patients, students, or citizens with specific needs to consumers. The latter two strategies—performance measurement and the transformation of citizens into consumers—play a particularly important role in NPM's ability to commodify the provision of public services.

Britain's NHS was not only a forerunner with regard to marketization. It was also an early adopter of performance measurements. The initial system that was introduced in 1983 was made up of seventy indicators, including eleven to assess clinical practice (Jowett and Rothwell 1988, 10–12).[17] The list of indicators was repeatedly revised and quickly expanded to several hundred items in the subsequent years. By the 1990s, close to 2,000 health service indicators were collected (Roberts 1990, 100–102). In the early 2000s, data were aggregated into league tables. At the height of this development, hospitals received between zero and three stars, reflecting their overall quality of care.

From 2009 onward, performance assessment was outsourced from the Department of Health to the formally independent Care Quality Commission. The commission currently rates hospitals according to five dimensions (safe, effective, caring, responsive, well led) and four levels of achievement (outstanding, good, requires improvement, inadequate).

However, the value of these assessments has been questioned after a report revealed substandard conditions at Mid Staffordshire Foundation Trust (Lewis 2016, 327). The issue was first raised by relatives of patients who died in the hospital. Apparently, the annual performance assessments had failed to alert the quality watchdogs. On paper, the hospital's performance had even been good enough to be granted the status of a Foundation Trust, which meant that Staffordshire hospital was no longer under supervision of the Department of Health. The public inquiry into the Staffordshire hospital scandal also revealed that the poor treatment standards were partly caused by managerial decisions to cut costs in order to achieve the financial (performance) indicators required to become a Foundation Trust (see Chapter 4).

Universities and faculty have also increasingly been subjected to performance evaluations. As in the healthcare sector, the quality of academic output is difficult to judge, except by other academics with similar expertise. This is the rationale behind the peer-review processes in academic research and publishing, as well as personal and institutional evaluations. However, while peer review is able to assess the conformity of academic work with certain quality standards, it cannot rank performance (i.e., it cannot say this academic, department, or university is better than another one). It also means that administrators are dependent on the judgment of academic professionals when assessing the performance of individuals or departments. For many administrators in the government and in universities, this was not a very satisfying situation (NPM is also about empowering managers at the cost of professionals such as doctors and university professors). Since the 1980s, universities have increasingly adopted quantitative measurements to replace or complement peer-review processes. In some countries, universities have done so voluntarily; in others, they were forced to do so by government reforms. Two measurements have become particular important: the number of publications in indexed journals as well as student evaluations.

One way to quantify academic output is simply to count publications (books, chapters, articles, etc.). The problem with this approach is that the number of publications says little about the quality of publications. An alternative method is the creation of citation indices.[18] The idea behind citation indices is that the importance of a journal can be assessed by counting how often its articles are cited in other publications. The more important, the more citations. And the more citations, the greater the journal's so-called impact factor (Vanclay 2012). In most academic disciplines, research output is meanwhile measured by the number of articles in high-impact-factor journals. This approach not only discriminates against other publications such as books; as most of the high-ranking journals publish in English, it also discriminates against other languages. What makes the assessment even more dubious is the fact that it is not academic bodies that determine which journals are included in the index and which are not, but private "science" businesses.[19] In fact, contrary to the academic principle of verifiability, the exact way in which impact factors are calculated is often a business secret. There are severe doubts that citation indices capture scientific quality (San Francisco Declaration 2012).[20] However, by determining the future of many academics, they have a profound impact on research. Researchers select their topics and research methods with an eye on possible publication in high-ranking journals, discouraging unconventional or radical projects (Busch 2017, 89).[21]

Another form of quantification of academic output are student evaluations of teaching (SET). While citation indices allegedly measure the quality of research, student evaluations are supposed to measure the quality of teaching. As such, they have become a common practice on campuses in North America, Europe, and other parts of the world (Spooren, Brockx, and Mortelmans 2013). At the end of each course, students receive the possibility to "grade" their teacher. Questionnaires cover different aspects of teaching, but usually also include an overall assessment (at UC Berkeley, students are asked to rate the "overall effectiveness of the instructor"). High student ratings are taken as evidence for a high quality of teaching, while low scores mean low quality.

There are two main objections against the quantification of teaching quality. First, student evaluations do not capture teaching quality. They capture if students like/dislike teachers, and there are many factors that impact their judgment that have nothing to do with teaching quality. Studies have shown that important factors are age, gender, the ways teachers are dressed, shared sense of humor, as well as the difficulty of exams (Stark and Freishtad 2014).[22] Second, it is statistically wrong to compare evaluations of different teachers and calculate averages because the evaluation scores are not numerical variables (Stark and Freishtad 2014). They look like numbers, but they are labels (the numbers could be replaced by descriptions such as "excellent," "very good," "good," "sufficient," "insufficient" without losing any information). And it doesn't make sense to average labels (a combination of "excellent" and "insufficient" does not amount to "good"). It is striking that universities consistently produce these averages against the better knowledge of their statistical departments (Stark and Freishtad 2014).[23] As in the case of research, student evaluations impact the way students are taught. Some authors link the grade inflation, i.e., the increasing average grade awarded at American colleges, to the growing importance of student evaluations. By giving students higher grades, faculty members hope to receive better evaluations (Stroebe 2016). [24]

In spite of the difficulties and, perhaps impossibility, to quantify quality, quantitative performance measurements are regularly used to grant or withhold tenure, to fire non-tenured faculty, and to allocate research funds and other financial resources. Together with other quantitative indicators, they are also used to rank universities in national and international league tables, such as the Times Higher Education Ranking and US News College Ranking.

With the introduction of markets and performance-based rankings, public service users are increasingly perceived as consumers. The main rationale for this model is that consumers are active and have a choice, whereas in the old system users were passive recipients of public-sector output (Clarke et al. 2007, chapter 2). Choice, according to NPM advocates, not only empowers users, but also forces providers to improve their services (Le Grand 2007, chapter 2). New Labour embraced this idea and made consumerism a central tenet of its public service reforms in Britain in the late 1990s and early 2000s (Needham 2007). The result is not only an erosion of the public sphere as something distinctive from the private (Marquand 2004). Consumerism also reduces public service users to citizens without a voice, as consumers can choose between different suppliers, but have little say in what is offered and under what conditions. By the same token, consumer status obscures the intimate and reflective relationship—what is sometimes called co-production—between service providers and users. Examples include the relationship between doctors and patients, or between teachers and students (Alford 2009). Contrary to consumer logics, money cannot buy a good education or good health when students are not participating in the learning process and patients do not follow instructions from their doctors. Ultimately, the most important effect of NPM is that once service users see themselves as consumers with a personal budget rather than as citizens with rights, they can much more easily be persuaded to pay for public services.

NPM's performance measurements promote fictitious commodification by subjugating quality to quantity.[25] At the same time, the transformation of service users into consumers makes them susceptible to formal commodification: as a consumer it is only natural to pay for a service. And as soon as services are paid for, it is also not unusual that better services cost more money, leaving those without money dependent on poor services.

Austerity

Austerity is an economic and social policy that aims to reduce government debt, and in some cases, even to create budgetary surpluses. While it has a long history, austerity regained popularity following the crisis of postwar capitalism in the 1970s (Blyth 2013, chapter 5; Teeple 2017). The crisis also marked the end of the golden age of Keynesianism in which John Maynard Keynes's insights into the relationship between demand and growth dominated economic and social policy in developed countries. For Keynesian economists, the state had a crucial role to play in creating demand through government spending. With the neoliberal counter-revolution in the 1980s, public debt was increasingly denounced as a problem threatening economic stability, even though it remained unclear exactly how and when debt undermined economic growth.[26] Given the significant historical and country-specific variation in national debt—US debt, for example, exceeded 100 percent of GDP by the end of the Second World War—it is also far from clear at what point debt levels become unsustainable (Blyth 2013, 10–12). However, since supply-side economic policies precluded tax increases as a way to reduce the deficit—in fact, several countries lowered taxes during the 1980s—the main effect of austerity policies were cuts in public expenditure.[27]

Welfare expenditure is a popular target of spending cuts. There is some debate among welfare state scholars about the significance of retrenchment (Pierson 1994; Starke 2006). Some argue that welfare expenditure (as percentage of GDP) has stagnated or even increased since the 1980s. For these scholars, welfare states have proven much more resilient than is generally assumed. The main reason for this resilience is popular support for welfare measures, which scares politicians off from introducing major cuts (Starke 2006, 105–106).[28] However, governments have proven able to overcome such fears when pressured by creditors and international organizations. The 1980s debt crisis in Latin America was, for example, followed by major cuts in welfare systems as part of the IMF's imposed structural adjustment programs (Hermann 2017a). More recently, the 2008–2009 financial crisis—which, due to massive bank bailouts and in the Greek case the failure to cut back the deficit in the boom years, became a sovereign debt crisis in parts of Europe—also led to major cuts in welfare programs (Hermann 2017b; Vaughan-Whitehead 2013; Farnsworth and Irving 2011).

Initially many countries responded to the 2008–2009 recession with Keynesian deficit spending. Yet in Europe governments quickly shifted from economic stimulation to financial consolidation. From 2010 onward, one country after another adopted austerity packages, in some cases, several packages in a row. Greece and Ireland presented the most ambitious plans, cutting public spending by 18 percent of GDP (Hermann 2017b, 52). These spending cuts had a major effect on welfare spending. Hence, while in 2009 social protection expenditure increased in the European Union, expenditure growth leveled out in 2010, started to decline in 2011, and continued to fall in 2012. This trend was especially pronounced in those countries that were most severely affected by the crisis (Hermann 2017b, 53). It should be noted that social protection spending usually goes up during times of crisis because of growing unemployment and increasing poverty. Measures included major cuts in public pension systems, a reduction of unemployment benefits, as well as the lowering of social assistance, family allowances, and housing benefits (Hermann 2013).

The drastic spending cuts also severely affected the provision of public services. In Greece, a more than 30 percent cut in healthcare spending translated into hospital closures and the elimination of 35,000 healthcare-sector jobs (Tzannatos and Monogios 2013, 278; Stuckler and Basu 2013, 84–85). Budget cuts also affected health prevention, with the consequence that HIV infections increased by 52 percent between January and May 2011 (Stuckler and Basu 2013, 77–78). David Stuckler and Sanjay Basu (2013, 114) conclude that "[h]ad the austerity experiments been governed by the same rigorous standards as clinical trials, they would have been discontinued long ago. . . . The side effects of the austerity treatment have been severe and often deadly." Greece may be an extreme case, but it is not an exception. Other countries in Europe, too, have reduced their healthcare spending in the wake of austerity. In fact, Aron Reeves and colleagues (2014, 4) have found in a study of healthcare spending in the European Union between 1995 and 2011 that, on average, a 100 US dollar reduction in tax revenue was associated with a 2.72 US dollar drop in healthcare expenditure.

In the United States, state-level expenditure cuts adopted in the aftermath of the financial crisis led to shrinking budgets for higher education. On average, states spent 20 percent less per student in 2014–2015 than they did in 2007–2008. In five states, the reduction amounted to more than 35 percent

(Mitchell and Leachman 2015). In the United Kingdom, too, government expenditure per student at higher education institutions has nearly been halved between 1990–1991 and 2010–2011. However, expenditure may increase substantially in the future when it turns out that students cannot pay back their government-backed student loans (Belfield, Crawford, and Sibieta 2017, 24–25).[29]

The welfare state has a de-commodifying effect by granting an existence that is partly independent from markets and the ability to buy and sell (see Chapter 7). By reducing welfare spending and cutting back public services, austerity reverses this process and advances (re)commodification.

Conclusion

Neoliberalism has pushed commodification through a variety of policies in recent decades. This chapter has focused on six major strategies. Privatization refers to the transfer of ownership of assets or access rights to resources from public to private entities. It also describes the private provision of public services. Examples include land grabbing, slum clearing, the sale of public assets and resources, PPPs, contracting out, and underinvestment. Privatization fuels commodification by eroding or eliminating public or communal alternatives to the private provision or usage of goods, services, and resources. Furthermore, private ownership typically means that the respective good can be sold on a market—which again implies that its value can be expressed in monetary terms. At the same time, private owners usually have an interest in maximizing the returns on their investments. Liberalization implies the termination of monopolies and the promotion of cross-border trade. As such, liberalization mainly affects sectors that were considered natural monopolies during the postwar period, including, among others, electricity, water, and public transportation. Liberalization typically results in several companies competing for customers, but it can also take the form that companies compete for exclusive yet temporary contracts. In addition, the opening of public-sector markets has also become an issue in international trade agreements. Liberalization enhances commodification by exposing private and public providers to competition. Faced with competition, providers try to cut costs and thereby alter the form and content of services as well their accessibility. While liberalization usually demands the adoption of new and frequently rather complex forms of regulation, deregulation aims at the elimination of norms and standards that limit the commodity character of goods and services exchanged on markets. As such, deregulation goes hand in hand with (re)commodification. Examples include the deregulation of labor and rental markets. In the case of financial markets, deregulation has fueled financialization with the effect that profit-making has largely been detached from the production of (non-financial) goods and services. By decoupling profit-making from the creation of (use) value, financialization can be seen as the most advanced form of commodification. Marketization is a process whereby new markets are installed in areas where none has existed before. The European Union has created a market for emissions trading which, subsequently, has turned emissions allowances into a commodity that can be bought and sold. In some cases, markets are installed in areas of social provisioning that have traditionally been dependent on planning and coordination and where users do not pay for services. Even though failing providers rarely disappear, marketization still puts pressure on hospitals and other public organizations and thereby contributes to fictitious commodification. NPM is a specific approach to managing public organizations. It embraces marketization, but also promotes commodification by introducing performance measurement into the provision of public services such as healthcare and higher education. Like prices, performance indicators impose a quantitative standard on qualitatively unique services, thereby subjugating their use values to an abstract metric norm. NPM also prepares the ground for commodification by turning public service users into consumers who are accustomed to paying for goods and services. Finally, austerity supports re-commodification by scaling back the welfare state and weakening welfare rights, as well as by underfunding the provision of non-commodified goods and services. As a result, people become more dependent on markets for access to what used to be public goods and services, as well as for obtaining the income necessary to pay for their living expenses.

4

Consequences of Commodification

Introduction

This chapter discusses the effects of commodification. It does so by elaborating twelve major tendencies associated with commodification. The tendencies are derived from various studies on the impact of commodification, including a large-scale study on the effects of liberalization and privatization of public services in Europe (Hermann and Flecker 2012a). The twelve tendencies were selected because they all have somewhat troubling effects, at least for those concerned with human prosperity, inclusiveness, equality, and sustainability. The purpose of this chapter is not to give a full account of the advantages and disadvantages of commodification. Rather, the purpose is to show that commodification is not only problematic when it affects certain goods, services, human attributes, and social behavior. As I will show in the following pages, commodification inevitably comes with a number of consequences that negatively affect the lives of a significant number of people and endangers the environment.

The examples I draw on are taken from six essential areas of human reproduction and the human-nature relationship: healthcare; (higher) education; public transport and utilities; housing; food; and agriculture, fishing, and forestry. Comparing changes in such a diverse range of activities is not without its problems since each sphere has its own dynamics and particularities. Scholars spend years studying each of them. Yet a major goal of this book is precisely to show that commodification processes have similar consequences in different social, economic, and ecological contexts. Of course, the national context, i.e., national culture, institutions, and class compromises, also plays an important role in explaining commodification processes and their specific effects. However, the focus here is on commonalities, and the examples are therefore taken from a range of countries, including, most notably the United States. Furthermore, the twelve tendencies are not equally important in each area and country. The evidence presented in the following pages is largely taken from cases where commodification has a substantial impact.

The Critique of Commodification. Christoph Hermann, Oxford University Press. © Oxford University Press 2021.
DOI: 10.1093/oso/9780197576755.003.0004

Exclusion of potential users

Commodification usually means that a good or service is given a price or a fee that a user must pay to take advantage of the related benefits. Individuals who cannot afford to pay the price are excluded from using the good or service. While it is widely accepted in capitalist economies that people must pay for goods and services, lack of access to essential goods and services is sometimes considered a problem. The United States is one of just a few developed countries that has a predominately private healthcare system. The private nature mainly stems from the fact that most Americans rely on private health insurance to cover medical expenses.[1] There is a public system (Medicare and Medicaid), but it covers only the elderly and some of the poor. Many Americans and their families receive health insurance through their jobs as a benefit granted by their employers. Others buy health insurance on the insurance market. The 2010 Affordable Health Care Act significantly expanded the population covered by health insurance through a mix of obligations and incentives, as well as an expansion of the public program. However, almost 30 million Americans, or more than 9 percent of the population, still lacked health insurance coverage in 2019.[2]

An exclusion rate of more than 10 percent among the non-elderly population is high compared to the predominately public systems in Europe and Canada. Even having private health insurance in the United States does not mean that all healthcare expenses are covered. Depending on the price and the buyer's ability to choose a doctor outside the insurer's network, the policy may only cover a certain percentage of the costs (until the adoption of the Affordable Care Act, some insurance plans included annual limits for total insurance payments). According to one study, as many as 31 million individuals, or 23 percent of the 19- to 64-year-old US population, were underinsured in 2014. This means that their out-of-pocket payments accounted for more than 10 percent of yearly household income, and more than 5 percent for households with low incomes (Collins et al. 2015).[3]

Access to higher education has also become increasingly dependent on the ability to pay. In the United States, students have always had to pay for private colleges, but public universities were free or at least relatively affordable in the postwar decades.[4] Average tuition for US public four-year colleges increased by a staggering 1,767 percent between 1971 and 2009 (Heller 2011, 16). Despite this rise, public universities are still more affordable (for in-state students) than comparable private institutions. In the United

Kingdom, too, studying has become an increasingly costly affair. Maximum tuition fees charged by British universities have increased from 1,000 pounds per year when they were first introduced in 1998 to 9,000 pounds in 2012 (Bolton 2016).

Even though tuition has increased dramatically, enrollment numbers have not fallen in the United States or the United Kingdom. The reason is that tuition hikes have been mediated by an expansion of student loans. Student loans allow students to pay for tuition and living expenses years after they have graduated. While playing a marginal role in the 1980s, federal student loans in the United States accounted for more than 1.5 trillion US dollars in 2018.[5] In the United Kingdom, student debt reached 105 billion pounds in the same year and is expected to reach 450 million pounds by 2050 (Bolton 2018). While the loans allow students from less fortunate families to obtain a college degree, they present a major burden for young adults, and some are never able to repay them. Every tenth US student of the 2015 cohort that started to pay back student loans defaulted on his/her federal student loan before September 2017.[6] However, when we expand the observation period, the default rate increases significantly (Scott-Clayton 2018). A study that followed students who started in 2003–2004 found that 27.2 percent defaulted within twelve years (National Center for Education Statistics 2017).[7]

Lack of access to utilities is mainly a problem in the developing world. In recent years, the privatization of public infrastructure or utility provision in developing countries has often been followed by an increase in fees or prices, especially for low-income households. Advocates of privatization have welcomed this step because in their view prior fees were often subsidized, undermining the proper functioning of utility markets (Nellis 2006, 17). Following the adoption of private business standards and practices by the country's national electricity provider, 9.6 million people in South Africa were affected by electricity cutoffs between 1994 and 2002 (Macdonald 2009, 26).[8] In Bolivia, the private acquisition of the municipal water network in the city of Cochabamba in 1999 was followed by a price hike of more than 35 percent. For many poor residents, this meant that they had to spend more than one-fourth of their household income on water, further constraining already tight household budgets. As a result, the local population started the so-called Cochabamba water wars, which ended with the deployment of military forces and with foreign investors leaving the country—and suing the government for 25 million US dollars in lost investments (Lobina 2000; Shultz 2003).

In Europe, the liberalization and privatization of electricity and gas did not result in similar dramatic cutoff rates and price increases. However, profit orientation has also increased pressure on staff of utility providers to be less understanding and accommodating when customers have problems paying their bills (Hermann and Pond 2012, 49). In the United Kingdom, further-more, rising energy prices have become a major problem for low-income households. In England, 2.55 million households, or 11.1 percent of all households, were affected by fuel poverty in 2016. This means that (because of poor insulation of their homes) they pay more for energy than average households, and after paying their bills their residual income slips below the poverty line (Department for Business, Energy and Industrial Strategy 2018).

For most people, access to housing also depends on the ability to buy a house or apartment or to pay rent. According to official statistics, 355,212 individuals were homeless in the United States in 2016, and 35 percent of the homeless population were families with children (US Department of Housing and Urban Development 2018). Unofficially, the number may be significantly higher. The British nonprofit Shelter estimates that 319,837 people were without a home in the United Kingdom in 2018 when people sleeping on the streets, in shelters, and in temporary accommodations pro-vided by the government were taken into account (Shelter 2018). The size of the homeless population would certainly be higher if it were not for family and friends taking in people who lose their homes or cannot find accom-modation. In the United States, 30 percent of all households were "doubled up" in 2011, which means that they encompassed more than two adults.[9] People often lose their homes when they lose their jobs, but in some cases the cause is also reckless mortgage lending or rapidly rising rents. People who can no longer afford to pay rent risk being evicted. According to Princeton University's Eviction Lab, 898,479 US households, or 2.34 percent of renter-occupied households, were evicted in 2016.[10]

Hunger is usually perceived as a problem of the developing world. A number of low-income countries have trouble producing enough food to feed their citizens. However, hunger also exists in advanced capitalist coun-tries. Yet here the problem is not a lack of food. The problem is that some people cannot pay for it. According to Alisha Coleman-Jensen et al. (2016), 15.8 million American households, or 12.7 percent of all US households, were food insecure in 2015. This means that some household members tempo-rarily suffered from a lack of food during the year. In 6.3 million households, the lack of food was more severe and resulted in a sustained deviation of normal eating patterns (Coleman-Jensen et al. 2016). While people suffer from hunger, about 30 percent of food in the United States is not eaten (Buzby, Wells, and Hyman 2014; Gunters et al. 2017). Retailers usually dump food that has not been sold, rather than giving it away for free. About 10 percent of the food supply on the retail level in the United States ends in the garbage, where it creates additional costs for waste disposal (Gunters et al. 2017; O'Neil 2019, chapter 9).[11]

Neglect of needs that are not backed by sufficient purchasing power or cannot be satisfied in a profitable manner

Lacking access to a good or service because of a lack of money is one thing. Lacking access because the respective good or service is simply not available is another. In a fully commodified system, goods and services are only offered when the provision promises sufficiently high profits. To be profitable, the revenues from sales must be high enough to justify investments in development as well as costs for production and distribution—including, in some instances, the maintenance of a costly infrastructure. This means that individuals may lack access to certain goods and services not because of an individual failure to pay, but because they belong to a group of citizens with insufficient collective purchasing power.

For example, if you happen to have a rare disease that affects less than 200,000 individuals in the United States, the pharmaceutical industry considers it unprofitable to develop drugs for your condition. They do in practice develop such drugs, but do so only because they receive subsidies from the US government (Angell 2005, 45).[12] Some diseases affect large numbers of people but are still neglected because those affected mainly live in low-income countries. Hence up to one billion people suffering from tropical diseases are abandoned by the pharmaceutical industry because their collective ability to pay is not large enough to justify investments in research and development. Researchers have revealed that of 1,393 new chemical entities marketed by the pharmaceutical industry between 1975 and 1999, only 16 were for tropical diseases and tuberculosis (Trouiller et al. 2002, 2188). Following growing pressure by the World Health Organization and others, efforts to tackle tropical diseases have been stepped up since the end of the 1990s. From 2000 to 2011, 37 out of 850 new therapeutic products developed were indicated for neglected diseases (Pedrique et al. 2013). However, the chance of a drug being brought to market for cancer or another first-world disease is still much greater than for a third-world epidemic.

To some extent, the spread of tropical diseases is caused by a lack of access to clean water and sanitation. According to a 2006 study, 78.5 percent of the richest quintile of low-income countries had access to water, but only 41.1 percent of the poorest quintile did. For sanitation, the numbers were 68.8 percent and 27.2, respectively (Estache 2006, 6). A more recent World Bank report covering eighteen low-income countries has confirmed this picture: the urban poor are two to three times less likely to have adequate sanitation than wealthy residents (World Bank 2016, viii). However, the same report notes that 74 percent of the poor in these countries live in rural areas, with many lacking access to proper water and sanitation infrastructures (World Bank 2016, viii).

While access to water and sanitation is usually not a major problem, rural households in developed countries are also disadvantaged when it comes to access to public infrastructures such as public transportation, postal services, and high-speed internet.[13] According to the Communications Commission (2020, 18), 22.3 percent of Americans in rural areas and 27.7 percent of Americans in Tribal lands lacked access to high-speed terrestrial internet in 2018. In contrast, only 1.5 percent of Americans in urban areas had to live without a fast internet connection (Communications Commission 2020). The neglect of profit-oriented companies should not come as a surprise: low-income households are more likely to fail to submit payments, and rural homes are costlier to connect to the network.

The economy's neglect of needs that are not backed by enough purchasing power can also be seen in the housing market. Here the problem is usually described as lack of affordable housing. Housing is deemed affordable when rent and utilities do not exceed 30 percent of household income. Many individuals and families are forced to pay more because their incomes are so low or costs are so high that 30 percent of household income does not pay for a market-based rent. According to the National Low-Income Housing Coalition (2017), there is a lack of 7.4 million affordable rental housing units for Americans living at or below the poverty line or living with 30 percent or less of the area's median income.[14] This means that 75 percent of poor households do not live in an affordable home. In the case of large metropolitan areas, the percentage increases to 88 percent (National Low-Income Housing Coalition 2017).

Focus on those needs whose satisfaction promises high profits, frequently at the cost of needs that are less lucrative

The neglect of needs that are not backed by sufficient purchasing power is complemented by a focus on those needs whose satisfaction promises high profits. The highest profits in healthcare are made by the pharmaceutical industry. This should come as no surprise, as it is much more profitable to sell a pill to millions of patients than to provide a medical service that involves the performance of large amounts of highly skilled labor.[15] However, even within the hospital industry, profit orientation affects the supply of treatments. For-profit hospitals tend to focus on more profitable interventions and to neglect less profitable treatments. A comparison between for-profit and not-for-profit hospitals in the United States shows that the former are more likely to provide open heart surgeries and less likely to offer psychiatric emergency care (Horwitz 2005, 794–795). While reimbursement rates for open heart surgery are relatively generous, payments for psychiatric emergency hardly cover the costs of care (Horwitz 2005, 792–793).[16] In a study that looked at 22 public hospitals that were converted into private for-profit institutions, Stefano Villa and Nancy Kane (2013) also found that the privatized hospitals dropped valuable but unprofitable services. While Villa and Kane (2013) did not find significant change with respect to uncompensated care, Kamal R. Desai, Carol Van Deusen Lucas, and Gary J. Young (2000) found in an earlier study covering 52 privatized hospitals that while private not-for-profit hospitals upheld the amount of charity care, private for-profit hospitals significantly cut back on unpaid care.

While for-profit hospitals in the United States focus on lucrative treatments, private healthcare companies in the United Kingdom almost exclusively perform highly standardized, low-risk procedures, usually in outpatient treatment centers. As part of the marketization of the NHS, the British government has invited private healthcare companies to supply elective treatments such as cataract surgeries and hip replacements (Player and Leys 2008). Low risk also means that private providers can turn away patients with more than one medical condition and direct them to an NHS facility (Turner et al. 2011, 526). Profit margins per elective surgery are relatively small, but overall profits are substantial because providers can exploit economies of scale (Turner et al. 2011, 525).[17] Hence while initially elective surgery may not have been the first choice of the private sector, it turned out to be a rather profitable business opportunity—whereas the one time a private healthcare company took over an NHS hospital, the business endeavor failed bitterly (Watt, Nicholas, and Ramesh 2015).

By contrast, in developing countries with a lack of funding for public healthcare, private for-profit companies often provide first-class (i.e., comparable with Western standards) health services for the rich or for families that pool all their financial resources to pay for treatment. However, in India there is also a highly developed healthcare industry that focuses on services for patients from high-income countries, including treatments that are not covered by the countries' health insurance schemes (Hopkins et al. 2010). The results are fertility clinics and centers for plastic surgery that almost exclusively treat foreign patients. In the literature, this phenomenon is described as "medical tourism."[18] While these cutting-edge facilities treat foreign patients with unpleasant but non-critical conditions, millions of Indians, including thousands with severe medical problems, struggle to receive adequate treatment.

Universities, too, have adopted new business models to increase revenues. American and English universities in particular, sometimes in cooperation with local institutions, have opened overseas campuses in order to attract wealthy students from developing countries (McBrunie and Ziguras 2006; McGettigan 2013, 121–123; Heller 2016, 173). In the United Kingdom, higher education has become a major export industry, accounting for an estimated 17.5 billion pounds, or 3.5 percent of all exports in 2011 (HM Government 2013, 5). At the same time, universities have increased admission numbers of international students who pay higher fees than domestic students. In the United Kingdom, foreign nationals make up almost 20 percent of all higher education students.[19] For the same reason, US public universities such as the University of California–Berkeley have increased the number of out-of-state students (Applegate 2012). To improve profitability, higher education providers also increasingly focus on popular programs or programs for which they can charge higher fees at the cost of less attractive or less business-relevant subjects. After opening a campus in Dubai, Middlesex University, for example, closed down its philosophy program (McGettigan 2013, 122–123).

The search for profit also shapes the private housing market. Instead of building affordable housing, developers focus on the creation of homes for above-average-income earners. A particularly popular activity in recent years has been the construction of condominium (condo) towers. They differ from traditional urban housing, as the apartments in these buildings are usually not owned by a landlord who rents them out to tenants for a living. Instead, condo apartments are either owned by the occupants or by real estate investors whose main interest is in preserving and increasing the value of their investment (see later discussion).

Condo towers frequently display glass facades and come with indoor amenities such as gyms, pools, and saunas. As such, they promise a specific kind of urban and upper-class lifestyle. Toronto is among the cities that have experienced a condo boom in the past twenty years. One study has shown that the residents in these buildings tend to be young (between 20 and 40 years of age), couples or singles without children and with an above-average household income (Lehrer and Widietz 2009, 95). Another study traced the owners of more than 5,000 apartments in 23 condo buildings in San Francisco. It found that about 40 percent of the owners do not live there. In some buildings the rate of absentee-ownership is more than 60 percent (Bond, Graham, and Redmond 2015). While some condos may be rented out—a few were even advertised on Airbnb—the authors assume that the majority of the owners are so wealthy they do not need the rental income; they just keep them as "collector's items" (Bond, Graham, and Redmond 2015, 100).

In food production, profit orientation has led to a replacement of fresh and artisanal food with industrially processed food. While most food is processed in one way or the other, primarily to make it durable, food processing reached a new stage with recent advancements in food science and technology. Rather than being the main component of the human diet, whole foods are now refined and used as ingredients—corn, for example, provides cornmeal, cornstarch, and corn sweetener—which are then assembled in various ways and combined with artificial substances to create new food items, many of which are ready to eat or can be turned into a meal with little preparation (Pollan 2006, 93; Monteiro et al. 2013). Ultra-processed foods provide a much higher rate of profit than traditional food products. The costs of the ingredients of processed foods usually make up a fraction of the retail price. In the case of ready-to-eat breakfast cereals, for example, the costs of the ingredients account for 12 percent of the retail price, while total production costs amount to 36.3 percent (Cotterill 1999). Unsurprisingly, breakfast cereals are considered a high-margin industry.[20]

Focus on short-term profits at the cost of long-term sustainability

The focus on profitability goes hand in hand with a focus on short-term profits. In healthcare, most experts agree that long-term improvements in health can best be achieved through preventive care, including workplace health and safety measures. Yet medical systems in advanced capitalist countries largely focus on curative care. There are several reasons for this fixation, and not all of them have to do with profit interests.[21] However, hospitals and doctors seeking to maximize profits have little interest in promoting prevention because their incomes depend on the treatment of sick patients (Kuttner 1996, 115).[22] Insurance companies, by contrast, have an interest in preventing the need for medical interventions, but they are also reluctant to invest in preventive care since in a private insurance market insurance holders may switch to another provider before the investment pays off (Kuttner 1996, 133).[23]

In the case of mental health, short-term thinking translates into the prescription of psycho-pharmaceuticals instead of the provision of psychotherapy (Kirsch 2010). This is not to say that psychotherapy is always more effective than psycho-pharmaceuticals in treating an urgent condition such as acute depression. Yet while antidepressants can help patients to cope with the condition, they do not tackle possible causes of the depression (assuming that depression is not simply the result of a chemical imbalance). Addressing underlying issues is precisely what psychotherapy attempts to do. According to several studies, the long-term effect of psychotherapy is much more favorable than that of antidepressants. Formerly depressed patients are less likely to relapse after psychotherapy than after treatment with antidepressants (Kirsch 2010, 158). However, antidepressants are the third most commonly prescribed medication class in the United States, with annual sales exceeding 10 million US dollars (Mojtabai and Olfson 2011). One particularly troubling study found that about two-thirds of antidepressants consumed in the United States are prescribed by doctors without any psychiatric diagnosis (Mojtabai and Olfson 2011, 1436).

The focus on short-term profits is especially problematic in the case of those public utilities that rely on infrastructures that need to be maintained and renewed on a regular basis. It is very tempting to save on these costs, because cuts usually have no immediate effects and possible problems emerge only years later, perhaps after the company has been sold to a new owner.

However, sometimes the lack of maintenance can cause major fatalities. For example, the national British railway system was split up and sold to private investors in the early 1990s (Funnel, Jupe, and Andrew 2009, 133). Railtrack became the company responsible for running and maintaining tracks, signals, bridges, and tunnels (whereas other companies were responsible for operating the trains). As an infrastructure provider, Railtrack had few opportunities to increase its profits without increasing prices. And prices were set by the rail regulator. One option was cutting expenses, including expenses for rail renewal. This was the main cause of a tragic train crash near Hatfield in October 2000 which cost four lives and left seventy passengers injured (Meek 2015 77). The train derailed after the track disintegrated into several hundred pieces. The inquiry that followed found that Railtrack knew about the unsafe state of the tracks for at least twenty-one months but had delayed repair work to postpone expenses (Funnel, Jupe, and Andrew 2009, 145–146).

While promising high profits for developers, condominiums towers may not be as durable as condo buyers assume. Some engineers predict that because of the extensive use of glass walls, these buildings will need major renovations fifteen to twenty-five years after being completed. In a report by the Canadian Broadcasting Corporation, the glass towers are called "throw-away buildings."[24] While only time will tell how durable the buildings really are, it is already clear that they are underperforming in terms of energy consumption. The glass facades create the need for additional cooling during the hot summer months, while demanding far more heating than conventional buildings in winter. Even if high energy costs do not bother the high-income earners who own apartments in condominium towers, the buildings nevertheless have a negative impact on environmental sustainability.

In agriculture, the prevalence of short-term profitability over long-term sustainability has led to major changes in agricultural practices, such as an increase in monocultures and the growing use of synthetic fertilizers and pesticides, as well as, more recently, the spread of genetically modified crops (Mazoyer and Roudart 2006, 385–389; see also later discussion). While it increases short-term output and therefore profits, industrialized agriculture tends to undermine the ecological foundations of farming. Among the main consequences are the degradation of soil and the depletion of water, the loss of biodiversity, and the promotion of climate change (Altieri 1998).

Short-term profit orientation has also put a major strain on marine ecosystems. Overfishing, i.e., the reduction of fish and other marine species to the point that they are extinct or cannot recover even if fishing stops, has led to the loss or near loss of several marine animals, plants, and specific habitats such as coral reefs. Analyzing the stock of some eighty marine species (globally and, if applicable, regionally), Jeremy B. C. Jackson (2008, 11459) comes to the conclusion that 91 percent are depleted, 31 percent are rare, and 7 percent are extinct. Among the best-known examples of overfishing is the Atlantic cod. Once a major source of food and income for thousands of fishermen and their families in eastern Canada, cod fishing in the Northern Atlantic collapsed in the early 1990s. Cod fishing changed in the 1960s with the arrival of factory trawlers, equipped with radar technology and large nets which are dragged on the ground rather than cast out (Roberts 2007, chapter 15). Yearly harvest rates (the percentage of stock that has been caught) subsequently increased from below 12 percent in the mid-1950s to 30 percent in the mid-1960s and 45 percent in the early 1990s (Rose 2004, 1555).[25] As a result, the stock of Atlantic cod was decimated to less than 5 percent of the historic maximum quantity (Frank et al. 2005, 1623).

Privatization of profits and collectivization of costs

Whenever possible, private for-profit businesses try to shift costs and the risks involved in producing and delivering goods and services or using natural resources onto the wider public. This should not surprise, as it leaves more profit for them. In economics, this process is called *externalization*.

One method for making the public pay for costs while privatizing profits are public-private partnerships (Whiteside 2015). PPPs are cooperations between a public entity and one or several private companies. As mentioned before, the British government has used special PPPs—PFIs and PF2s—for the creation of a wide range of public infrastructures such as hospitals, schools, and prisons (see Chapter 3). A series of studies have shown that the total costs for PFI/PF2 projects are significantly higher than if the same facilities had been paid directly for and constructed by the government. According to a report commissioned by the House of Commons in 2011, the costs for a privately financed hospital accumulated over the life span of the project are approximately 70 percent higher than if the money were to have been borrowed and invested by the government (House of Commons 2011, 18). The National Audit Office (2018, 15) estimates that the costs for PF2 schools are about 40 percent higher compared to schools directly paid for by the public.[26]

Not surprisingly, many PFI hospitals struggle to break even. In 2015–2016, two-thirds of trusts were in deficit (National Audit Office 2015).[27] As described in the following, hospitals responded to the additional costs by reducing bed numbers and cutting staff.[28] While hospitals are struggling, private partners make considerable profits. A study that looked at 125 PFI contracts signed by private companies and an NHS entity has found that the private partners made a total of 831 million pounds in pre-tax profit between 2010 and 2015 (Centre for Health and the Public Interest 2017). The pre-tax profits accounted for 8 percent of the NHS payments to these companies. In 13 contracts, pre-tax profits accounted for more than 20 percent of the funds, and in one contract it was a staggering 31 percent. Five percent of NHS payments (480 million pounds) were paid out to the companies' shareholders. According to the authors, the deficits of the hospitals covered in the study could have been reduced by just under a quarter if the pre-tax profits of the PFI partners had instead gone to fund patient care (Centre for Health and the Public Interest 2017).[29]

While privatizing profits, the private partners have no problem leaving the public with the tab if the project turns out to be a business failure. While it surprised investors by achieving solid surpluses in the second half of the 1990s—through outsourcing and delaying maintenance—Railtrack ran into financial difficulties after the Hatfield accident and had to be bailed out by the government to the tune of 1.5 billion pounds. Significantly, right before the breakdown, the company was still paying 138 million in dividends to its shareholders (Bowman et al. 2013, 70–71).[30] Another example of the externalization of costs is a failed PPP between a consortium of several private corporations and the London Underground. The consortium was awarded a thirty-year-long contract to maintain, renew, and upgrade nine London underground lines in 2003 (Funnel, Jupe, and Andrew 2009, 159–160). After it became clear that the company could not fulfill its contractual obligations without losing money, the private owners simply stopped investing and carrying out the required work. The government had to step in and provide emergency funding to guarantee the proper functioning of the Tube system. According to the National Audit Office (2009), the Metronet failure cost taxpayers up to 410 million pounds.

Another form of shifting the costs of profit maximization onto the wider public is pollution. In many instances, private companies do not or only partially account for the environmental consequences of their business activities. As mentioned before, industrialized agriculture puts a major toll on ecological sustainability. The growing use of fertilizers has increased the amount of nitrogen and phosphorus in many inland and coastal waters in the United States and other countries (Schindler and Vallentyne 2008). In addition, the shift to factory farming, with hundreds if not thousands of animals kept in limited spaces, has created an oversupply of manure which, if not safely stored, periodically contaminates water (Schindler and Vallentyne 2008, 188–189). The inflow of excess nutrients has a major impact on underwater vegetation. A common effect is the rapid growth of alga, which eventually decomposes and, in this process, uses up oxygen. The oxygen, then, is missing for the growth of other underwater plants and animals (limnologists call this process "eutrophication"). In some cases, the lack of oxygen results in hypoxia or dead zones. One of the largest dead zones in the world hovers in the Gulf of Mexico (Schindler and Vallentyne 2008, 241–243). According to the US National and Atmospheric Administration (2017), the Gulf dead zone reached a record 8,766 square miles in the summer of 2017. This is about the size of New Jersey. The main reason is the influx of pollution from highly intensive agricultural production along the Mississippi River (Schindler and Vallentyne 2008, 241–243).

The lumber industry has also shown little concern for the wider effects of deforestation. The most dramatic deforestations currently take place in the Amazon rainforest. The Amazon rainforest is not only a massive source of lumber, it is also unique refugium of biodiversity (Malhi et al. 2008, 169). This has not prevented logging companies from chopping down millions of trees, sometimes illegally. According to Brazil's National Institute for Space Research (INPE), 371,319 square kilometers (143,367 square miles), an area larger than Germany, was been cleared between 1988 and 2008.[31] Since the completion of the Trans-Amazonian Highway in the early 1970s, about 19 percent of the rainforest has been lost (Dutra Aguiar et al. 2016, 1823). Deforestation has caused more than a loss in biodiversity; the elimination of carbon storage capacity and the transformation of forest into agricultural land used for cattle and soybean production has also meant that more carbon dioxide is released into the atmosphere, which in turn fuels global warming and climate change—with knock-on effects for other ecosystems around the world (Fearnside 2005).

Standardization and homogenization

While advocates of liberalization, deregulation, and privatization promise greater choice for customers, commodification inherently promotes standardization. The simple reason for this is that a certain degree of stand-ardization of output is a precondition for markets to function and for the exploitation of economies of scale. Standardization, in turn, implies a loss of diversity and, hence, an increase in social and cultural homogeneity. Yet homogenization can also be the result of deregulation and the establishment of new market norms, pushing out those who cannot pay or who do not gen-erate high enough profits.

Peter Conrad (2007, 6) has described medicalization as a process by which non-medical problems are defined as medical conditions—typically diseases or disorders that merit medical treatment. The definition of a medical condi-tion necessarily requires some form of standardization, ideally based on some measurable indicators. For the pharmaceutical industry, the setting of norms for a disorder such as hypertension is immensely important since the lower the threshold that indicates high blood pressure, the more blood-pressure medication can be sold (Greene 2007, chapter 2). Yet while the definition of diseases necessarily involves some form of standardization, the treatment of patients has traditionally been rather flexible. True, surgeons use standard procedures taught in medical schools and published in medical handbooks, but each patient presents a somewhat unique case with a specific history and varying symptoms. The fact that patients present rather unique cases makes the comparison of costs difficult. The response to this phenomenon was the creation of a catalogue of typical hospital treatments, or what became known as *Diagnosis Related Group systems* (DRGs; Kuttner 1996, 123).

DRGs were developed in the early 1970s by a group of researchers at Yale University. The purpose was to explain why hospitals charged widely different costs for comparable treatments. Because they knew little about cost control, the medical researchers sought support from a business school professor. The resulting conversation illuminates the main purpose of the standardi-zation process (Mayes 2007, 32–33). The business school professor asked the researchers what the products of a hospital are. The doctors responded that hospitals treat patients—to which the business school professor replied "and Ford makes cars, but there's a big difference between a Pinto and a Lincoln." The business school professor, subsequently, explained that in order to con-trol costs, one needs a product definition (Mayes 2007, 32–33). This is pre-cisely what the DRGs attempt to do. The initial catalog included 487 different treatments and listed the average resources needed to carry them out. The standardization of hospital treatments not only allowed funding organiza-tions to control costs by paying prefixed or prospective prices for medical procedures; it also enabled private health insurance and health maintenance organizations to shop for the best deal among various hospital providers and as such was a precondition for the development of a competitive healthcare market.

Higher education has experienced a parallel push for standardization. On the one hand, internationalization has meant that more and more universities around the world have adopted British and American higher education standards and practices, including, for example, the bachelor's/master's-degree structure (Gibbs 2013).[32] On the other hand, the use of new technologies and the spread of online learning have led to a standardization of courses. Learning platforms promote a certain course structure with a predetermined set of resources and tools. The fact that the same structure and partly even content can be used for multiple courses greatly adds to the attractiveness of online learning. However, the standardization of courses not only allows for the exploitation of economies of scale; it also means that once developed, the courses can be taught by interchangeable teachers (Noble 2001, 32–33). This, in turn, gives universities the option of expanding the number of adjunct faculty at the expense of tenure-track professors. It is therefore not surprising that profit-oriented online-colleges have a much higher proportion of non-tenured faculty than regular nonprofit colleges (see later discussion).

To some observers, glass-walled condominium towers also look astonishingly similar to one another. Developers promise a New York–style living experience in places far from Manhattan. More significant in this case are the effects of gentrification. As mentioned before, gentrification is a process by which low-income neighborhoods become a target of real estate investment. As a result, existing residents are often displaced because they can no longer afford to live in these areas (but renter protection laws can severely slow down this process). Because of high living costs, new residents tend to be above-average income earners, and in the United States, they also tend to be white (in other countries they are primarily non-immigrant). A study that looked at neighborhoods in three major Canadian cities found that gentrification goes hand in hand with a decline of low-income households (Walks and Maaranen 2008). Especially in areas that were completely gentrified, the proportion of low-income households (defined as households with a yearly income of 50,000 Canadian dollars or less per year) declined from 77 percent to 49.5 percent between 1971 and 2001. As many of the low-income residents were recent immigrants, the cities and neighborhoods also lost much of their ethnic diversity (Walks and Maaranen 2008).

In the food industry, standardization takes the form of fast-food restaurants. These facilities stand out because of the comparably short cooking time required to churn out meals. Moreover, the fact that most of the components of fast food come from a common food supplier ensures that the respective meals offered taste exactly the same regardless of whether they are ordered in Los Angeles, or New York, or anywhere else in the United States, and perhaps even in the world (in spite of the fact that the locations may be run by different franchise partners). To underline the standardization and homogenization of food, restaurant members of the same chain share not only a menu, but a similar design. With the commodification of food in advanced capitalist societies, fast-food chains have gradually replaced traditional restaurants. According to a 2013 survey, one in five Americans eats fast food several times a week (McCarthy 2013). An estimated 11.3 percent of the daily calories consumed by adults in the United States stem from fast food (Fryar and Ervin 2013).

Commodification-related standardization has also left its mark on nature. William Cronon (1991, 116–118) has shown that the classification and standardization of agricultural output was pivotal for the development of the nineteenth-century Chicago commodity exchange. To take the example of wheat: grading of wheat according to specified indicators of quality not only gave faraway buyers some degree of security that their purchase met their expectation, thereby extending the reach of the market; it also made it possible to mix wheat from different producers, allowing larger purchases of the same commodity and making storage and logistics much easier and cheaper. Improvements in storage and logistics, including the use of large grain elevators, cemented Chicago's position as leading trading spot for wheat in the United States in the second half of the nineteenth century (Cronon 1991, 116–118). With American lumber increasingly shipped across the country in second half of the nineteenth century, lumber buyers, too, were looking for assurance of the quality of their purchases (Cronon 1991, 177–178). But without a dominant trading center, it proved more difficult to establish uniform standards. Lumber grades were already widespread in the 1860s, but their scope was regional and they were only weakly enforced. However, in the 1890s, efforts to establish an effective national standard made significant progress when the Mississippi Valley grading system became a reference point for much of the US lumber industry (Cronon 1991, 177–178; Davis 1983, 368). A more recent example of the standardization of natural resources is the measure of wetlands (Robertson 2004 and 2006). Rather than categorizing wetlands according to different grades, scientists have invented a standard measure that makes it possible to compare highly diverse wetland ecosystems (see Chapter 2). Ironically, units of ecosystem function are supposed to reflect the degree of biodiversity that can be found in a particular wetland, assuming that the more biodiversity of a wetland, the greater its ecological value.

Bureaucratization and expansion of management/administration

Supporters of liberalization and privatization not only promise more choice, but also claim that the private sector is able to produce the same goods and services more efficiently than any government. However, commodification can actually increase costs because the creation of markets and the documentation of output creates the need for more bureaucracy, while the adoption of private-sector business practices frequently involves an expansion of management or administration and an increase of managerial/administrative salaries.

The costs of commodification can clearly be seen if we compare different healthcare systems. The United States has both the most privatized system among the advanced capitalist countries and the most expensive one (while underperforming in a number of health indicators).[33] A significant part of the high costs of American healthcare stems from the higher administrative costs generated by a private insurance market as opposed to a public or single-payer system. A comparison of the US and Canadian healthcare systems found that in 1999, health administration costs accounted for 31 percent of healthcare expenditure in the United States and 16.7 percent in Canada (Woolhandler, Campbell, and Himmelstein 2003, 772). A more recent study has compared administrative costs on the hospital level (Himmelstein et al. 2014). Here, too, the United States leads among the countries included in the sample. Administrative costs make up 25.3 percent of hospital expenses in the United States, while accounting for only 12.4 percent in Canada (Woolhandler, Campbell, and Himmelstein 2003, 1589–1592). These higher administrative costs primarily stem from the fact that US hospitals deal with various insurance providers with specific regulations and cost standards. However, even within the United States, for-profit hospitals tend to have higher administrative expenses (27.2 percent of all hospital expenses) than not-for-profit (25 percent) and public hospitals (22.8 percent) (Woolhandler, Campbell, and Himmelstein 2003, 1589–1592). The same study also shows that in the United Kingdom, the proportion of administrative personnel increased from 13.8 percent of all hospital staff in 1980 to 23.9 percent in 2009 (Woolhandler, Campbell, and Himmelstein 2003, 1589–1592). The increase took place while successive market reforms were being introduced in the English healthcare system (see Chapter 3). In addition to boosting administrative staff, commodification has also meant that nurses have to perform more and more bureaucratic tasks, leaving less time to spend with patients (Flecker and Hermann 2012, 116–117; Gordon 2005, 237).[34]

The growing importance of management and administration in commodified healthcare can also be seen in managerial/administrative salaries. According to one newspaper report, the salaries of the CEOs of leading American healthcare corporations far outstripped those of surgeons. However, even the average salaries of hospital administrators are considerably higher than those of general physicians. Furthermore, hospital CEOs earn on average more than six times what is earned by staff nurses. These high salaries are believed to contribute to the comparably higher administrative costs of American hospitals described earlier (Rosenthal 2014).

Healthcare is not the only sector where administrative costs have crept up. The adoption of private business strategies has also meant that administrative staff has increased at many universities. A study that looked at 193 research universities in the United States found that the number of full-time administrators per hundred students grew by 39 percent between 1993 and 2007, while the number of employees engaged in teaching, research, or service grew by only 18 percent (Green, Kisida, and Mills 2010). The same study shows that inflation-adjusted spending on administration per student increased by 61 percent over the same period, while instructional spending grew by just 39 percent (Green, Kisida, and Mills 2010). An analysis of staff development at the University of California confirms this trend: Here managerial staff increased between four and five times as fast as total university employment rates between 1995 and 2005 (Newfield 2016, 177–179). A similar development took place in Britain, where managerial and professional staff increased by almost a quarter between 2004–2005 and 2014–2015 (Taylor and Underwood 2015). And this is not a specific feature of public and nonprofit universities. It is merely an adjustment to private-sector practices: private for-profit colleges in the United States spend more on advertising, marketing, recruiting, and admission than they do on teaching (see later discussion).

There is another parallel with healthcare to be found here: While the number of administrators is growing, teaching faculty are also increasingly burdened with administrative tasks, including an increasing amount of performance-related documentation, which, in turn, is used to foment the status of the respective institution (see Chapter 3). It is not difficult to imagine that the excellence of a university might be better served were the same time used for teaching or research. In addition, universities, like healthcare systems, have seen increasing administrative salaries. According to the *Chronicle of Higher Education*, executive compensation for presidents at US public colleges can be as high as 2 million US dollars a year, whereas in private colleges it can be more than 5 million US dollars (Bauman, Davis, and O'Leary 2020). Vice chancellors at British universities have also experienced a significant boost, earning on average 275,000 pounds per year in 2017 (Khomami 2017).

Sacrificing quality for profitability

The maximization of profits can also come at the cost of lower product quality. A series of company case studies of European public service providers has shown that companies facing competition or the pressure to increase profits tend to reduce costs by cutting labor expenses (Hermann and Flecker 2012b, 201–202). While in some cases cost reductions can be achieved through the introduction of new and labor-saving technology, in labor-intensive services such as healthcare there are severe limits to the replacement of people by machines (as explained by William Baumol in his work on the service-sector cost disease). Hence in services where labor costs make up the major part of production costs, cost-cutting strategies are often effectuated through the deterioration of employment and working conditions (Hermann and Flecker 2012b, 201–202). However, especially in labor-intensive services such as healthcare, the quality of service also depends on a motivated and resourceful workforce that is not constantly disgruntled or at the brink of collapse.

Of course, quality is something that is difficult to define, and individual perceptions of quality indicators can differ considerably. However, several studies have shown that there is a close relationship between patient satisfaction and staffing levels in hospitals and nursing homes (Kutney-Lee et al. 2009). This should not surprise: The fewer patients a nurse has to take care of during a work shift, the more time he/she can spend with an individual patient. Nonetheless, increasing patient-to-nurse ratios is a widespread method of reducing hospital expenses. Hence for-profit hospitals in Germany tend to have fewer nurses per patient than their public counterparts (Hermann 2009b, 139). In the United States, for-profit nursing homes tend to employ fewer nurses per resident than not-for-profit or public homes and, subsequently, have more quality issues (Harrington et al. 2001). Sometimes hospital operators also try to reduce costs by substituting less skilled for higher skilled nurses. Here, too, studies show that lower staff qualification also tends to mean lower quality of care (Aiken et al. 2017).

A 2013 public inquiry revealed that a shortage of skilled nursing staff was an important reason for the unusually high mortality rates and poor treatment standards at Stafford hospital in England (Mid Staffordshire NHS Foundation Trust Public Inquiry 2013). Although it was part of the NHS, Stafford hospital adopted the status of a foundation trust, which gave it more autonomy. This allowed the hospital, among other things, to engage in public-private partnerships, but also included the responsibility to balance their budget (see Chapter 3). In anticipation of this new responsibility, the managers unleashed a drastic savings program which, among other things, included a deferral of hiring of urgently needed nursing staff in the lead-up to the crisis, which may have caused hundreds of unnecessary deaths (Mid Staffordshire NHS Foundation Trust Public Inquiry 2013; see also Campbell 2013).

In addition to understaffing, another cost-cutting strategy applied at Stafford, and at many other hospitals in the United Kingdom and in other parts of the world, is to outsource auxiliary services such as cleaning, catering, and janitorial work. In particular the outsourcing of cleaning has come under growing criticism. Outside cleaners, underpaid and under pressure to meet their quotas, tend to clean less thoroughly than in-house cleaners, increasing the risks of hospital infections (Davies 2009). A study that looked at methicillin-resistant Staphylococcus aureus (MRSA) infections in 126 acute hospital trusts in Britain found that hospitals with outsourced cleaning services had significantly higher MRSA incidents than those in which cleaning was carried out by internal staff (Toffolutti et al. 2017, 66–68).

While many leading universities and colleges in the United States are private, they are not-for-profit institutions. For-profit colleges, by contrast, are among the worst institutions when it comes to the quality of higher education. As in healthcare, for-profit schools lower costs by increasing the number of students per teacher. Because of the potential to increase student-teacher ratios, several for-profit colleges focus on online learning and the provision of online degrees (Deming, Goldin, and Katz 2012, 140–141). A report for the US Senate Committee on Health Education Labor and Pensions (2012) has revealed that more than half of the students who enrolled in thirty for-profit colleges in 2008–2009 left without a degree or diploma within a median of four months. One reason is that for-profit colleges specifically target underprivileged students with low high school scores but with eligibility for federal student loans (Deming, Goldin, and Katz 2012, 148). Another factor is that for-profit schools have much higher student-teacher ratios than not-for-profit universities and colleges. According to the previously mentioned study, for-profit colleges only spend 17.2 percent of all revenues on instruction—less than on advertising, marketing, recruiting, and admission, and less than was registered as pre-tax profit in 2010 (US Senate Committee on Health Education Labor and Pensions 2012). In addition, instruction costs are kept low through the use of part-time faculty; 80 percent of the teachers employed at the thirty colleges included in the study had a part-time contract. In five schools, the part-time rate was more than 90 percent (US Senate Committee on Health Education Labor and Pensions 2012). Part-time not only means few hours; it also means no tenure. The resulting job insecurity certainly does not increase the motivation of the teachers.

Food producers also face a dilemma: more agricultural output usually means a lower quality product (Pollan 2008, 118–124). As described before, the industrialization of agriculture has dramatically increased output through the use of synthetic fertilizers and pesticides, genetically modified (GM) crops, as well as antibiotics and growth hormones. However, there is evidence that these techniques have a negative impact on the quality of plants and livestock. On the one hand, there is the risk of residual chemicals and drugs in the food stemming from the use of these substances. While the risk itself is rarely contested, scientists debate whether the amounts are large enough to negatively affect the health of consumers. Genetic engineering of crops makes it possible to achieve high yields while forgoing the use of pesticides. But the long-term effects of GM food are also hotly debated. Based on a review of published literature in scientific journals, José L. Domingo (2007) concludes that the evidence for the harmlessness of GM crops is rather thin.[35] In order to avoid the risks associated with industrial farming, an increasing number of consumers in rich countries buy organic products.

At the same time, the use of chemicals also affects the nutritional value of plants. Several studies from the United States and the United Kingdom show that nutrient content in fruits and vegetables has declined considerably over the last fifty to seventy years (Davis 2009). The decline of minerals, vitamins, and protein is explained by the boost in output per acre over the same period. The result is what some scientists have called the "dilution effect" (Davis 2009). Other studies have compared the (micro)nutritional content of conventional and organic plants. Some studies showed significant differences, while others have not. However, after looking at thirty-three studies with a total of 908 comparisons of micronutrients, Duncan Hunter et al. (2011) came to the conclusion that micronutrient content in organic plants tends to be higher than in plants grown with conventional methods.

Manipulation and speculation

In some cases, private providers of goods and services even manipulate human needs in order to increase sales. The pharmaceutical industry responds to needs by developing drugs for existing medical conditions, but pharmaceutical companies are also actively involved in the identification and approval of new diseases for which they can provide drugs. Critics call this practice "disease mongering" (Moynihan, Heath, and Henry 2002; Moynihan and Cassels 2005). Several authors have documented cases where the pharmaceutical industry has spent millions of dollars to convince doctors, health administrators, and potential patients that one or several symptoms make up a specific disease that can be treated. Examples include restless leg syndrome, female sexual dysfunction, and social anxiety disorder. In order to increase awareness of new diseases, pharmaceutical companies develop educational programs in which potential patients are told that what they thought of as a normal albeit unpleasant condition—such as shyness or baldness—is actually a disease and that there is medicine to cure it (Moynihan and Cassels 2005).

Defining a disease is a complex process; not only have definitions changed over time, but they also differ between countries. New diseases are therefore often contested. Furthermore, there is a history of health administrators and doctors ignoring certain forms of pain and refusing to help patients with unknown medical conditions. Yet the point here is not to engage in medical controversy. The argument is that the pharmaceutical industry has no problem inventing profitable diseases and using all available marketing strategies to boost drug sales (Kalman 2009).

The food industry, too, manipulates human needs. The food industry uses large amounts of salt, sugar, and fat to make its ultra-processed food tasty and to sell it to consumers. Deprived of nutrition such as fiber, protein, minerals, and vitamins, ultra-processed food tends to have a low nutritional value (Albritton 2009, 117); moreover, if eaten in large quantities, it can also cause serious health problems, such as obesity, diabetes, and heart disease (Monteiro et al. 2013; Bowman et al. 2014; Paeratakul et al. 2003). While the food industry argues that it only delivers what consumers want, it spends millions of dollars in advertising to make sure that consumers know that they should long for ultra-processed food (Nestle 2007, 21–22). A significant part of the advertising is specifically targeted to children who are accustomed early on to the taste of artificial food and drinks at the expense of more nuanced natural tastes (Nestle 2007, 176–180). The result is what has been described as an obesity epidemic. About a third of all American children between ten and seventeen years of age are obese or overweight.[36] A fifteen-year study with 3,000 participants who consumed fast food on a regular basis has shown a clear relationship between fast-food consumption and weight gain (Pereira et al. 2005).

Commodification not only opens the doors for manipulation, but also invites speculation. Speculation played an important role in the California electricity crisis of 2000 and 2001. Electricity wholesale prices increased more than five times between 1999 and 2000, while in some months prices were fifteen times higher than in the same month of the preceding year. As wholesale prices reached record levels (at one point a megawatt hour cost 400 US dollars), households and businesses suffered from rolling blackouts (Blumstein, Friedman, and Green 2002 25, 28; Palast, Oppenheim, and MacGregor 2003, 147–150; Weare 2003, 1–2).

The crisis had a number of causes, including complex yet incomplete regulation of a newly liberalized sector that allowed market participants to make money by gaming the system (Blumstein, Friedman, and Green 2002, 30–31; McLean and Elkin 2004, 264–283).[37] However, there is also a more profound problem at stake because power generators, especially if they are also active in electricity trading, can earn more money by shutting down existing power plants than by building new ones (Palast, Oppenheim, and MacGregor 2003,

149). Hence in the lead-up to the crisis, demand for electricity increased while supply stagnated or declined. Owners of generating plants showed little interest in investing in new facilities, and several generators ran their plants below full capacity (Blumstein, Friedman, and Green 2002, 33; Weare 2003, 15–19). Traders further exploited this shortage by betting that prices would increase before offering available electricity (McLean and Elkin 2004, 267). According to the Independent System Operator, the organization set up for managing the state's high-voltage transmission network, electricity generators and traders made more than 6 billion US dollars in extra profits due to market manipulation and speculation during the crisis (Thompson 2001).

Speculation is even more common in the housing sector. With commodification, homes have increasingly become an object of investment rather than places to live (Harvey 2014, 20–21; Madden and Marcuse 2016, 4). Since the value of a real estate investment depends on supply and demand, developers are careful to limit supply since too much supply would drive down the prices of their objects.[38] On the demand side, a shortage of housing drives up prices. But this is only the beginning. Increasing property prices, then, attract investors who do not need the space for living, which further adds to demand and drives up prices. Fast-rising prices, in turn, make real estate investments even more attractive and increase interest from non-institutional investors who buy a second or third home because the costs partly pay for themselves through rising property values (e.g., a home that was bought for 500,000 US dollars is worth 600,000 a few years later). This is why regular people ended up owning five or six houses in the run-up to the 2008 crisis. Like a Ponzi scheme, the system works as long as everybody believes in increasing prices. However, as soon as a large enough group of investors or lenders start to doubt that the prices match property values, the scheme is in trouble and the housing bubble bursts. As a result, people lose not only their investments, but in some cases also their homes. Those with a problematic credit history may even have trouble finding apartments to rent (Madden and Marcuse 2016).

Speculation is also an essential element in markets for agricultural products. Investors pay a fixed price for products that will be harvested in the future, betting that the price at the time of the harvest will be higher than what they have paid in advance. They can also sell future harvests at current prices, expecting that prices will fall. In order to limit risks, investors often bet on opposite outcomes. To make things even more opaque, investors frequently acquire future options rather than committing to the purchase or sale of a commodity. In fact, only 2 to 3 percent of contracts on commodity markets are physically settled (Schmidt 2016, 46).

Some form of speculation in commodity markets is widely seen as beneficial as it provides the market with liquidity and stability (yet price volatility may be the result of an increasingly industrialized agri-mono-culture that produces for international markets). However, speculative investments in commodity markets have increased dramatically since 2000. The amount of money flowing into commodity markets increased from six billion US dollars in 2000 to 270 billion in 2008 (Schmidt 2016, 59). The financialization of commodity markets was driven by the growing interests of institutional investors such as pension funds, hedge funds, and sovereign wealth funds (De Schutter 2010). They were looking for new investment opportunities after the 2000 dot.com crash. The interest was partly fueled by research findings that showed an inverse relationship between equity and commodity markets. When equity prices increase, commodity prices decrease, and vice versa. Commodity investments, hence, seemed a perfect hedge against slumps in equity markets (Schmidt 2016, 63).[39]

As a result of the growing interest of institutional investors, the number of future and option contracts outstanding at commodity exchanges increased from less than 15 million in 2000 to close to 50 million in 2007 (Flassbeck et al. 2011, 15, figure 4). Increasing investments in commodity markets, subsequently, drove up commodity prices and, along with other factors such as the growing demand for crops for biofuel production, resulted in a major increase in food prices (Wahl 2009).[40] World food prices rose by 83 percent between 2005 and 2008, with corn prices nearly tripling. Rice prices increased by 170 percent, and wheat prices by 127 percent. Growing food prices, in turn, drove at least 40 million more people in the developing world into hunger (De Schutter 2010).

Growing inequality

Because access to a good or service depends on the buyer's ability to pay, commodification necessarily produces inequality between those with and without money, or between the rich and the poor.[41] Unsurprisingly, it is primarily poor or low-income households that lack access to healthcare, higher education, public utilities, housing, and food (see earlier discussion).

For example, 36.2 percent of non-elderly families in the United States with a household income of less than 40,000 US dollars lacked health insurance coverage in 2019, while only 8.3 percent of those with an income of more than 40,000 US dollars were uninsured (Kaiser Family Foundation 2020, table 1). Given the racial and ethnic inequality in the United States, it should not surprise that African Americans and Hispanics tend to have worse access to healthcare than whites (Agency for Healthcare Research and Quality 2017).

Access to higher education in the United States also varies considerably according to income: While 82 percent of 18- to 24-year-olds from the top family income quartile attend college, only 45 percent of those in the bottom quartile do so (Pell Institute for the Study of Opportunity in Higher Education 2015). Furthermore, an analysis of Pell Grant recipients (these are grants for low-income students) shows that low-income students are more likely to attend two-year as opposed to four-year colleges and to enroll in private-for-profit institutions (Pell Institute for the Study of Opportunity in Higher Education 2015). As discussed earlier, the latter are notorious for their low teaching quality and high dropout rates. Here, too, social inequality is underpinned by racial and ethnic disparities, with the effect that African American and Hispanic youth are less likely to obtain a college degree than white Americans (Ryan and Bauman 2016; see also Krogstad and Fry 2014). To some extent, the exclusion of low-income families from higher education is the result of discrimination in primary and secondary education and the fact that many (public) schools in low-income neighborhoods in the United States are grossly underfunded (Rothstein 2013). However, even among high school students with high test scores, the likelihood that children from high-income families obtain a college degree is still more than twice as high as those from low-income households (Mettler 2014, 26).

Access to certain goods and services is only one part of the story. Commodification not only excludes those who cannot pay, it also creates goods and services whose quality differs according to their price. This means that consumers with plenty of money can buy better goods and services than those with limited funds. Hence high-income earners can buy better food, including organic products, while low-income households are stuck with industrially produced food (Albritton 2009, 93). Because of its high energy density, ultra-processed food seems a cheap alternative to conventional food and especially fruits and vegetables (Drewnowski 2004). Yet because ultra-processed food is less satiating and even addictive, potential savings are turned into actual losses as people end up eating more food than they need to cover their demand for energy. The paradoxical result is that it is primarily low-income families and their children who suffer most from diseases such as obesity (Wang and Beydoun 2007).

In housing, too, lower prices are usually associated with lower building quality, or in some cases even substandard housing. About 75 percent of cases of severe and moderate housing inadequacies affect households with an income of less than 60,000 US dollars per year.[42] Studies have shown that poor housing quality negatively affects the development of low-income children (Levine et al. 2013). In education, too, quality has its price. With few exceptions, leading educational institutions in the United States also charge the highest fees, making it even more difficult for students from poor families, as well as racial and ethnic minorities, to access them (Carnevale and Van der Werf 2017). Raij Chetty et al. (2017, 1) have found that more students from families in the top 1 percent of the income scale attend "Ivy-Plus" colleges than students from the bottom half of the income scale.[43] Only 3.8 percent of students are from families in the bottom income quintile. "As a result," the authors note, "children from families in the top 1 percent are 77 times more likely to attend an Ivy-Plus college compared to the children from families in the bottom quintile" (2017, 1).

There is also considerable evidence that the privatization of public services promotes inequality (Hermann 2016, 12–15). First, price increases demanded by private operators affect lower-income households more than high-income earners: for those of low incomes, these increases make up a larger proportion of their household budget. As mentioned previously, increasing energy prices in Britain have meant that a growing number of households are suffering from fuel poverty. Some experts have argued that increasing energy costs are the result of higher oil prices, rather than privatization.[44] However, Massimo Florio (2013, 176, 217) has shown in a European-wide study that it is the publicly owned electricity and gas providers that charge the lowest prices in the liberalized European markets. Second, privatization typically comes with a diversification of prices. For example, British households on prepaid meters pay more per kilowatt hour for electricity than debit payers (Waddams Price and Young 2003, 112). According to a newspaper report, the difference can amount to 300 pounds per year (Lunn 2013). Homes with prepaid meters are usually occupied by people who fail a credit check or have significant debt with the supplier. In other words, poor residents tend to pay more for electricity than the rest of the population.

In South Africa, the deregulation of the health insurance market and the privatization of hospitals in the 1980s allowed for the continuation of a highly unequal healthcare system after the end of apartheid. Sixteen percent of the population have private health insurance and use private doctors and hospitals, whereas 84 percent have no insurance and rely on the public system for hospital care (Mayosi and Benatar 2014, 1345–1346). Yet while the private system provides care that is comparable to "Western" standards, the public system is grossly underfunded. Hence the 8 million South Africans with private insurance are cared for by 70 percent of the country's doctors, whereas the 40 million without insurance, including several million HIV patients, are attended by the rest (Mayosi and Benatar 2014, 1345–1346). In South Africa, too, social inequality is racially structured: Whereas the majority of white South Africans have private insurance and enjoy private healthcare, the majority of black and colored South Africans have no choice but to go to a public hospital when they need treatment (Mcintyre et al. 2006).

Marginalization of non-profit-based motivations, and the erosion of solidarity

With commodification, profit-orientation becomes the most important motive for social action, over all other social values and orientations. As discussed in Chapter 2, representatives of the moral critique of commodification strongly criticize this consequence as the intrusion of market norms and monetary valuations into areas of social life that are traditionally governed by other standards or conventions. Since profits are typically increased at the costs of competitors, profit orientation implies a certain degree of selfishness. Selfishness is the opposite of altruism, or the willingness to help others in need without expecting something in return. In many societies, altruism is a highly respected attitude, and even capitalist societies appreciate the availability of volunteers who work for no or very little pay (arguably capitalism wouldn't work without unpaid work, including vast amounts of domestic labor performed by women).

Yet altruism is often fueled by religious beliefs and the promise of a return for altruistic behavior in the afterlife. More often, people help out other people in the belief that they will be helped if needed. This attitude is called solidarity. Perhaps the most developed form of solidarity is the modern welfare state. Millions of people pay taxes or contribute to social insurance funds in the expectation that they will receive benefits if they need it. A revealing example of how commodification undermines solidarity are recent pension reforms. Most developed countries have public pension systems in which people who are currently employed pay through their ongoing contributions for the benefits of those who have retired. Typically, public pension systems also include some measure of redistribution, as high-income earners contribute proportionally more than low-income earners. However, in recent decades many governments have encouraged the establishment of private pension schemes to compensate for cuts in public pensions (Ebbinghaus 2015; Ebbinghaus and Gronwald 2011; Etxezarreta and Festić 2009; Huber and Stephens 2000).[45]

Private pensions no longer demand solidarity. Benefits in defined contribution plans are based on what people have paid into an individual pension account over the course of their working career—plus interest and possible gains from investing by pension funds (minus the costs for "managing'" pension funds and accounts). There is no redistribution in the system, and the state no longer has an obligation to make sure that citizens receive a minimum pension that allows them a decent existence when they are too old to work. A lack of retirement income becomes an individual problem caused by the failure to put sufficient money in the pension account. Yet decades of wage stagnation, the expansion of low-paid jobs, and cyclical unemployment mean that many people simply do not have the funds to build retirement income (Ellis, Munnel, and Eschtruth 2014). However, the absence of solidarity also means that retirees' income depends on the value of their pension fund's investments. And as the 2008–2009 crisis has shown, a stock market crash can drastically reduce the value of the fund and force people to work far beyond their planned retirement date (Munnel and Rutledge 2013).[46]

Another motive that is threatened by commodification is use-value orientation. Use-value orientation refers to the interest of a producer in creating something that is useful and functional in order to solve a tricky problem, or to help somebody and make him/her feel better. Allegedly, competition ensures that in capitalist economies the best output is produced with the least input. However, as countless workers can attest, management is primarily interested in making a profit, and the best product is not always the one that guarantees the highest returns. Workers are therefore frequently confronted with caps on resources they are allowed to use for a specific job, task, or project. This should not surprise us, as the fewer resources workers use, the greater the company's potential profit.[47]

For Richard Sennet (2009), use-value orientation mainly takes the form of crafts(wo)manship. According to Sennet crafts(wo)men are workers or owners

of small workshops who are primarily interested in doing a good job and creating something that they can be proud of, rather than in making money or
out-competing a competitor; in other words, "they are dedicated to good work
for its own sake" (2009, 20). The term "craftsmanship" is usually associated with
skilled manual labor and, perhaps, with artisanal forms of production. However,
Sennet notes that crafts(wo)manship goes beyond skilled manual labor and
can be found in a large variety of jobs, including software developers. Software
programmers who are engaged in improving the freely available Linnux operating system do so not because of the financial reward—they are not paid; they
do so because they believe in the product and they are proud to contribute their
skills and knowledge to an exciting project (Sennet 2009, 24–25). Yet competition and profit orientation leave less and less room for this sort of quality-driven
work, resulting in what Sennet describes as the demise of crafts(wo)manship.

In the public sector, the same attitude is sometimes called *public-sector
ethos*. In this case, workers are not only doing a good job; they are also
working for the community or for a larger public interest, rather than for
a profit-making company. In a number of cases, public-sector workers
even accept lower wages (compared to private-sector workers with comparable skills) to do something that benefits society.[48] Investigating several
cases where IT staff has been outsourced from local governments in Britain,
Simone Dahlmann (2008, 157) found that the majority of interviewees would
have liked to remain in the public sector in spite of the lower salaries and
limited career opportunities they confronted. One IT professional even considered retraining as a healthcare worker to move back to the public system
where she would no longer have to "fill 'shareholder pockets.'" However,
public-sector workers also struggle with growing workloads and quantitative
performance measurements, making it increasingly difficult to do their jobs
properly. Nurses, for example, have grown increasingly frustrated because
they cannot spend sufficient time with their patients and comforting patients
is no longer seen as part of their job (Gordon 2005, 369–370). This is one
reason why 17.5 percent of new nurses in the United States leave their first
job within one year of starting work (Kovner et al. 2014).

More commodification

Commodification tends to promote more commodification—if not hindered by social forces and de-commodifying policies. The fact that people

have accepted that a certain good or service costs something rather than being freely available, and that the price varies according to quality, quantity, and other factors, makes them susceptible to more products being turned into commodities. At the same time, the conversion of freely available goods and services into commodities or the deepening of the commodity character of existing commodities—including the substitution of goods for services—often creates new opportunities for profit-making. In other words, commodification processes reinforce each other, with the result that people and societies become more and more dependent on the acquisition of commodities to facilitate their reproduction (de-commodification processes have the opposite effect).

It is not by accident that the United States has the most commodified healthcare system among the world's most advanced economies, and at the same time the highest expenses for prescription drugs. Per capita expenditures for prescription drugs in the United States were 30 percent higher than in Canada and almost 60 percent higher than in the United Kingdom.[49] To some extent, higher US pharmaceutical spending is the result of higher drug prices (Kesselheim, Avorn, and Sarpatwari 2016). However, there is also evidence that Americans consume more drugs. According to a 2013 Commonwealth Fund (2015) survey, average Americans took about a third more prescription drugs than average Germans or French. National statistics show that more than two-thirds of Americans between ages 45 and 64 use at least one prescription drug on a regular basis; almost half use up to four different drugs (National Center for Health Statistics 2017, 25). The percentage would likely be higher if the millions of Americans without insurance were to receive prescription drug coverage. The lack of coverage and the high co-payments demanded by insurance providers result in the somewhat absurd situation that the United States has at the same time the highest usage rate of prescription drugs in the world while also having the highest percentage of adults who skip prescriptions or doses for cost reasons (Sarnak et al. 2017).[50] It is important to note that high drug spending has no positive effect on health outcomes. On the contrary—death from overdoses of prescription drugs, especially from painkillers, tranquilizers, and stimulants, is a major cause of death in the United States.[51]

The overreliance on pharmaceuticals is only one feature of a highly commodified healthcare system. Another one is the widespread use of medical devices. Unsurprisingly, the United States is also leading in per-capita expenses for medical devices, surpassed only by Switzerland. The United

States spent between 20 and 40 percent more for medical devices in 2011 compared to both Germany and France (Skinner 2013). As a result, the United States has four times more magnetic resonance imaging (MRI) machines and three times more computed tomography (CT) and positron emission tomography (PET) scanners per million inhabitants than Canada (Squires and Anderson 2015). These numbers may not tell the whole truth. In a public healthcare system, the government can coordinate the availability of expensive medical equipment so that every citizen has a chance to use one if needed. In the private US healthcare system, this is not possible. And given the undersupply of medical services in rural America—following a wave of rural hospital closures since 2010, an estimated 4.4. million rural residents live in a county without a hospital—Americans in urban centers receive even more MRIs, CTs, and PET scans (Probst, Ebert, and Crouch 2019). In other words, while Americans see a doctor less frequently and are admitted to a hospital less often than people in countries with public healthcare systems, they are more frequently "scanned" when they see a doctor (Probst, Ebert, and Crouch 2019; see also Rice et al. 2013, 176–178). As with the consumption of prescription drugs, the frequent use of this technology does not necessarily result in better health outcomes. As mentioned before, the United States lags behind its economic peers for most health indicators. However, the medical device industry certainly benefits from a healthcare system that seems to be more prepared to invest in machines than in doctors and nurses.[52]

The recent increase in student fees at colleges and universities was accompanied by a similarly dramatic expansion of student debt. This, in turn, created new opportunities for profit making. According to Charlie Eaton et al. (2016, 526), American households spent 34 billion US dollars for interest associated with student loans in 2012. Until 2010, even public loans were collected by a private "loan-servicing" company.[53] In addition, some student loans are turned into student-loan-backed securities and are sold to private investors—similar to the mortgage-backed securities described later in this chapter (Soederberg 2014). By the end of 2018, 170.2 billion US dollars of student debt had been "securitized" in such a manner.[54] Following a similar path, the British government has started to sell securitized student debt to private investors (Warrel and Thomas Hale 2017).

At the same time, the expansion of US student loans has provided for-profit colleges with a new business model. As mentioned previously, for-profit-colleges largely focus on low-income students whose student loans are used to pay for tuition. Enrollment in for-profit colleges increased by three times between 2003 and 2011. Net profits over the same period increased from one to five billion US dollars (Eaton et al. 2016, 524–526). Yet while the schools make considerable profits, loan default rates among their former students are significantly higher than for public and nonprofit institutions. In the fiscal year 2017, the percentage of students who started to pay back their federal student loans in the previous three years and subsequently defaulted on payments was 9.7 percent. Among students from private for-profit colleges, the default rate was 14.7 percent.[55] Another study that analyzed default rates over a twelve-year period starting in 2003–2004 found that more than half of students from private for-profit colleges defaulted at least once on their payments (Woo et al. 2017).

Similarly, the elimination of public-sector monopolies in the European Union had a number of knock-on effects which deepened the commodity character of what are still referred to as public services. Officially, the EU policy was only about the introduction of competition and choice in sectors such as electricity, gas, postal services, and to some extent rail transport. While the policy change required member states to stop subsidizing former monopolists and to grant market access to alternative providers, the directives did not address the issue of public ownership (the European Union does not have the mandate to prescribe forms of ownership). However, while competition only evolved slowly—unsurprisingly, given the network character of these industries—member states quickly started to privatize the former monopolists, not least because they thought that a private company would be better suited to exploit new business opportunities (Hermann and Verhoest 2012, 20). German Post is a case in point: today, the former national postal service provider is predominantly privately owned and has become one of the biggest global logistics providers, with a presence in more than 200 countries.[56] Almost 70 percent of its earnings come from its subsidiary DHL, a US company that had specialized in express air freight before it was acquired by German Post in the late 1990s (Deutsche Post 2017, 5).

Confronted with growing pressure from competitors and private shareholders, the former monopolists did more than just internationalize. They also started to restructure their traditional businesses. Common strategies in this respect include the creation of subsidiaries and the outsourcing of activities (Flecker and Hermann 2012, 109–112). Both measures save costs because workers employed by subsidiaries or subcontractors are usually paid lower wages. Hence German Post not only went global, but it also set up forty-nine regional subsidiaries for parcel delivery in Germany. Workers in these subsidiaries earn significantly less than those employed by the parent company (Handelsblatt 2016). At the same time, the Post subsidiary DHL uses hundreds of subcontractors to deliver express mail across Germany. In a 2011 study, Hajo Holst and Ingo Singe (2011, 60) found that independent deliverers were paid between 70 and 90 cents per delivered item. On average they made five euro per hour. The legal minimum wage in Germany was 8.50 euro per hour when it was first introduced in 2015. The self-employed deliverers made up for their low hourly wages by working up to 15 hours per day (Holst and Singe 2011, 60).

The deregulation of housing markets and the privatization of public housing have further deepened the function of real estate as an asset, as opposed to a place to live (Madden and Marcuse 2016, 26–35). The elimination of rent control, the erosion of tenants' rights, and the lack of an alternative to the private rental market have not only increased rents—rent for urban primary homes in the United States tripled between 1980 and 2017[57]—they have also encouraged former tenants to buy homes and become property owners in order to escape spiraling rent and to shelter from the prospect of being evicted on short notice.[58] Growing demand for home ownership has, in turn, fueled real estate prices, with the result that new homeowners often have to take on excessive debt in order to be able to buy a home. Outstanding US mortgage debt increased from less than four trillion US dollars in 1990 to more than 14 trillion in 2008.[59] And it was not only that: a growing proportion of mortgage interest is no longer fixed but fluctuates according to the market rate.

Meanwhile, interest is only one source of revenue in the mortgage industry. With the lifting of regulations that made sure that lending primarily served homeowners in the postwar decades, US mortgage debt has been turned into a financial product that is sold to investors around the world (Madden and Marcuse 2016, 32). In this process, several parties make a cut: the lender who underwrites the initial mortgage contract; the agency that collects the payments; the securitizers that sort mortgages according to maturity, locality, risk of default, and other criteria and package them in mortgage-backed securities or collateralized mortgage obligations; the rating agencies that confirm the security of the resulting financial products; as well as the dealers and traders who sell the securities to banks and financial investors. Securitization of mortgages is not new.[60] However, the total value of mortgage-backed security issuances increased from less than

500 million US dollars in 1996 to more than 3.2 trillion dollars in 2003 (McConnell and Buser 2011, 179).

The commodification of agriculture has fueled the commodification of food and vice versa. The shift from poly- to monoculture cultivation of plants provided the food industry with the cheap inputs for its industrially processed food. In turn, the use of a limited number of plants as the source of most food ingredients—hundreds of US supermarket products contain some ingredient derived from corn—made it even more attractive for farmers to specialize in single-plant cultivation. In the United States, 70 percent of the land used for planting crops is used for corn, soybeans, and wheat (National Agricultural Statistics Service 2016). At the same time, concentration meant that farmers dealt with an ever-smaller number of large customers, driving down prices and therefore creating the need to increase output.

Yet one problem of monoculture farming is precisely that soil fertility tends to decline while the susceptibility for infestation increases (Altieri 1998). Here the chemical and biotech industries come into play: They have provided farmers with large amounts of fertilizers, pesticides, and increasingly GM crops. In spite of growing environmental concerns, the amount of money spent on pesticides in US agriculture increased five times (in real terms) between 1960 and 2008. However, the 12 billion US dollars spent in 2008 is significantly lower than the 15.4 billion spent in 1998 (Fernandez-Cornejo, Nehring, et al. 2014, 9). Even more dramatically, the proportion of corn harvested from genetically engineered plants increased from 25 percent in 2000 to 90 percent in 2013. Soybeans and cotton are also frequently grown from GM crops, with the result that in 2013 about half of total land used to grow crops in the United States was used to grow GM plants (Fernandez-Cornejo, Wechsler, et al. 2014, 9).

The relentless drive toward commodification did not stop here: The production of low-cost staples such as corn provided animal farmers with a cheap source of animal feed which, in turn, made them partly independent from the use of land to feed their livestock. In the United States, more corn is fed to animals than is used for human diets.[61] The result is so-called concentrated or confined animal feeding operations (CAFOs) where hundreds if not thousands of animals are contained in limited spaces for the production of meat, milk, or eggs (PEW 2008). According to the Union of Concerned Scientists (2008, 2), CAFOs only account for 5 percent of all US animal operations, but they produce more than 50 percent of America's meat. Even though antibiotics had been added to animal feed for some time to promote animal growth, these overcrowded spaces have made antibiotics even more attractive to farmers because they limit the transmission of diseases. Factory farming therefore greatly expanded the market for antibiotics. In the United States, more antibiotics are consumed by animals than by human beings (Barrett and Armelagos 2013, 104). The use of antibiotics in animal farming has become so commonplace that the Centers for Disease Control (2013, 11) warns of the growing threat of antibiotic-resistant infections for humans and urges the phasing out of antibiotics in animal food production.

Nevertheless, commodification had another trick up its sleeve: the low-cost meat produced by concentrated animal feeding operations created cheap inputs that allowed fast-food restaurants to offer hamburgers, chicken wings, and other meals at prices that are significantly lower than those of traditional restaurants. And because of their success, fast-food chains became the largest customers of meat producers. Today, McDonalds is the largest purchaser of beef, and KFC is the largest buyer of chicken in the United States. Their enormous demand for cheap meat, in turn, has spurred the expansion of factory farming (Smith 2016, 17, 136).

Conclusion

The purpose of this chapter has been to show that commodification has a number of problematic consequences. The fact that goods and services are given a price that consumers have to pay when they want to possess or use them means that those who do not have sufficient money are excluded. Exclusion is particularly problematic if the goods and services in question are essential for survival as a human being. However, exclusion is not always the result of the inability to pay. Needs can also be neglected because the individual is part of a social group with insufficient collective purchasing power. Because goods and services in a commodified system are only produced when they generate sufficiently high profits, the collective purchasing power of potential consumers must be high enough to justify investments in the development and provision of commodities. The neglect of unprofitable needs is complemented by a focus on those needs that promise particularly high profits. For private investors, the time they have to wait for returns on their investments in critical. This is why commodification entails a focus on short-term profits. Short-term profitability often comes at the cost of long-term sustainability. A major victim of short-termism is the environment.

While focusing on profitability, private companies routinely shift the burden of costs associated with their businesses on to the wider public. Governments then have no choice but to jump in and take over the activities of failing providers who deliver essential services. Externalization also greatly affects the environment and produces ecological crises.

Contrary to the promise of greater choice in markets with multiple private suppliers, commodification in fact entails a process of standardization and homogenization. The reason is that for markets to function there has to be a clearly defined and comparable output that can be bought from competing suppliers. In addition, producers often increase profits by exploiting economies of scale—and economies of scale depend on an advanced degree of standardization. Contrary to popular wisdom, commodification can even fuel bureaucratization and the expansion of management or administration. Here the main reason is that the administration of markets and the documentation of chargeable outputs create bureaucratic work that is either carried out by additional personnel or shifted onto existing staff—usually at the cost of other more essential tasks. Especially in labor-intensive services, strategies to increase profitability frequently imply the worsening of the work and employment conditions of non-managerial staff and, consequently, a deterioration of service quality.

Finally, commodification also invites manipulation and speculation. This often has dramatic effects for those dependent on given goods and services. Together, the exclusion of those who cannot pay and those who belong to specific social groups, the focus on profitable needs at the expense of unprofitable demands, as well as increases in prices and the variation of price according to quality, fuel another development that is characteristic of commodification: growing inequality. Self-interest and profit-orientation become the main reason for economic activities, undermining alternative motives of human action such as solidarity and use-value orientation. Most importantly, commodification tends to produce more commodification, as commodification processes reinforce one another, with the result that people and societies become more and more dependent on the commodified goods and services. Because commodification is an ever-expanding process, it is not only problematic when it affects certain forms of production or spheres of life. Instead, commodification always produces winners and losers, and the winners are overwhelmingly those with plenty of money.

5

Limits to Commodification

Introduction

While capitalism depends on commodification, no society has ever existed in which everything is really for sale. So far, in every known society, some goods, services, emotions, or actions have been provided for free, disregarding the profit motive. This raises questions about how much commodification societies can take or, put differently, where the limits of commodification lie. As mentioned previously, many critics of commodification believe that it has gone too far in recent decades, but few explicitly address how much commodification is enough. This chapter presents major arguments that imply limits to commodification. Based on the nature of the limits, four broad categories of boundaries can be identified: social limits, political limits, systemic limits, and ecological limits. The chapter discusses each group in a separate section and ends with a brief conclusion.

Social limits

Michael Walzer (1983, 100–103) has compiled a list of what he calls "blocked exchanges" and what can be described as "no-goes" for commodification. At top of the list is the ban on trade in human beings. When humans are the property of other humans, they become slaves, and slavery is widely considered as incompatible with the basic human rights granted in modern societies (see Chapter 1). For Walzer, other no-goes include institutions that are indispensable to the functioning of modern democracies, such as the sale of political power (votes) and political offices, exemptions from military service, jury duty, and other forms of communally imposed work (1983, 100–103). In addition, citizens enjoy certain rights that are inalienable, including the freedom of speech, religion, and assembly; marriage and procreation rights; and the right to leave a political community. Honors and prizes should not be for sale, since they lose their meaning if they can be obtained for money. The

The Critique of Commodification. Christoph Hermann, Oxford University Press. © Oxford University Press 2021.
DOI: 10.1093/oso/9780197576755.003.0005

same holds for love and friendship. Walzer (1983) also argues that basic welfare services such as police protection and primary and secondary education should be free and therefore cannot fully be commodified. He, furthermore, urges the establishment of a minimum set of social protection, including an eight-hour workday, minimum wages, and workplace health and safety regulations. Such regulations are necessary to protect workers from the outcome of what Walzer calls "desperate exchanges."

Morals, rights, duties, social protection, and social welfare are all social norms that stand outside of market logic. What are sometimes described as the moral limits of markets are really social boundaries of commodification. However, since social norms are subject to change, boundaries can also shift. Arlie Hochschild (2003, chapter 2) calls the shifting boundary of commodification "commodity frontier." Several of the things that were considered outside the market sphere a few decades ago have become subject to market exchange and are now readily paid for—including, as Hochschild points out, various household activities (2003, chapter 2). Yet for Michael Sandel (2012, 10–11) a tipping point is reached when a market economy transmutes into a market society. "A market economy is a tool . . . for organizing productive activity. A market society is a way of life in which market values seep into every aspect of human behavior. It's a place where social relations are made over in the image of the market."

The distinction between market economy and market society resembles Karl Polanyi's claim that with the establishment of an economy that is exclusively governed by market signals—what he calls self-regulated markets—society becomes a mere adjunct to the market (Polanyi 1957). Hence, "[i]nstead of economy being embedded in social relations, social relations are embedded in the economic system" (1957, 57). Subsequent scholars have called this process dis-embedding (e.g., Lie 1991).[1] While in pre-capitalist societies, economic activities were governed by all kinds of non-market-based social norms—customs, law, religion, and, perhaps, morals—such regulations disappear with the establishment of self-regulated markets. In self-regulated markets the profit motive, which played a marginal role in pre-capitalist forms of production and distribution, becomes the sole guiding principle for human behavior and economic organization.[2] Another consequence of dis-embedding is that once established, the self-regulated market affects ever more aspects of social life. As a result, even goods that were never intended for sale become commodities that are traded on markets. Above all, these include labor, land, and money. For Polanyi, labor is a human activity and as such cannot be separated from the human individual, stored, and mobilized independently; land is nothing other than a form of nature which is not a human product, and money is a measure for purchasing power rather than a product with intrinsic value. Since their commodity character is utterly socially constructed, Polanyi calls them fictitious commodities (1957, 72). However, as fictitious commodities, they, too, are subordinated to the market logic.

While sharing these concerns about the subordination of social relations to market forces, Polanyi goes beyond Sandel and other moral critics of commodification when he argues that a society governed by self-regulating markets is not only undesirable but also unsustainable. At the very beginning of his major work, *The Great Transformation*, Polanyi notes that the idea of a self-adjusting market is a crude fiction. "Such an institution could not exist for any length of time without annihilating the human and natural substance of society; it would have physically destroyed man and transformed his surroundings into wilderness" (1957, 3). This does not mean that certain social forces—what Polanyi calls the "liberal creed"—have not tried. The result was a series of devastating social and economic crises that plagued the capitalist world in the late nineteenth and early twentieth centuries, the rise of fascism and the two world wars. Polanyi substantiates his thesis by describing the consequences of the establishment of markets for the fictitious commodities of labor, land, and money. He argues that without any legal or moral protections, workers would be either exposed to indiscriminate exploitation or left to starvation. In both cases, the consequences would be devastating for those who have no alternative to the sale of their labor power. As a commodity, land, too, would be reduced to a mere resource in the production process and subsequently exposed to over-exploitation, with the result that the ability to produce food would be destroyed. The trade in money, finally, would result in periodic shortages and surfeits of money, which would be as disastrous for modern businesses as floods and droughts were in primitive societies (1957, 73).

Polanyi's warnings about the disastrous effects of self-regulated markets met with renewed interest after the Great Recession, as deregulated financial markets were widely held responsible for the worst economic downturn since the 1929–1932 crash. Among others, Nancy Fraser (2014) uses Polanyi's framework to make sense of the 2008–2009 crisis. Following Polanyi, Fraser argues that the crisis was not only a financial crisis. Instead, once again, the (re-)commodification of labor, land, and money stood at the heart of the economic and social collapse. Yet Fraser also expands Polanyi's perspective by focusing not only on labor, land, and money, but also on the broader categories of social reproduction, nature, and the financial system (2014, 542). According to Fraser, societies are facing a triple crisis. First, there is the crisis of social reproduction. This includes not only high levels of unemployment and precarious jobs, but also a shortage of care as families struggle to provide care for their children, the elderly, and the disabled (2014, 550–551). As the state has largely abandoned the responsibility to provide adequate social services, some families rely on migrant workers to look after dependent family members. Yet these migrant women often lack a formal employment contract and are usually paid below minimum wages for what used to be uncommodified domestic labor. They are often forced to leave their own children in the hands of other family members, neighbors, or even without supervision. This means that far from being solved, the problem of social reproduction is only handed down to the most vulnerable groups in society (Fraser 2014).

Second, the environmental problems Polanyi alluded to have become a full-fledged ecological crisis. With the invention of genetic modification of crops and the patenting of DNA, the commodification of nature has proceeded beyond anything Polanyi could have imagined (see Chapter 4). The depletion of natural resources and the pollution of the environment have brought the planet to the brink of collapse (Fraser 2014, 552–553; see also the section on ecological limits later in this chapter).

Third, rather than providing financial stability, deregulated financial markets have become a constant source of insecurity. In the twenty-first century the trade in currency has been surpassed by the trade in derivates and other so-called securities. Yet rather than making financial investments more secure, securitization has fueled speculation and has left the financial system even more vulnerable to market fluctuations (Fraser 2014, 553–554). Neoliberalism, or the second coming of the nineteenth-century faith in the "self-regulating market" (2014, 543), responded to the triple challenge with more rather than less market: the commodification of care work, markets for carbon emissions and other environmental "bads," as well as the invention of new financial products such as credit default swaps. Yet, not surprisingly, the reinvention and expansion of what Polanyi has called the "satanic mill" has only resulted in another economic and social disaster.

While from a Polanyian perspective it is obvious that societies cannot be "commodities all the way down" (the title of Fraser's article), it is less clear how much commodification societies can take. There are two competing interpretations: On the one hand, there are authors who use Polanyi to argue for what can be called a social-democratic program for taming markets. Fred Block is a representative of this approach. He and his coauthors go to great lengths to separate Polanyi from Marx and to argue that Polanyi's notion of embedding refers to the political regulation of markets (e.g., Block and Sommers 2014, chapter 3). There is also a more radical position, however, which argues that because of the need to commodify labor, land, and money, capitalism is ultimately prone to fail (a system in which labor is not a commodity can hardly be called capitalism). Michael Brie (2015, 22), for example, notes that Polanyi saw only two solutions to the disaster caused by self-regulated markets: fascism and (democratic) socialism. Not surprisingly, given his political history, Polanyi was strongly in favor of the second (Brie 2015). Both interpretations can be backed with references from Polanyi's writings (as is the case with other authors, Polanyi's work is not free from an occasional lack of clarity and possibly contradictory statements). In my view, Polanyi's repeated references to the separation of the economic and political spheres—a unique feature of capitalism that did not exist in pre-capitalist societies or in fascism or socialism—suggest that societies need more than regulation to overcome this division (Polanyi 1957, 71). Polanyi repeatedly mentions economic planning and the social control of the means of production as viable strategies to re-embed the economy in society (1957, 257).

Political limits

Not only did Polanyi assume that self-regulated markets would result in economic and social annihilation; he also argued that this process could not go unchallenged. "Inevitably society took measures to protect itself" (Polanyi 1957, 3). The result is what Polanyi calls a double movement (1957, 130): Every move to expand the market is met by a countermovement to push back against the intrusion of market forces into the fabric of social life. According to Polanyi, attempts to create a market society through the commodification of labor, land, and money in the late eighteenth and early nineteenth centuries were met by a series of pushbacks, such as the adoption of the Factory Acts, the introduction of tariffs on agricultural products, and, ultimately, the departure from the gold standard in the 1930s (1957, chapter 11).[3] Developments after the Second World War brought an even more regulated form of capitalism with the emergence of the welfare state, the exclusion of agricultural products from the General Agreement on Trade and Tariffs, as well as the establishment of the Bretton Woods system for monetary and exchange-rate management.

However, the automatic nature of the countermovement proposed by Polanyi has been questioned by the absence of an effective push for re-embedding following the wave of (re)commodification unleashed by neoliberalism since the 1970s. While there is no shortage of opposition to neoliberalism—including, among others, movements against globalization, privatization, precarization, and inequality—these struggles have so far failed to turn the tide. Many expected that the 2008–2009 crisis would mark the end of neoliberalism and the beginning of a new progressive era, but more than ten years after the crisis there are few signs of fundamental change. Given the experience of recent decades, it looks as if Polanyi was too optimistic. This may be due to the specific time period he based his analyses on (Brie 2015, 27–28). It may be due to his disregard for Marxist political economy and its emphasis on the imperative of accumulation (Burawoy 2010, 301–302). Yet it is also due to an underdeveloped analysis of class and social forces.

Polanyi assumed that only a small group of capitalists would benefit from the growth of self-regulated markets, whereas the vast majority of the population would suffer from what he described as cultural degeneration (Polanyi 1957, 161–162). De-commodification therefore represented the general interest of society (whereas struggles against exploitation exclusively served the interest of the working class)—uniting the heterogenous groups fighting for various protectionist measures. Hence "no single groups or classes were the source of the so-called collectivist movement, though the outcome was decisively influenced by the character of the class interests involved. Ultimately, what made things happen were the interests of society as a whole" (1957, 161–162). While Polanyi goes into great depth to explain the success of the countermovement, he has little to say about how the highly particular interests of the supporters of laissez-faire capitalism became so dominant in the late eighteenth and early nineteenth centuries. What is missing, in other words, is an explanation of how social groups and their interests become hegemonic. Of course, it was Antonio Gramsci who thought very thoroughly about this problem. According to Gramsci, the state apparatus, cultural institutions, and public intellectuals, as well as class alliances and compromises, play a key role in what he described as a hegemonic project (Forgacs 2000, chapter 6).

Precisely because of the hegemonic nature of politics, interests do not have to be universal to become dominant and, conversely, universal interests can remain marginal. The neoliberal counterrevolution and its program of re-commodification were not successful because it represented the universal interest of society—quite to the contrary. It was successful because it was a hegemonic project (Albo 2007). As such, it represented the interests of a rel-atively small group of wealthy individuals—the so-called one percent—but it succeeded in gathering support among various social groups, including reli-gious groups that were not so much attracted by economic liberalism than by social conservatism (Brown 2006). Thatcher and Reagan, to take two leading politicians of the neoliberal era, not only pushed for economic liberalization; at the same time, they also promoted anti-liberal family and social policies (Cooper 2017). Following Gramsci, several authors currently think about the potential of hegemonic projects to counter neoliberal commodification (Evans 2005; Brand 2005).

Polanyi's enthusiasm for the universal character of the countermovement not only meant that he missed the critical importance of hegemony. It also meant that he paid too little attention to the specific motives for what he called collectivist struggles. This is surprising, given that he was well aware of the reactionary and anti-democratic nature of some of the movements against the expansion of markets.[4] As mentioned previously, Polanyi also noted that there are two major solutions to the failure of the market society: fascism and socialism. The main difference between the two is that the first neglects the possibility of freedom, while the other one embraces freedom and promises a form of freedom that goes beyond the market freedom promoted by laissez-faire liberals. For Polanyi the freedom of capital owners is based on the un-freedom of wage earners. While capital owners dictate prices and choose to invest, wage earners merely cope with the consequences of these decisions. In contrast, socialism, through conscious regulation and control of the economy, offers the possibility of combining civil liberty with social justice (Polanyi 1957, 256). Yet while criticizing the liberals' narrow understanding of freedom, Polanyi paid little attention to non-market-based forms of op-pression, such as social hierarchies and racial exclusion. It is the disregard for the latter that keeps Polanyi from seeing that markets can actually have liberating effects when they do away with oppressive social norms, such as, for example, the patriarchal family and the confinement of women to un-paid household work.[5] In a similar way, Georg Simmel (2004, 285–287) has argued that money has a liberating effect because it frees individuals from personal ties such as, for example, the tie between serf and master. Fraser (2014, 547–548) therefore suggests distinguishing between struggles against commodification that defend or challenge forms of social domination and those that do not. It is only the former that promises a progressive alternative based on de-commodification.

Polanyi's disinterest in non-market-based forms of social domination is matched by a disregard for struggles against exploitation, which, at best, play a subordinate role in his account of the countermovement. Instead, resistance against commodification is mainly sparked by what Polanyi describes as cultural injuries, including damaging the social status of those affected (1957, 157). Beverly Silver (2003, 16–20) distinguishes between Marxist and Polanyian types of labor unrest, the former focusing on limiting exploitation and the latter on maintaining social security in the wake of expanding labor markets. Both played a significant role in the more than one hundred years of labor protests that Silver covers in her analysis, but their importance varies over time. For example, workers and their unions at times fought for shorter work hours to have more free time, while at others they mainly did so to fight unemployment—assuming that shorter hours meant that the same amount of work could be distributed among a larger group of workers (Hermann 2015a, chapters 8 and 9). However, in both cases their motive was economic rather than cultural. After more than two hundred years of capitalist expansion, resistance against commodification is overwhelmingly the result of economic facts. The citizens of Cochabamba who started the so-called water war against the privatization of the municipal water system did so primarily because the increase in water prices threatened their material existence—not their social status (see Chapter 4). The hundreds of protests against the failure of the government to deliver public services in South Africa that take place every year are also mainly driven by the desire to improve living conditions in townships (Ngwane 2011). Even resistance against land-grabbing and gentrification in various parts of the world is as much economically motivated as driven by the desire to preserve communities and cultures.

Furthermore, in a capitalist economy, commodification is a precondition for exploitation. It is only because labor is a commodity that capitalists can extract surplus value without relying on extra-economic forces. In reality, commodification and exploitation often go hand in hand. The liberalization and privatization of public services in Europe, for example, have meant that quality and prices can vary according to the purchasing power of customers, and those who cannot pay are more quickly cut off (see Chapter 4). It has also meant that public service workers have lost job security and many have taken wage cuts, while newly hired workers are often confronted with precarious employment conditions (Hermann and Flecker 2012b). Not surprisingly, the public-sector trade unions are at the forefront in the struggle against privatization, including, in the European case, the staging of a highly successful European citizens' initiative against the commodification of water (Hermann, Kubisa, and Schulten 2012).[6] In California it was the nurses' union that successfully fought for the introduction of minimum hospital staff-to-patient ratios—first in collective agreements and then in state legislation (Gordon, Buchanan, and Brethorst 2009, chapters 1 and 2). The staff-to-patient ratios not only maintain acceptable working conditions, they also protect patients from errors caused by overworked staff, while giving them a chance to talk to a person familiar with their case. It is precisely coalitions between workers and consumers or between consumers and environmentalists that can make struggles against commodification hegemonic.

In sum, two main conclusions can be drawn from Polanyi's idea of the countermovement. First, there are political limits to commodification as people tend to resist the negative consequences caused by self-regulated markets. However, the success of the countermovement depends on the hegemonic nature of the struggles against commodification. Second, de-commodification is a strong motive for social resistance and can unite various social groups, including producers and users of public services. Yet resistance alone does not guarantee a progressive alternative to commodification. For that to happen, de-commodification must be linked to liberation from oppression. An effective way to end social domination is the promotion of democratic participation and cooperative decision-making in all spheres of life, including economic, political, and personal matters.[7] Socialist feminists have argued this for a long time. Of course, this would also end the separation of the economic and political sphere discussed earlier.

Systemic limits

In addition to confronting social and political boundaries, commodification also faces systemic problems. Systemic limits differ from social and political ones inasmuch as opposition to commodification does not arise from outside the market system, either as a result of social necessity or political reflex; rather it is the market system, or more precisely capitalism, that is threatened by continuous commodification. In Marxist terms, it is the logic of capitalist accumulation that produces a limit to commodification. Polanyi's prediction that self-regulated markets ultimately destroy labor power and natural resources can also be seen as a systemic failure—but one that can easily be remedied by (political) regulation. Other systemic failures are much harder to fix, or can only be delayed rather than solved.

Rosa Luxemburg has pointed to such a problem. Her starting point is a critique of Marx's schema of the expanded version of capitalist reproduction. According to Marx, capital accumulates as capitalists invest parts of their profits in new production, including more machines and more workers, which, in turn, leads to more output and more profits, some of which, again, are reinvested. The problem with this model, according to Luxemburg, is that as a closed system there is not sufficient demand to take up the additional output.[8] Workers can only consume parts of their social output because otherwise there would be no surplus value and no profit. Yet capitalists, too, must leave parts of the profit unconsumed so that it can be reinvested. As a result, expanded reproduction creates more and more products, while at the same time restricting demand for the growing output.

For Luxemburg there is only one solution to this problem: capitalism needs non-capitalist outlets to absorb the surplus created by expanded reproduction (Luxemburg 2003, 346). "The decisive fact is that surplus value cannot be realized by sale either to workers or capitalists, but only if it is sold to such social organizations or strata whose own mode of production is not capitalistic" (2003, 332). This means that capitalism depends on a non-capitalist outside to grow and prosper. Yet what makes things even more difficult is that in order to absorb the excess supply, these non-capitalist economies must be commodified—i.e., their economies can no longer be self-sufficient. Instead, the members of these societies must be rendered dependent on the acquisition of commodities to reproduce themselves.[9] The result is what is widely discussed as imperialism. Hence "[i]mperialism is the political expression of the accumulation of capital in its competitive struggle for what remains still open of the non-capitalist environment" (2003, 426). The United Kingdom, among others countries, has an impressive record of making its colonies dependent on goods manufactured in the "motherland."[10] However, the colonies not only provided an outlet for capitalist surplus production; they also supplied the capitalist center with cheap raw materials, agricultural products, and labor power. As a result, capitalism tends to undermine the non-capitalist outside it depends upon.

Following Luxemburg, David Harvey calls the mode by which capital incorporates non-capitalist resources and forms of production accumulation by dispossession (see Chapter 1). However, rather than assuming a lack of demand as the main driver for expansion, Harvey (2003, 138–139) emphasizes the need to find new opportunities for investments to keep capitalist accumulation going. The problem, in other words, is not under-consumption but over-accumulation (2003, 138–139). The focus on investment rather than demand also means that capital can use existing non-capitalist resources or forms of production within capitalist social formations for its expansion. From this perspective, the main reason for privatization is that the sale of public assets provides investment opportunities for surplus capital. In addition, capital can actively manufacture a non-capitalist social and territorial formation inside capitalism through spatial reconfigurations (2003, 141). Urban decay or the demise of industrial districts entails a systematic devaluation of existing assets. Spatial devaluation also means de-commodification—even though the people who live in the abandoned spaces often suffer from the lack of economic activity. Yet over time devalued spaces can provide the ground for new investments (2003, 151–152). A prime example of this phenomenon are American inner cities which were largely abandoned in the 1960s and 1970s in the wake of postwar suburbanization, only to experience a dramatic comeback in the 1990s and early 2000s as the target of gentrification. According to Harvey (2003, 151), "[r]egional crises and highly localized place-based devaluations emerge as the primary means by which capitalism perpetually creates its own 'other' in order to feed upon it."

Others have pointed to the role of internal colonization as a mode of absorbing surplus value.[11] Following Luxemburg, Burkhart Lutz (1984, 57–61 and 216–217) has argued that Fordist expansion during the postwar period was sustained by the commodification of working-class reproduction through the expansion of mass consumption—including the acquisition of detached family homes, cars, washing machines, TV sets, etc. Commodification also increasingly affected leisure time with the development of tourism, the expansion of television, and the creation of theme parks (Schmid 2013, 26). However, because the expansion was based on the commodification of previously uncommodified aspects of working-class life, it eventually had to come to an end. The result was the crisis of the 1970s, ending what Lutz has called "the short dream of everlasting prosperity" (the title of his book).

For Klaus Dörre (2015a, 42–43), financialization is another form of internal colonization and as such is an indispensable component of the neoliberal expansion that has dominated economic development since the 1980s. The provision of credit allows working-class households, at least for some time, to consume more output while their share of the social product is declining. Financial markets, at the same time, provide new space for accumulation through the creation of new investment opportunities such as asset-backed securities based on mortgages, consumer loans, or student debt. Through the privatization of pension systems, even the retirement income of ordinary workers becomes the object of financial accumulation. In addition, internal colonization can also target existing non- or not fully capitalist modes of social provisioning, such as healthcare, education, or unpaid care work (Dörre 2013, 89–90). According to Dörre (2016, 227), each phase of capitalist expansion must be accompanied by a new wave of colonization. Ursula Huws makes a similar argument when she describes how the commodification of a previously uncommodified social sphere, such as household reproduction, results in the invention of a whole series of new products—washing machines, detergents, dryer sheets, etc.—that can be sold to consumers (see Chapter 1). Several authors see nature as new frontier for commodification (Smith 2006; Burawoy 2010, 309–310; Dörre 2015b, 261–264). Biotechnology and the patenting of DNA have greatly expanded the possibilities for turning natural substances into commodities, while at the same time the rights to pollute are sold as carbon credits (see Chapter 3). In turn, the preservation of ecological resources such as a rain forest becomes a business.

Not everyone believes in the creative powers of commodification. The problem is that commodification tends to create additional costs. And these costs must be covered by the social product, leaving fewer resources that can be reinvested. For example, as soon as care work becomes a paid activity, families must earn sufficient income to cover the additional expense. This is why not all families can afford to employ domestic workers, and why those who can often use undocumented migrants and pay them less than minimum wages to do the job. This is also why even some die-hard capitalists are in favor of public healthcare and education, knowing that the private alternative creates more costs that can eat into their profits.[12] Perhaps nature is the best example: the more that nature is commodified, the more it costs (some scholars argue that nature can only be saved by putting a price on natural resources). For Maria Mies (1986, 33–34) and her colleagues from the Bielefeld

School of Feminism, women's unpaid and uncommodified domestic work—which in the developing world includes subsistence farming—is at the same time an expression of patriarchal oppression and a precondition for capitalist accumulation. As such it will not vanish anytime soon.

In sum, capitalist accumulation undoubtedly benefits from the existence of non-commodified environments and social strata, both as potential for expansion and as a source of cheap inputs in the accumulation process. However, the drive for expansion and the preservation of cheap inputs are often mutually exclusive. Hence for Harvey (2003, 152–153), capitalist accumulation is accompanied by a simultaneous process of de- and re-commodification or a constant re-drawing of the limits of commodification. Yet because it is hard to know beforehand if the profits from more accumulation outweigh the costs of more commodification, the boundaries are also the result of trial-and-error processes as families and businesses struggle with the consequences of additional expenses. Furthermore, what looks like the boundaries of commodification can also be understood as barriers that can be overcome by capitalist innovation. According to Dörre (2016, 227–228), it is the overcoming of these barriers that gives capitalism its specific dynamic. Yet the fact that capital has repeatedly demonstrated its ability to overcome barriers to accumulation by opening up new terrains for commodification does not mean that this process can go on forever. As discussed in the following section, the global ecosystem may present an ultimate barrier that cannot be overstepped without fatal consequences.

Ecological limits

The ecological boundaries of commodification are also systemic in the sense that they present barriers to capitalist accumulation, but their specific nature and growing importance warrant special treatment. Commodification here is mainly understood as the first step in the process of accumulation, assuming that natural resources that are paid for are deployed in a capitalist accumulation process. The fact that the holders of some resources are paid not to use them does not contradict this assumption. The value of carbon, wetland, and other credits depends on these resources being used up in the accumulation process. There are several barriers that emerge when natural resources become inputs in the accumulation process.

First, there is the finite nature of some natural resources that play a critical role in the capitalist accumulation process. Perhaps the most important non-renewable resource is petroleum. It takes several hundred thousand years to create petroleum from organic material. This means that there will be no additional oil in the foreseeable future when the existing reserves have been depleted. Petroleum is the most important modern source of energy, and as such represents the lifeline of the modern transportation system with its cars, trucks, buses, and airplanes. It is also a critical ingredient in many chemical processes, including the production of fertilizers. The main advantage of petroleum versus other fuels is that comparatively little energy needs to be invested to obtain vast amounts of energy in return (Altvater 2006, 39). In addition, oil and the various petroleum-based fuels can relatively easily be shipped, stored, and distributed to the final consumer.[13] As such, oil has proven an extraordinary useful ingredient in the capitalist accumulation process. Elmar Altvater (2006, 54) therefore calls the growth model that emerged in the 1920s and was consolidated after the Second World War "fossil fuel capitalism" (the importance of oil for the advanced capitalist economies can also be seen in the enduring conflicts over the control of oil, especially in the oil-rich countries of the Middle East).

US petroleum consumption increased by three times between 1950 and 2013 (Ratner and Glover 2014, 8). In 2017, the United States consumed a total of 7.26 billion barrels of petroleum products, or about 19.88 million barrels per day.[14] However, with accelerating oil consumption, the amount of remaining reserves has shrunk. Marion King Hubbert (1962) has predicted that there will be a point in time when the total amount of known oil reserves starts to decline. The invention of new extraction methods such as hydraulic fracturing and the exploitation of unconventional sources such as tar sands have proven initial predictions too pessimistic, and peak oil production has been pushed further into the future. This does not, however, mean that oil reserves are infinite. Furthermore, petroleum is not the only natural resource whose quantity is limited. A number of minerals used in the production of high-tech goods such as smart phones are close to or beyond their peak points (Diederen 2009). Given the growing scarcity of non-renewable resources, alongside the lack of fertile land and clean water, Birgit Mahnkopf (2013) suggests that we are not only approaching peak oil; we are approaching "peak capitalism."

Second, even if petroleum and other natural resources do not vanish in the foreseeable future, the costs for extracting these resources are expected to rise. The result is what Jason Moore (2015, Conclusion) has described as the end of cheap nature. In spite of the shale boom, US gasoline prices in 2012 were more than twice as high as in 1972.[15] And alternatives such as biofuels or other forms of renewable energy are even more expensive. Even the cost of food, a major factor for the reproduction of the labor forces, has increased since 2000 after declining over much of the postwar period (not least because of high oil prices). According to Moore, capitalist growth depends on cheap nature, and every major expansion in capitalism has been accompanied by a reduction in the price of key resources. Hence the Fordist expansion in the postwar decades was not only fueled by the invention of mass production, but also by the discovery of major oil fields (Moore 2015, 96–97). Higher costs for energy and other inputs in the production process will likely put pressure on profits, which may result in lower investments. This does not necessarily mean the end of capitalism. But it certainly means that future capitalism will look quite different from the one that we are used to (*Das Ende des Kapitalismus wie wir ihn kennen* [The end of capitalism as we know it] is the title of Altvater's 2005 book).

A third limit arises from the incompatibility between the temporality of capitalist accumulation and the temporality of the reproduction of nature (Moore 2015, 97–98). The accumulation process is driven in part by an acceleration of turnover time. Ever more goods are produced, consumed, and disposed in ever shorter time periods (Harvey 1990, chapter 17; Altvater 2005, 75–78). On average, smart phones in the United States are replaced every two and a half years, and Americans buy a new piece of clothing every 5.5 days (Schor 2010, 29).[16] In some cases, producers even build in artificial breaking points in order to limit the life cycle of their products (see Chapter 2). Shortening turnover time is one way in which capital makes sure that demand remains high. Time also plays a crucial role in nature's reproduction cycle. Renewable resources need time to regenerate. Trees, for example, need time to grow before they can be cut down and used for lumber. And growing environmental pollution can increase recovery time. Capital has succeeded in reducing the reproduction cycles of some agricultural products through the use of fertilizers and growth hormones. But in many cases, natural reproduction cycles cannot be manipulated. This is true in particular for the absorption of human pollution and waste. It can take several hundred years for carbon dioxide to disappear from the atmosphere and for plastic to degrade in the ocean (Archer et al. 2009; Kershaw et al. 2011). The growing tension between decreasing turnover time and stagnating or increasing reproductive time leads to a situation in which an increasing number of natural resources are no longer reproduced. Hence capitalist accumulation not only depletes non-renewable resources, but also destroys the basis for the reproduction of renewable inputs in the accumulation process.

A fourth boundary is the cumulative effect, or the chain reaction that is set in motion by ecological degeneration (Foster, Clark, and York 2010, chapter 6). Nature is a highly complex system, and human interference with natural processes can have unintended consequences. The colonial settlers who brought animals and plants from Europe to the New World sometimes triggered a chain reaction that brought indigenous flora and fauna to the verge of extinction. While these were in the past local or regional events, the expansion and acceleration of accumulation has meant that today unintended effects can have a global dimension. Perhaps the prime example is climate change. Climate change is the result of rising average temperatures on Earth, which, in turn, is chiefly caused by a record-high concentration of greenhouse gases in the atmosphere. Greenhouse gases such as carbon dioxide are mainly produced by human activity, such as the burning of fossil fuels (but also deforestation and the disappearance of "green sinks"). Climate change, in turn, causes extreme weather events, such as heat waves and cold snaps, record rainfalls and record droughts, as well as tornadoes and other storms—which, subsequently, cause floods, wildfires, and other environmental damage (including decimating harvests, which drives up food prices). Wildfires, in turn, destroy ecosystems that are important for the absorption of greenhouse gas emissions, while producing additional carbon dioxide through wood burning. According to some estimations, California wildfires, which have increased in frequency and size in recent years, more than undo the state's widely lauded initiative to reduce greenhouse gas emissions (Baker 2017).

In sum, nature creates an ultimate boundary for commodification and accumulation, but as Marx already noted, the limit is elastic (Burkett 1999, 142–143). Yet the elastic nature of the barrier also presents a major risk: Precisely because we do not know how much depletion, pollution, and destruction nature can take and what the cumulative effects of the various forms of ecological degeneration are, there is a real possibility that the limit will be overstepped and ecological devastation will reach a point of no return. Unfortunately, trial and error does not work for ecological limits. Once destroyed, nature cannot simply be restored. It takes dozens or hundreds of years for natural resources to recover. This must not mean the end of capitalism, but disastrous de-commodification will come at a huge social cost and will make it even more difficult to develop a progressive alternative.

Conclusion

The social limits of commodification include morals, rights, duties, and various forms of market regulations. They are necessary to protect society and certain aspects of social life from the consequences of markets and their imperative to undermine any valuations that are not based on money and the maximization of personal gain. In the view of moral critics of commodification, societies deprived of non-market values such as human rights, justice, honorability, welfare, and democratic citizenship are highly undesirable. Polanyi goes further when he argues that societies governed by self-regulated markets are in fact unsustainable. According to Polanyi, unregulated markets lead to social devastation. This is particularly true when dis-embedding affects the fictitious commodities of land, labor, and money. Polanyi pointed to the economic and social crises of the late nineteenth and early twentieth centuries to substantiate his claim. Several authors argue that the Great Recession, which shocked the world economy in 2008–2009, was also the result of dis-embedding, especially of financial markets. However, while it is clear from a Polanyian perspective that societies cannot survive when they are fully commodified, there is some debate about where exactly the limits of commodification lie. While for some it is enough to regulate markets, for others effective re-embedding demands nothing short of a move beyond capitalism and the establishment of what Polanyi has called democratic socialism.

Polanyi warned not only of the devastating effects of self-regulated markets, but he also argued that society has a quasi-natural reflex to protect itself from market-based intrusions into the social fabric. The resulting double movement means that commodification inevitably faces political limits. Polanyi, furthermore, argued that the interest of the countermovement is universal, as it represents the interests of the vast majority of the people who suffer from self-regulated markets. And the universal character would ensure that the countermovement is ultimately successful. Polanyi thereby greatly underestimated the role of hegemony, which can allow a minority to impose its interests on a majority and to block majority interests from becoming dominant. His admiration for the universal nature of the countermovement also blinded him to the reactionary character of some of the initiatives against the expansion of markets and caused him to overlook the liberating effects that markets can have when they do away with non-market-based forms of hierarchy and exclusion. Some authors therefore argue that a progressive alternative to market society cannot be based only on de-commodification, but must also aim to end all forms of social domination and marginalization.

A third group of limits to commodification are systematic in the sense that they do not arise as external limits to markets, but rather as intrinsic boundaries of the accumulation process. Luxemburg argued that capitalism needs a non-capitalist outside to survive. However, at the same time, it constantly destroys the outside by commodifying it. Subsequent authors have emphasized the possibilities for creating and exploiting outsides within capitalist systems through the privatization of public goods and services, the colonization of uncommodified spheres of social life, as well as spatial reconfiguration. In any case, the result is not only a constant re-drawing of the limits of commodification, but also sustained attempts to overcome existing barriers by opening up new terrains for commodification. However, since commodification comes with costs, limits can also be the result of social trial-and-error processes.

A fourth group of limits emerge as a result of the ecological destruction caused by commodification and accumulation. These limits follow from the fact that certain natural resources which are critical for the capitalist accumulation process are of a finite nature and will therefore run out at some point in the future. Even before these non-renewable resources are depleted, accumulation will likely run into problems because of the rising costs of natural resources. While in the past capitalism repeatedly found new ways to keep costs low, it increasingly looks as if the era of cheap nature will come to an end. Another challenge stems from the tension between the speed-up in accumulation and the stagnating or increasing time necessary for nature to reproduce itself. Because nature increasingly lacks the time to reproduce itself, accumulation does more than deplete non-renewable resources; it destroys renewable inputs into the accumulation process. Finally, the complexity of nature and natural processes means that human interference can have unintended consequences and can cause chain reactions with dangerous outcomes. The fact that intrusions into the world ecosystem can trigger chain reactions with unknown outcomes also means that humanity can easily overstep the ecological limit without realizing it. Perhaps herein lies the greatest danger to the capitalist system and to commodification.

6

Rediscovering Use Value

Introduction

Commodification, as argued in Chapter 2, can best be understood as subjugation of use value to exchange value. The distinction between use value and exchange value goes back to ancient Greek philosophy and played a prominent role in political economy until the later part of the nineteenth century. Adam Smith famously noted that water has an enormous use value, but hardly any exchange value, whereas diamonds have a large exchange value, but for most humans they are not particular useful. However, by the end of the nineteenth century, use value has largely been replaced by (marginal) utility as the universal measure of the value of goods and services. The near erasure of use value from economics and the social sciences more broadly meant that even critics of neoclassical economics, including representatives of the moral critique of commodification, assume that there is only one economic value and that this value can be expressed in money. To make things even worse: even within Marxist scholarship, which continued to insist on the duality of use value and exchange value, use value was largely marginalized, as some scholars argued that the transformation of use values lies outside the scope of critical political economy. However, the concept of use value attracted renewed interest with the accelerating ecological crisis: While nature has little if any (marginal) utility, it has an enormous use value. At the same time, nature's use value is inherently collective: it provides the collective basis of life and human flourishing.

This chapter pursues three goals. First, it rediscovers use value as a key concept of economic and social thought. Second, it argues why (marginal) utility is inadequate to capture the value of goods and services, including, most notably, the value of nature. Third, it emphasizes the need for a collective valuation of goods and services, resulting in what can be described as social and ecological utility. The chapter starts with a look at the antique roots of use value and then proceeds to a discussion of use value and exchange value in the work of classical political economists such as Smith and Marx.

The Critique of Commodification. Christoph Hermann, Oxford University Press. © Oxford University Press 2021.
DOI: 10.1093/oso/9780197576755.003.0006

The next section describes the emergence of utility as alternative to use value, followed by a presentation of marginal utility as a universal measure of value in neoclassical economics. The subsequent section presents major arguments in the Marxist debate about the role of use value in critical political economy. The following part discusses the value of nature and presents arguments for a collective assessment of social and ecological utility. The chapter ends with a brief conclusion.

The antique roots of use value

The idea that a good, or what was later described as commodity, has two sorts of value—exchange value and use value—goes back to Aristotle. In *Politics*, the Greek philosopher notes that "[o]f everything which we possess there are two uses. . . . For example, a shoe is used for wear, and is used for exchange; both are uses of the shoe" (Aristotle 1988, 12). For Aristotle, furthermore, the use for exchange is a secondary, improper form of usage, since "a shoe is not made to be an object of barter" (1988, 12). Rather than fulfilling a human need, use for exchange becomes the basis for profit-making and for the accumulation of wealth—something Aristotle depicts as unnecessary and not honorable, alien to what he perceives as a largely self-sufficient household economy. This does not mean that in his mind the exchange of goods should be rejected. In common with later work by Marx and others, Aristotle makes a distinction between the exchange of goods that a community has in abundance and exchanges for goods it needs, and exchange purely for gain. The first sort of barter "is not part of the wealth-getting art and is not contrary to nature but is needed for the satisfaction of men's natural wants" (1988, 12). Things started to change when money was introduced as a means to facilitate exchange. With the invention of coins as medium of exchange, the barter of necessary articles was increasingly displaced by exchange for profit-making (which Aristotle describes as the art of retail trade). Karl Polanyi (1957, 53–54) noted that Aristotle's distinction between production for use and production for gain or money-making is "probably the most prophetic pointer ever made in the realm of the social sciences." According to Polanyi (1957, 53–54), "[o]nly a genius of common sense could have maintained . . . that gain was a motive peculiar to production for the market, and that the money factor introduced a new element into the situation, yet nevertheless as long as markets and money were mere

accessories of an otherwise self-sufficient household, the principle of production for use could operate."

For Aristotle, the idea that money represents economic wealth is somewhat alien because money is "not useful as a means to any of the necessities
of life and, indeed, he who is rich in coin may often be in want of necessary
food" (1988, 13). Hence monetary riches or exchange-based wealth are an
unnatural form of wealth. As such, this stands in contrast to the natural art of
wealth-getting, which is part of what Aristotle describes as household management or what today can be called a largely self-sufficient economy (Booth
1993, 27).[1] True wealth, accordingly, cannot be represented by money; it
consists of the necessary things that allow for a life free of toil and full of enjoyment, in short, a good life created by a use- rather than exchange-value-
oriented economy (Aristotle 1988, 13; Booth 1993, 191–192). Georg Simmel
(2004, 176) later noted that "money is a claim upon society," or, we could add,
a claim on society's true wealth, i.e., on the use values created in a particular
community. While Aristotle's claim about natural and unnatural wealth has
a strong moral connotation, the insight that true wealth or the amount of
goods needed for a good life is limited proved to be an extremely prophetic
statement in the light of the twenty-first century's looming ecological crisis
(Aristotle 1988, 11; see later discussion).

Classical political economy and the distinction between use and exchange value

Adam Smith is usually credited for introducing the distinction between use
value and exchange value in modern political economy. However, Smith
was not the first modern scholar to follow Aristotle's lead. François Quesnay
(1963, 90), a French economist whom Smith met during a stay in Paris,
had already used the example of diamonds to argue that the "least useful
of items of exchangeable wealth, almost always has a market value which
greatly exceeds the market value of wealth in form of food" (market value
here means the same as exchange value and refers to the price a specific good
receives when being exchanged on the market).

However, Quesnay also notes that in exceptional circumstances, such
as in the case of a severe famine, the market value of food can exceed the
value of diamonds. In such an exceptional case, "it is the use value which
determines . . . its market value" (1963, 90). Generally, however, use values

have little impact on exchange values. "The fact that one item of wealth yields more gain than another . . . does not derive from their use values" (1963, 90). Furthermore, while use values tend to remain constant depending on people's needs, exchange values fluctuate according to changes in market prices. This means that the price of a specific good "is not regulated at all by men's needs" (1963, 90). This is a very strong statement and stands in stark contrast to the utilitarian approach and the concept of marginal utility discussed further later in the chapter.[2]

Anticipating the discussion of public goods, Quesnay, furthermore, notes that not all goods constitute marketable wealth, or have exchange values: "[T]he air which we breathe, the water which we fetch from the river, and all other goods or forms of wealth which are in very plentiful supply and available to everyone, are not exchangeable" (1963, 89). Marx later argued that it is the specific characteristic of commodities that they have exchange and use values, while non-commodified goods only have use values (see later discussion). In a similar manner, Quesnay stresses, "we should not confuse all goods which are suitable for men's subsistence, use, and enjoyment, with those items of marketable wealth which are of benefit because of their value in trade" (1963, 89).

Smith follows Quesnay by using diamonds as an example, but then compares diamonds to water rather than to food. The result is the famous diamond-water paradox: "Nothing is more useful than water: but it will purchase scarce anything. . . . A diamond, on the contrary has scarce any value in use; but a very great quantity of other goods may frequently be had in exchange for it" (Smith 1900, 21). While water satisfies an essential human need—humans cannot live without water—diamonds merely appeal to human sensibility and may initiate some positive feelings, or what economists describe as a state of pleasure (Smith 1900, 138). According to Smith, "the demand for . . . precious stones arises . . . from their beauty. They are of no use, but of ornaments" (1900, 138). The distinction between usefulness and beauty is important because what is considered to be beautiful and what is not are culturally determined (there may be some cultures where diamonds are not considered an object of beauty). As will be described in the following, the distinction between usefulness and beauty was later obscured with the invention of the concept of utility as an alternative to use value.

However, Smith was not so much interested in use values as he was in exploring "the principles which regulate the exchangeable value of commodities" (1900, 22). In the subsequent elaboration, Smith identifies two main characteristics that determine the exchange value or the price of goods sold on the market. On the one hand is the human "toil and trouble" for acquiring the good (1900, 22), or, in other words, the labor expended for the production of the respective object or a product of similar value which can be exchanged for it. On the other hand is the degree of scarcity. The scarcer a good, the higher its exchange value.[3] "Cheapness is in fact the same thing with plenty. It is only on account of the plenty of water that it is so cheap . . . and on the account of scarcity of diamonds . . . that they are so dear" (Smith 1896, 157).

Whereas Smith emphasizes the contradictory nature of use and exchange values—particularly useful goods have often little exchange value, and items with high exchange values are typically not particularly useful—Karl Marx starts his critique of political economy by pointing to the dual character of commodities—as bearers of use value as well as exchange value. For Marx, a commodity has a twofold nature: use value and exchange value (1990, 131). In fact, it is this dual character that distinguishes commodities from other goods that are produced for self-use rather than use of others. The dominance of commodity production, subsequently, distinguishes capitalism from other economic systems. There are a number of goods which only have use values, but no exchange values. Marx mentions air, virgin soil, natural meadows, or what we today would describe as nature. In addition to natural resources, goods also lack exchange value when they are produced for self-use. "[A] man who satisfies his own need through his product creates use-value, to be sure, but not a commodity. In order to produce a commodity, he must produce . . . use-value for others, social use values" (1990, 131).

Marx, furthermore, notes that use values and exchange values differ fundamentally in the way they can be assessed. While exchange values can be captured quantitatively, most commonly in units of money, use values can only be grasped qualitatively. "Wheat, for example, is a distinct use-value differing from the use-values of cotton, glass, paper, etc." (Marx 1970, 27). What makes things even more complicated is that the same object can have different use values: A diamond, for example, can be used as an ornament, but it also can be used for cutting glass. Because use values differ qualitatively, it is impossible to tell if one use value is greater than another. In a strict sense we therefore cannot say that water is more useful than diamonds. Water and diamonds satisfy different needs. All that we can say is that one need is more important for human survival and flourishing than the other. It is only through exchange on markets that a quantitative relationship between two qualitatively different goods is established.[4] Hence "[a]s use-values, commodities differ above-all in quality, while as exchange value they can only differ in quantity" (Marx 1990, 128; see also Chapter 2).

While the nature of use values and exchange values differs fundamentally, there is nonetheless a link between the two sorts of value: not only do commodities need use values to be sold in capitalist economies, but use values must also enable capitalists to sell the respective commodities for a profit. This means that the use values produced for one's own needs (as needs of the household, the community, or an even larger collective) may not be the same as use values produced for exchange. In the first case, use value is the whole purpose of production; in the second case, production is geared toward the creation of exchange value.

Marx does not explain, however, what exactly this means for use values or the usefulness of goods and services created for human reproduction. At best, he hints at the consequences of commodification when he writes about the alienation of workers in the capitalist mode of production (see Chapter 2). Instead, he notes that "[t]he use-values of commodities provide the material for a special brand of knowledge, namely the commercial knowledge of commodities" (1990, 126).[5] This statement, as discussed in the following, has created considerable confusion and controversies among Marx's followers and has caused some to argue that the nature and transformation of use values lays outside Marx's critique of political economy. However, capitalism differs from other social systems inasmuch as the purpose of the economy is not the creation of use values and the satisfaction of human needs; the purpose of economic activity is to create exchange values and to maximize profits. Use values are only a means to achieve this goal.

Utility as alternative to use value

There is an alternative interpretation of (use) value that goes back at least to Nicolas Barbon. The English economist notes that the value of all goods arises from their usefulness. "Things of no use have no value" (Barbon 1905, 13). Barbon then argues that goods are generally used to satisfy the necessities and wants of individuals. So far, Barbon's argumentation is still in line with later interpretations of Smith, Ricardo, and Marx. However, Barbon further notes that human beings generally have two different kinds of wants: the wants of the body and the wants of the mind (1905, 4). The wants of the body are necessities of life and concern such things as food, clothing, and lodging.

The wants of the mind are not necessary for human reproduction and concern the possession of certain objects such as diamonds, pearls, and precious stones. However, even though the satisfaction of the desires of the mind is not essential for human survival, they still imply human wants. And the "appetite of the mind" is as natural to the soul as "hunger to the body" (1905, 4). For Barbon, therefore, it makes no sense to distinguish between the value of goods that satisfy necessities of the body and those that satisfy desires of the mind; both goods have value, and their value is expressed in their respective prices (1905, 15).

Barbon makes three further observations that are relevant for the debate on use values and exchange values. First, while the necessities of the body are limited—one should only eat until one is satiated—the desires of the mind are boundless. "Man naturally aspires, and as the mind is elevated, his senses grow more refined, and more capable of delight" (1905, 14). As a result, "his desires are enlarged, and the wants increase with his wishes" (1905, 14). Second, desires of the mind (but not the necessities of the body) change over time, with the result that "things grow out of use, and so lose their value" (1905, 15). In today's terminology, we could say that the value of certain goods depends on the current state of fashion. Third, for Barbon the desire to possess something mainly because it cannot be possessed by somebody else is perfectly legitimate. Things that are rare and difficult to obtain are "general badges of honor" and the value of diamonds and other precious goods is therefore precisely that they convey honor to their owners (1905, 15). It is for this reason that scarce goods are more valued and achieve higher prices than commodities which are plentiful in supply. More than a hundred years later, Thorstein Veblen (2007; first published in 1926) criticized the desire of the rich to distinguish themselves from the poor as "conspicuous consumption."

Jeremy Bentham picks up where Barbon left off. He distinguishes between different needs and the values of the objects that satisfy these needs (Bentham 1954, 84). Barbon's needs of the body become essential and invariable values, deriving from such goods as foods, clothes, lodging, etc. Wants of the mind become variable, fancy, or superfluous values whose sole purpose is to further the enjoyment of the purchasers—including luxury goods, amenities, and conveniences. However, Bentham goes beyond Barbon when he argues that most objects have both variable and invariable value (1954, 84). The example he gives are pineapples. Pineapples have a variable value as a source of nutrition; but pineapples also have fancy value as a source of enjoyment. And this is the reason why pineapples are much more expensive than potatoes and "nobody in England will eat pineapples otherwise as a luxurious dessert" (1954, 84). In Bentham's words: The "value of the article as means of subsistence is absorbed and lost in its value of enjoyment" (1954, 84).

The next step in Bentham's argumentation is then to ask if it is possible to draw a distinction between invariable and variable values, or between what is necessary and what is superfluous. And his answer is: "I do not think so" (1954, 85). Bentham goes on to argue that what is considered necessary and superfluous varies from individual to individual, and for the same individual from one time to another. The obvious conclusion is that there is only one value and it should be left to the individual to judge the value of a particular good at a given point in time. Utility (which at this point no longer means the same thing as use value) subsequently becomes the impartial value of commodities. For Bentham (1907, 2), "utility is meant that property in any object, whereby it tends to produce benefit, advantage, pleasure, good, or happiness."[6] Bentham later contemplates how utility can be measured, but only gives some very general hints, such as the idea that the amount of utility depends on the intensity and duration of pleasure (1907, 29).[7]

The triumph of marginal utility

While utility (ability to please; benefit-giving power) had emerged as alternative to use value (usefulness), it was only with the marginalist revolution in economics that the term "use value" largely disappeared as an object of academic contestation. William Jevons (1879), the main proponent of the marginalist revolution in England, criticizes Smith and other classical political economists for failing to discriminate between total utility and the final degree of utility (or terminal utility) that an object confers to its owners—what Heinrich Gossen (1854, 85) had called the value of the "least atom" of the respective good.[8] According to Jevons, the acknowledgment that the utility of a good tends to decline the greater the quantity of it that a person possesses perfectly explains Smith's alleged water-diamond paradox: "Many commodities which are most useful to us are esteemed and desired but little. We cannot live without water, and yet in ordinary circumstances we set no value on it. Why is this? Simply because we usually have so much of it that its final degree of utility is reduced nearly to zero" (Jevons 1879, 57). It is only when water becomes scarce as, for example, during a drought, its final degree of utility starts to increase (1879, 86). However, the absence of scarcity does not always mean that the final degree of utility sinks to zero. This holds for goods that are consumed until one is satiated, including food and water. Echoing Barbon and Bentham, Jevons argues "the more refined and intellectual our needs become, the less are they capable of satiety" (1879, 86).

There is some debate as to who actually invented the term "marginal utility" (Howey 1972, 296–298). What is clear is that Alfred Marshall (1890, x) started to use it in *Principles of Economics* because he believed that it was more to the point than Jevon's final (degree of) utility.[9] Marshall also ends the debate about measuring pleasure and pain by declaring that the price of a commodity is the measure of its marginal utility (which means that marginal utility is effectively the same as exchange value). However, for neoclassical economists, marginal utility does not just explain prices and solve the water-diamond paradox; the assumption that marginal utility follows a predictable curve also allows for the application of mathematical models to predict the individual behavior of millions of economic agents—and as such became the basis for an attempt to recast economics as natural science (Milonakis and Fine 2009, 97).[10]

The main difference between use value and marginal utility is that while the former captures the ability of a good or service to satisfy human needs, the latter presents the price an individual is willing to pay to obtain an additional unit of a specific good or service. The purchase may give the owner pleasure, but it can be socially useless and ecologically harmful. For example, some people may derive pleasure from driving a Ferrari, but as a means of transport a Ferrari is quite impractical and, given its speedy acceleration, even dangerous.

Hence with the shift from use value to marginal utility, usefulness is no longer a social issue or, consequently, an issue of social contestation.[11] Instead, it becomes a matter of personal taste, or what Joseph Schumpeter (1954, 190) calls a "fact of individual psychology." However, with the invention of marginal utility, use value largely disappeared from economic discourse in the twentieth century, and, subsequently, from the social sciences more broadly. The triumph of marginal utility even means that critics of neoclassical economic reasoning, such as Margret Radin and Elizabeth Anderson, can only think of (marginal) utility when they criticize economic valuation.

Marxist use value controversies

While forgotten in mainstream economics, use value continues to play a role in the work of those economists who follow Marx's framework.[12] However, while most Marxists acknowledge the existence of use value as opposed to exchange value, there are different views with respect to the importance of use value in Marx's work and the associated question of whether an analysis of use values should be part of a Marxist political economy. Rudolf Hilferding (1919, 9) argues that use value represents the natural dimension of commodities, or their material aspect, whereas exchange value captures the social dimension, or their appearance as social relation. Accordingly, use value is the object of study of natural sciences, whereas exchange value is investigated by the social sciences, including the field of economics. Following Hilferding, Paul Sweezy (1946, 26) states that political economy is a science of the relations between people. "Marx excluded use value . . . from the field of investigation of political economy on the ground that it does not directly embody a social relation."[13]

The main opponent of the exclusionary view is Roman Rodolsky. He cites a series of passages from Marx's writings to demonstrate that Marx was far from suggesting that scholars should exclude use values from a critical analysis of capitalist political economy (Rodolsky 1977, chapter 3). Perhaps the strongest evidence for the inclusionary view can be found in Marx's *Marginal Notes on Adolph Wagner*.[14] Therein Marx strongly rejects Wagner's association of his view with those economists who suggest that use value should be removed from (economic) science. According to Marx, only an "obscurantist who has not understood a word of *Capital*" can come to such a conclusion (1975, 198). He subsequently clarifies that his statement, according to which use value is the subject of the study of merchandise, was intended to point readers who wanted to know more about use values to a useful source. He was suggesting that what the German economic professors had to say about the issue was mostly twaddle (1975, 198–199). In contrast to Wagner's interpretation of his work, Marx (1975, 200) insists that "for me use value plays an important role in economics completely different [than it did] in previous political economy." Henryk Grossman (1977, 44) subsequently concludes. "[t]he Marxist critique is directed against the abstract-value mode of study of political economy."

However, the refutation of the exclusion of use value from political economy had little impact on subsequent Marxist theorizing, let alone empirical research. In economics, most Marxists continued to analyze contradictions and shifts in capitalist societies in quantitative terms (most notably by analyzing the development of the profit rate) and paid little attention to the qualitative side of capitalist transformation, including the transformation of use values. An exception is Harry Braverman's (1974) *Labor and Monopoly Capital*, in which the author describes the degradation and deskilling of work in capitalist factories. This process can also be read as the transformation of the use value of labor power. Use value also figured prominently in the 1980s domestic labor debate. Some feminists argued that women performing unpaid labor in the household produce use values, but not exchange values. And because they only produce use value, their contribution to national wealth is largely ignored by mainstream and Marxist economics (Hermann 2015a, 37–38). However, the lack of exchange value has also meant that domestic work has been much less intensified than factory work, and the time spent on household labor declined only gradually over the postwar period (Hermann 2015a, 99–102). Qualitative aspects of life under capitalism also played a role in studies on the shift from modernism to postmodernism (Jameson 1991; Harvey 1990) and from Fordism to post-Fordism (Lutz 1984; Hirsch and Roth 1986; Ash 1994). Recent studies also looked at changes in housing, along with food and agriculture (Albritton 2009; Madden and Marcuse 2016; Holt-Gimenez 2017). Most importantly, use value experienced some kind of revival in light of the accelerating ecological crisis and the question of the value of nature.

The value of nature

With the growing critique of environmental destruction in the last third of the twentieth century, nature has increasingly become a focus of value discussions. In the neoclassical understanding of value, nature has no value because it has no marginal utility. The reason is that nature until recently was plentifully available. Following Jevon's argumentation, even though nature is essential for the survival of human beings, its marginal utility is zero because there is so much of it (by contrast, some natural resources such as oil are rare and therefore have a significant marginal utility—which has made them a source of considerable wealth). And because its marginal utility is zero, nobody (and especially no profit-maximizing corporation) wants to pay for nature. This has the somewhat contradictory effect that the more nature is destroyed, the more valuable it becomes (e.g., the more water is contaminated, the more valuable clean water becomes). The problem is that when destruction reaches a certain tipping point, nature can no longer reproduce itself, with disastrous effects for local and global ecosystems (see Chapter 5). Hence the moment when marginal utility of nature finally becomes large enough to warrant paying for it, it may very well be too late to save the planet as we know it.

This is essentially the dilemma that conventional environmental economists are facing.[15] Their response is to find ways to put a price on nature before it is too late. In other words, what they do is to derive marginal utility by imposing a price, rather than deriving a price from marginal utility (see, for example, Helm 2015; Helm and Pearce 1991; May and Seroa da Motta 1996). Yet putting a price on nature, or transforming nature into a commodity, is more complicated than it sounds. In order to have a price there needs to be a market, and in order to have a market there has to be a clearly defined good with exclusive and transferable property rights. Yet nature is precisely not a clearly defined good; it is a system with many components that, depending on the location, is never exactly the same and persistently changes (what is widely appreciated as biodiversity). What makes things even more complicated is that local habitats rarely exist in isolation and are dependent on other ecosystems. At the same time, the collective nature of many natural resources makes it difficult to limit access to nature to those who are able and willing to pay a price (how can we, for example, limit access to air?).

In spite of these difficulties, some attempts to create markets for environmental goods, which sometimes look more like environmental bads, have been successful. The European Emissions Trading System is one example. As discussed in Chapter 3, since 2003 companies can buy and sell emissions rights on a European-wide market. Another example is the trade in wetland credits, which is fairly common in the United States. However, trading environmental goods on markets means that the value of nature is determined by supply and demand, rather than its ability to sustain human life and maintain diverse ecosystems. For example, the value of a ton of carbon dioxide on the European emissions market collapsed in the wake of the 2008 economic crisis, while the ecological crisis deepened (as discussed in Chapter 5, nature's temporality differs from the timing of economic cycles). Contrary to marginal utility, the use value of nature doesn't fluctuate; it remains the same and it continues to be crucial for human survival. And while the price of nature increases the more of it that is destroyed, the same destruction causes a diminishment of ecological use value.

For some environmentalists, including those who identify with deep ecology, nature has intrinsic value, i.e., value that exists independently from human needs (e.g., Jacobs 1991, 74–77).[16] Intrinsic value is derived from social norms (e.g., the beauty of nature), moral considerations (e.g., animals and other organisms have the same rights to inhabit the planet as human beings), or spiritual feelings (e.g., nature as God's work). Yet understanding the utility of nature as intrinsic value raises at least three issues. First, as with all moral norms, it is unclear who decides what is valuable and merits protection and what does not. Second, intrinsic value is the same for all forms of nature. Grasslands have as much intrinsic value as rain forests. Yet if we accept this equation, there is little reason for protecting rainforests from being turned into grasslands. Third, if nature has only intrinsic value, this means that humanity could exist without it. This is a highly questionable proposition. Understanding nature as use value, in contrast, stresses the dependence of human beings on natural resources. The main use value of nature is that it provides the basis for life (Altvater 1990). From this perspective, rainforests are particularly useful because they are a major source of biodiversity and an effective instrument for absorbing carbon dioxide emissions (see Chapter 4). This is why rainforests need special protection. However, intrinsic value shares with use value the quality that the value of nature cannot be expressed in dollars and cents. As such, both stand in contrast to the concept of marginal utility.

Social and ecological utility

Understanding the value of nature as use value not only means that the value of nature is limited; the use value of nature is also inherently collective. On the one hand, nature is an encompassing system that cannot be separated and partialized without destroying or at least severely damaging its functioning. On the other hand, there is little benefit from nature if one is the only human being who can enjoy it. In fact, if you are the only human being in a natural habitat—like Robinson Crusoe on the Caribbean island—nature can be very dangerous.[17] Nature is no exception. Many and perhaps most goods and services created under capitalist relations of production have collective value; they provide a collective solution to a social need. Examples include transportation, education, and healthcare.[18] The denial of collective benefit is one of the most significant consequences of the adoption of the concept of marginal utility.

Polanyi (2016, 403) differentiates between individual and social utility.[19] Many products which seem to be useful from an individual perspective are useless or even harmful from the perspective of society as a whole (2016, 403). An example is transportation: While automobiles may be useful for an individual or a small group of individuals to get from point A to point B, automobility has become a major burden for people and the environment in many urban centers around the world. Not only are drivers stuck in traffic for hours; freeways take away much needed green space and pollute neighborhoods with emissions and noise. In addition, frequent traffic accidents cause injuries and sometimes even death. And because fuel-based transportation is one of the largest sources of greenhouse-gas emissions, automobility is also a major driver of climate change. Hence from a social and ecological perspective, automobility causes more harm than good. In contrast, a comprehensive and well-functioning public transport can provide mobility without destroying neighborhoods and the environment. In Polanyi's (2016, 404) terminology, public transport has a higher social—and we can add ecological—utility than automobility.[20] However, as pointed out in Chapter 2, investors still favor automobility because of the much higher profits that can be obtained from selling cars. Hence commodification not only implies the subjugation of use value to market/exchange value; it also involves the promotion of individual utility at the cost of social and ecological utility.

To come back to the example of transportation: car manufacturers are not selling just any cars; they are interested in selling cars that promise particularly high profits. In recent years, car manufacturers in the United States, but also increasingly in Europe, have focused on the sale of sports utility vehicles (SUVs).[21] SUVs are generally bigger and heavier than medium-sized passenger cars, include more special features, and, hence, sell for a higher price. However, because they are heavier, they also produce more emissions. According to the International Energy Agency (2019), growing SUV sales have eradicated gains from fuel efficiency and the spread of electric cars, and are the main reason for the increase of carbon dioxide emitted by passenger cars in the past decade.[22] Some automobile manufacturers meanwhile offer electric SUVs. Electric SUVs produce no emissions (the power generator that supplies the car with electricity may) but heavier cars need larger batteries and the production and disposal of batteries come with a heavy cost for the environment.[23] However, more weight is not only damaging for the environment. In connection with higher bumpers, it also means that SUVs, including electric versions, are more dangerous for other drivers, bikers, and pedestrians (Anderson and Auffhammer 2014).[24] And because of increasing safety concerns, more people, including those with small children, buy SUVs. In short, SUVs are a classical example how in a profit-driven economy, individual utility trumps social and ecological utility. Polanyi states that a capitalist economy not only creates "use values whose rank ordering is inferior from a social perspective," but in some cases the profit-logic even produces "counter-value" (2016, 405). Polanyi mentions the production of weapons and alcohol as examples of a counter-value, but given their social and ecological costs, SUVs may also fall under this category. What an economy that promotes social and ecological utility might look like will be discussed in the next chapter.

Conclusion

According to neoclassical theory, the value of a good or service is expressed in its price, and the price reflects its marginal utility. Utility is understood as the ability of the respective good or service to please its owner/consumer, and marginal utility captures the utility derived from the last unit of the respective good. Diamonds, from this perspective, are more expensive than water because of their greater marginal utility—regardless of the fact that human beings can live without diamonds but cannot live without water. The latter has occupied political economists for several hundred years. The general assumption has been that commodities have use values and exchange values and that water has a large use value but a small exchange value, whereas diamonds have a large exchange value but a small use value. Marx even argued that it is the specific character of capitalism that production is geared toward the creation of exchange values and the maximization of profits, rather than the creation of use values and the satisfaction of social needs. However, with the invention of marginal utility, use value largely disappeared from economics apart from the Marxist fringes. Yet while Marxists routinely mentioned use value, there were some controversies about the extent to which use value should play a role in Marxist political economy. Some argued that the analyses of use values belonged to the field of natural sciences. Others insisted that Marxism differed from classical and neoclassical economics precisely by putting emphasis on use value or the qualitative side of economic transformation. However, few Marxists actually investigated how use values were transformed in capitalist economies in the postwar decades.

More recently, use value has received new attention in the debates about the value of nature. From a marginalist perspective, nature has no value because it has no marginal utility. Moreover, destroying natural resources actually increases the value of nature because it transforms nature into a scarce good. In contrast, Marxists emphasize that nature has plenty of value; it's just use value and not exchange value. And while destroying nature increases its marginal utility, it shrinks its use value. The use value of nature is that it provides the basis of life and human flourishing. As such, the value of nature is the same regardless of supply and demand for environmental goods, and it is inherently collective. Nature is not alone. Other goods and services, too, have collective use values. The collective nature of use values demands for a collective assessment, resulting in social and ecological utility. However, because of the greater potential to make profits, capitalist economies favor individual utility over social and ecological utility. Commodification, hence, also implies the subjugation of social and ecological utility to individual utility, with potentially harmful effects for society and the environment.

7

Alternatives to Commodification

Introduction

So far, the book has shown why commodification is problematic and laid out
some of the negative consequences of commodification processes for people
and the environment. This chapter explores alternatives to commodification,
which ultimately means alternatives to capitalism. By mapping an alternative that does yet not exist, the chapter is necessarily speculative—but it is
speculative based on a thorough analysis of the nature and consequences of
commodification. De-commodification imposes limits on the commodity
character of goods and services traded on markets, but it does not provide for
an alternative. Following an understanding of commodification as the subjugation of use value to market/exchange value, an alternative must seek to
"free" use value and reinstate it as the prime goal of production. Or, put differently, an alternative to commodification must focus on satisfying human
needs rather than the expansion of private profit. Three elements are crucial for the promotion of use value: democratization, sustainability, and solidarity. The chapter discusses each of these elements in a separate section.
It then brings the three elements together into an alternative vision that is
called *use-value society*. The last section lays out some important characteristics of a use-value society and discusses its relationship to the more traditional concept of socialism.

De-commodification

The opposite of commodification is de-commodification. As noted in Chapter
1, it was welfare state theorists who introduced the term "de-commodification" in the 1980s. Claus Offe (1984, 61) describes de-commodification as "the
withdrawal and uncoupling of an increasing number of social areas and social
groups . . . from market relations." For Gøsta Esping-Andersen (1987, 86), de-
commodification captures "the extent to which individuals and families can

The Critique of Commodification. Christoph Hermann, Oxford University Press. © Oxford University Press 2021.
DOI: 10.1093/oso/9780197576755.003.0007

maintain a normal and socially acceptable standard of living regardless of their market performance." Esping-Andersen, subsequently, sets out to measure the extent of market independence provided by different welfare states, resulting in his influential welfare state typology, consisting of liberal, conservative, and social democratic welfare states (1990, 26–28). Both Offe and Esping-Andersen derive their understanding of de-commodification primarily from Karl Polanyi (see Chapter 1). As discussed in Chapter 5, Polanyi was a fierce critic of commodification and especially of the commodification of land, labor, and money. In *The Great Transformation*, Polanyi (1957) argues that the abolishment of the Speenhamland System, an eighteenth-century social safety net in England, was crucial for the commodification of labor power, as workers were deprived of an alternative to selling their labor on the emerging labor markets. While Polanyi does not discuss the merits of welfare states—according to his wife, Ilona Duczynska, Polanyi was not a fan of welfare states, not even of the Swedish one—modern welfare states can be seen as an advanced version of Speenhamland, mitigating the dependence of workers on labor markets (Dale 2010, 370–371).[1]

Polanyi may have been ambiguous about the merits of welfare states, but he certainly was in favor of the creation of a public sector and the provision of public services. He discusses the role of what we today call public services when he compares Speenhamland to the system of social service provisioning established by the city of Vienna after the First World War (Polanyi 1957, 286–288). The "crown jewel" of what became known as Red Vienna was the municipality's public housing program, which provided adequate housing for thousands of workers and their families who had previously been dependent on a private housing market, which was, much like today's housing market in many urban centers, unable to provide affordable and acceptable housing (see Chapter 4).[2] Red Vienna was not the only example of a development that later has been described as "municipal socialism" (Sheldrake 1989). In the early twentieth century, the creation of publicly owned and operated infrastructures facilitating access to gas, electricity, water, and sanitation, as well as the provision of essential services such as healthcare, education, and public transportation, were increasingly seen as a government responsibility (not least because the private sector often neglected such services because of a lack of profitability). In German this responsibility is called *öffentliche Daseinsvorsorge*, which can be translated as "common assurance of basic conditions of existence." In short, public services also provide independence from markets and may in fact be more important for de-commodification than cash benefits (Bambra 2005; Hermann 2016).

While the welfare states and public services provide some degree of independence from the market, de-commodification can also be the result of the regulation of markets. Polanyi (1957, 202) specifically mentions the adoption of protective legislation, such as a series of reforms that were introduced during the New Deal era in the United States and which subsequently "started to build a moat around labor." Apart from the introduction of social security, which provided only for a minimal and incomplete safety net, New Deal legislation also established minimum wages, standard work hours, as well as a legal framework for collective bargaining (Wagner Act). For Polanyi (1957, 251), such legislation is path-breaking because "[t]o take labor out of the market means a transformation as radical as was the establishment of a competitive labor market. The wage contract ceases to be a private contract except on subordinate and accessory points. Not only conditions in the factory, hours of work, and modalities of contract, but the basic wage itself, are determined outside the market." Hence de-commodification not only means the existence of an alternative to the labor market, but also can refer to the regulation of labor markets through employment legislation and collective agreements. In both cases, employers' discretion to hire and fire and to negotiate individual wages and work hours is limited, resulting in a restriction of the commodity character of labor (Hyman 2007, 13). Several authors have described the development of the standard employment relationship in the postwar decades, providing for continuous full-time employment, a family wage, as well as healthcare, pension, and other benefits, as a form of de-commodification (Bosch 2004; Rubery and Grimshaw 2016). Others have used the concept of social wage to emphasize that the employment relationship is no longer only an exchange of labor for money, but comes with a series of entitlements that guarantee workers and their families some level of social protection and a stake in social progress (Saunders 1994).

While scholars use the term "de-commodification" mainly in connection with welfare states and labor regulation, other regulations, too, can hinder the free play of market forces and thereby have an impact on the commodity character of the goods and services traded on markets. For Polanyi, the countermovement against self-regulating markets included not only social regulation, but also the abandoning of the gold standard and the introduction of agricultural tariffs (see Chapter 5). Polanyi does not discuss the Bretton Woods system of monetary management that was established after the Second World War. *The Great Transformation* was published in the same year as the negotiations were staged at the New Hampshire resort. However, scholars have described the resulting international monetary system as embedded liberalism (Ruggie 1982). While few people have described it in this way, the Bretton Woods system can also be understood as a form of de-commodification—as an agreement to put a break on the free flow of capital and market-based exchange rates (for an attempt to understand international relations in terms of de- and re-commodification, see Laxer 2006). In a similar way, the New Deal financial regulations introduced in the United States in the 1930s significantly constrained the leeway of financial actors, including interest rates that could be charged for certain loans and mortgages (Krippner 2011, 60–63). To a certain extent, even product regulations and product admission processes, mainly introduced to protect consumers and the environment, can be seen as a form of de-commodification. What all these regulations have in common is that they limit the producers' discretion to sell whatever they think "the market" is buying. In other words, they reduce what Fred Block (1990, 56) has described as a society's degree of "marketness."

Finally, de-commodification can also be the result of production for self-use. While being the main motive of production in pre-capitalist societies and the world's remaining non-capitalist communities, production for self-use has been increasingly marginalized in the last two hundred years with the expansion of capitalism and commodification. However, subsistence farming still plays an important role in many developing countries, and because it provides some degree of independence from capitalist world markets, it can also be seen as form of de-commodification (Waters 2007). Meanwhile, people in advanced capitalist countries have shown some interest in growing their own vegetables, and creating, repairing, or simply reusing things, rather than buying new commodities on a market (for urban gardening, see Tornaghi and Certoma 2019). In some cases, individuals join forces and form cooperatives to create goods and services that they commonly need. There is also a history of artists who produce art for themselves, their friends, and their communities, rather than for an art market. In these cases, de-commodification, or more accurately anti-commodification, can be part of an alternative subculture or lifestyle.[3]

De-commodification is important because it provides people without money with some degree of security and independence, and, as a result, decency in a market society. De-commodification is also beneficial because it reduces inequality. It is no accident that the most commodified societies also tend to be the most unequal ones, and recent waves of re-commodification have resulted in escalating inequality.[4] Most importantly, de-commodification is crucial to raise expectations. First of all, people who have experienced a well-functioning public service such as effective public healthcare or reliable public transportation know that there is an alter-native to the market (this is the reason why so many allegedly individual-istic Americans support the government-run Medicare program). Second, people who do not have to struggle to make ends meet or live under constant fear of losing their homes as a result of losing their jobs can start to contem-plate what would constitute a "good life" and how society could provide it. They may even find time to meet with others to discuss visions and strategies to get there.

However, de-commodification necessarily faces limits in a capitalist so-ciety. Labor may be de-commodified, but labor cannot cease to be a com-modity. If labor is no longer a commodity, then capitalism comes to an end. To put it simply: without proletarians there can be no capitalists. The de-commodification of labor power can therefore only be partial. The same holds for welfare states: Esping-Andersen (1990, 23) had a vision in which welfare states would allow citizens to "freely, and without potential loss of job, income, or general welfare opt out of work when they themselves con-sider it necessary." While this may have been the case for a brief moment in the most developed welfare states in the early 1970s, subsequent waves of welfare state retrenchment have made sure that non-working is not an at-tractive alternative to having a paid job. Furthermore, even social democratic welfare states have linked benefits to work obligations in a turn that some authors have described as a shift from welfare to workfare (Peck 2001).[5] Even in the case of public services, experience has shown that the state provision of essential services is only acceptable if it does not endanger private profit making. One way to restore profitability in the light of an expanding public sector is precisely to enforce accumulation by dispossession (see Chapter 1).

Democratization

While de-commodification provides a cushion against the worst effects of markets and profit making, it does not present an alternative to capitalist commodification. As argued in Chapter 2, commodification implies the subjugation of use value to market value. An alternative, hence, must focus on rejecting market value and reinstating use value as the prime objective of economic activity. In other words, production must be redirected toward the satisfaction of needs rather than the maximization of profit. Production for need rather than profit was a dominant characteristic of pre-capitalist societies and still is in the few indigenous communities that have not been affected by commodification. In these mostly agricultural societies, goods and services are mainly produced for self-use, resulting in what are sometimes called subsistence economies. Yet, because production focuses on self-use rather than the use of others, such economies typically display a very limited division of labor and an absence of complex machinery and other labor-saving technology. This, in turn, results in low productivity and economic stagnation. While Polanyi, perhaps in his capacity as anthropologist, shows some admiration for pre-capitalist societies, Marx was an admirer of the dynamic character of the capitalist mode of production. Some Marxists subsequently concluded that capitalism is a necessary stage in the transition to socialism (not least because higher productivity means more time can be used for non-work-related activities and enjoyments).

Yet given the ecological destruction caused by both industrial capitalism and industrial communism, some eco-socialists advocate a return to a more subsistence-oriented form of economic life (Mies 1986). In addition, there are also environmentalists who criticize the destructive nature of the Western imperial mode of living (Brand and Wissen 2017). However, for many, and perhaps for the majority of the population in the Western world, a subsistence economy is not a very attractive alternative to the status quo. The challenge, hence, is to develop an alternative that focuses on needs but provides for more than the mere necessities of life (Mészáros 1994, 526). To come back to an example used by Polanyi: Red Vienna did more than just provide workers with a roof over their heads; the municipal housing projects built were qualitatively superior to rentals available for workers on the private housing market.[6] It is this superiority that caused Polanyi (1957, 287) to argue that the Vienna system was an attempt to transcend the market system altogether.

The next challenge, then, is how to maximize use value. While market/exchange value can be measured in units of money, the nature of use value is precisely that it cannot be expressed in quantitative terms (this is why all attempts to introduce performance measurements in the delivery of public services must ultimately fail—see Chapter 3). In other words, while we can measure prices and profits, we cannot measure usefulness, or the suitability of a good or service satisfying a need. This does not mean that we cannot assess usefulness. It only means that an assessment must be based on a qualitative evaluation, comparing different options to satisfy a specific need or a bundle of related needs and their consequences, not only for consumers but for society and the environment. In short, usefulness and use value can only be properly assessed in some form of democratic decision-making process. At the same time, democratic decision-making processes enable collective valuations of goods and services.[7]

The democratization of the economy is a long-standing demand of those who are opposed to both the market and central planning. Economic democratization has two components: on the one hand, the shift toward self-managed enterprises, and on the other hand, the introduction of democratic planning. Self-management typically involves some kind of democratic decision-making process in which a majority of workers decide what is produced and how production is organized, including the division of labor and renumeration. Democratic planning differs from authoritarian planning insofar as it is not top administrators who set production targets for the whole economy and pass them down in a chain of command; instead, planning is part of a participatory process in which various groups with an interest in the outcome take part in a collective decision-making process.

There are different visions of how exactly these participatory processes can be organized. Michael Albert (2003) proposes a largely decentralized approach involving workers' and consumers' councils organized on the local, regional, and national levels that are in permanent (re)negotiations about production goals and the related distribution of resources. Pat Devine (1988) suggests the creation of Negotiated Coordination Bodies that intermediate between national and regional planning commissions and self-managed production units. Sam Gindin (2018) attributes a special role to sectoral councils not so much as bodies of intermediation, but as a counterweight to both the interests of the central planning board and of the autonomous workplace collectives. In Gindin's model, mediation between worker and consumer interests, along with the articulation of other relevant concerns, takes place in community councils (2018). What all these models have in common is that they give workers, consumers, and other groups with a stake in social reproduction a voice in collective decision-making processes, rather than reducing them to passive subjects who can choose between different and perhaps equally unsatisfying products. It also means that all consumers have the same voice, regardless of individual purchasing power.

Given that workers and consumers—in fact, most workers are consumers and vice versa—have an interest in the usefulness of products, it is not difficult to imagine that use-value orientation could play a prominent role in the various negotiations and mediations that take place as part of the coordination process. However, existing participatory models tend to focus on the coordination between supply and demand and related inputs and outputs in the production processes. What is often missing is a forum for more profound discussions about what constitutes a "good life," what needs are important, and what would be the best way to satisfy them (taking into account the wider consequences of specific forms of consumption). In other words, the question is not only how many electric cars we need and what we need to produce them; the question is also whether we want cars as the main form of transport, or if we want alternative forms of mobility such as public transportation.

In addition, the rather complex process of adjusting supply and demand involves the danger of prolonging existing arrangements at the cost of innovation. Yet maximizing use value requires constant efforts to improve existing goods and services to satisfy needs. In Albert's (2003, 128–135) model, product innovation is the result of ongoing negotiations between producer and consumer councils, but innovation has its own dynamic and it may not be helpful that every step in the process needs democratic approval. An alternative approach could focus on the institutionalization of a process of use-value maximization that includes a specially trained group of use-value promoters (replacing today's managers), as well as an ongoing exchange between developers and potential users (substituting for what is currently known as market research). While ultimately production decisions should be made in a democratic fashion, there can still be some leeway for experimentation and adaptation in the production process. There should also be some room for failure, as not all innovations will be successful.

The main argument against democratic planning is that the extent of the participatory processes involved makes it inefficient. And most people can think of better ways to spend their time than sitting in endless meetings. Conventionally, efficiency is understood as the amount of output created by a given input. The more output, the greater the efficiency (it can also mean that the same output is produced with less input). In some industries we can count pieces of output, but in most sectors of the economy, output is measured as the market price of what has been produced. In other words, efficiency depends on market value (the lack of market value for public goods and services makes it difficult if not impossible to determine public-sector productivity).[8] It should therefore come as no surprise that the maximization of market value results in growing efficiency, even if higher profits are attainted through lowering product quality.

For example, fast-food chains are more efficient than traditional restaurants, even though the food has little nutritional value and even endangers the health of consumers. Hospitals which limit patient stays to little more than the duration of an operation are highly efficient, even though a significant number of patients have to come back for further treatment because they have been released too early. In much the same way, online universities are more efficient than traditional universities, as one professor can virtually teach a thousand students or more. But students tend to learn less than in traditional settings where they sit in a classroom and interact with an actual teacher. In contrast, fire brigades per definition are inefficient if there are no fires to put out; prisons are inefficient if there are no prisoners to lock up; and doctors are inefficient if there are no patients to be treated. Yet people usually prefer the absence of fires, criminals, and epidemics to a more efficient public service. In short, what is needed is a new understanding of efficiency that focuses on outcome rather than output—including outcome for the environment. Accordingly, participatory processes should be judged with respect to their contribution to preferable social and environmental outcomes, rather than the market value of output. Taking time to find the right solution may very well pay off in the long run.

Technology can play an important role in facilitating democratic planning (Hahnel 2020, 301–302). On the one hand, new forms of communication can help to organize decision-making processes with a large number of participants who do not necessarily live in the same community. On the other hand, advanced data processing enables planners to cope with large amounts of data, refuting the assumption that economic planning is doomed because the planning authorities will not be able to collect and process all of the relevant information. If digital enterprises such as Facebook can store and process the data of more than two billion users, planning commissions should be able to compute the relevant information regarding all economic actors in a regional economy. Of course, circumstances can change and agents can change their minds, but this is also a problem in a market economy. Capitalist enterprises also must plan ahead, and their plans do not always match demand—as can be seen by the large amounts of food disposed by supermarkets on a daily base (see Chapter 4).

Furthermore, not all production needs participatory planning. Not all markets negatively affect use value. Mostly it is large and, perhaps, international markets with large investor-owned corporations that exclusively care about profits that tend to maximize market value at the cost of use value. In contrast, local producers selling their products on local markets without being threatened by price competition usually care about the usefulness and the quality of their goods and services. Hence it makes little sense to democratically plan decentralized agricultural production. A local farmer's market is a perfectly fine instrument to distribute local fruits and vegetables. The same holds for local shops, restaurants, and other community-based service providers (I am afraid that democratically planned bars and clubs will not be very attractive). Local businesses should still be self-managed—in fact, there are already thousands of co-ops that provide goods and services for local markets—but there can also be room for local entrepreneurs who do not want to be part of a collective. In any case, the red line should be drawn where market exchange and profit maximization start to marginalize use-value orientation.[9]

Even labor can be allocated through markets, most likely through some form of internet platform, as long as workers' existence does not depend on the sale of their labor power. However, as in capitalist societies, the development of skills, knowledge, and experience, i.e., the formation of the use value of labor, demands long-term planning and the creation of adequate public institutions that provide education and training. Furthermore, in a democratically planned economy, workers would no longer be dependent on private capital and its profit-driven investment decisions to deploy their skills and experience; instead they would be able, and perhaps even encouraged, to use their own imaginations and capacities and form their own companies to produce useful goods and services (one of the most problematic features of capitalism is the waste of the skills and experience of workers who become unemployed because some form of production no longer generates sufficient profits).

Sustainability

While people in a democratic economy are free to commonly decide what is produced and how it is produced, they need to take into account the consequences of specific forms of production and consumption for the environment and for future generations who want to live on this planet. In order to preserve existing ecological resources and biodiversity, production and consumption must be sustainable. The concept of sustainability goes back to the management of renewable resources such as forests and fisheries. Essentially it means limiting the use of a specific resource to the ability of the resource to renew itself—i.e., to cut only as many trees as can grow back over a certain period of time. Sustainability became increasingly popular with the publication of the Brundtland Report in 1987 (World Commission 1987). Therein the World Commission on Environment and Development proposed sustainable development as a strategy to cope with the growing ecological destruction and the need for a capitalist economy to grow. The idea was to make economic growth more sustainable by decoupling it from the use of natural resources—through, for example, the use of more energy-efficient technology. In other words, the plan was not a move to an actually sustainable economy; the plan was to make the existing economy less environmentally damaging (Jackson 2009, 67). The idea received a new push after the 2008 crisis when a number of scholars, politicians, and international organizations proposed the adoption of a Green New Deal to stimulate sustainable growth (Hermann 2015a). However, so far efforts to make growth more sustainable have largely failed, with the effect that the ecological crisis has severely intensified in the past few decades.

Some have argued that growth itself cannot be sustainable because even if it uses fewer inputs, the production of more output still requires additional natural resources (Sachs 1999, chapter 5). Herman Daly (1977) has proposed a model of an economy that breaks with the growth imperative and instead aims at maintaining a certain level of economic activity. The goal, then, is to make the stagnating economy ecologically sustainable. In order to do so, two conditions must be met: natural resource extraction must be limited to the extent that resources renew themselves, and total waste emissions cannot be allowed to exceed the natural absorption capacity. In short, throughput is limited to the lowest feasible flow of energy and matter. The result is what Daly calls a steady-state economy (1977)[10]. However, a steady-state economy also implies a steady stock of people—which, again, requires some form of population control and, perhaps, the adoption of authoritarian measures. Furthermore, the number of people that can live on the planet depends on the amount of resources used per person. Critics have argued that current living standards in the Global North depend on billions of people in the Global South suffering from material deprivation. According to the Global

Footprint Network, Americans need two countries of the size of the United States to provide the biocapacity to sustain current living standards (Kelly, Burns, and Wackernagel 2015). Hence, rather than a steady-state economy, what is needed is an economic contraction in the Global North, making space for some material improvement in the South. This is more or less the position of scholars who identify with the degrowth movement (see, for example, Martinez-Alier et al. 2010). Interestingly, both the steady-state economy and the degrowth society imply a quantitative notion of economic activity. Simply shrinking the economy may make it sustainable in ecological terms but can come at enormous social costs. In my view, the priority should not be downsizing; the priority should be qualitative change. Or put differently: the goal should not be to lower living standards; the goal should be to change modes of living (for more elaboration of this point, see the section on use-value society later in this chapter).

The big question, of course, is whether capitalism can be sustainable. As mentioned in Chapter 2, the primary purpose of a capitalist economy is to increase profits. Profits can be increased by acts of dispossession or by exploiting privileged access to markets. However, in capitalism profits are typically increased by expanding surplus value. Surplus value can be increased by cutting wages and expanding the workday, but there are boundaries to this sort of surplus maximization, set by the fact that a day only has 24 hours and the labor force needs to be reproduced. Alternatively, capitalists can also increase surplus by introducing labor-saving technology and by combining it with new and increasingly cheap forms of energy. However, higher productivity means more output, and in order to realize the surplus inherent in mass-produced commodities, consumption must also grow. Growing consumption, in turn, fuels economic growth, usually measured as increase in the gross domestic product (GDP). In a capitalist system the failure to grow quickly turns into a crisis. In 2009, a 5 percent drop in GDP in the United States and other countries caused a massive social disaster, with millions losing their jobs and homes. In the wake of falling auto sales, the "big three" auto manufacturers had to be bailed out by the US government, even though the fall in auto sales was actually good news for the US environment. Faced with the worst crisis since the Great Depression, neoliberal politicians and central bankers around the world rediscovered Keynesianism and pumped billions of dollars into the faltering economy. Negative growth results in negative investments, which, in turn, mean fewer jobs and incomes, which cause further cuts in investments. The result is an accelerating downward spiral. This is precisely what John

Maynard Keynes saw when he looked at the Great Depression and what caused him to argue that in times of severe crisis the government has to step in and create demand to get the economy going (Crotty 2019, chapter 4).

Keynes also emphasized the role of expectations. In a capitalist system, investments are based on expectations about future developments, but, of course, the future is unknown. To make things even worse, investors, including investments funds that administer the money of wealthy clients, compete for the highest returns on capital. The results are investment decisions which are at times quite irrational, driven by what Keynes (2007, 158–162) has described as "animal spirits." However, the same decisions are responsible for capitalism's extraordinary dynamism and the massive economic change that took place over the past two hundred years. In contrast, a zero-growth economy demands a constant amount of investment, replacing outworn stock and, perhaps, steering the economy on a more sustainable path. Such a scenario seems highly unlikely in a profit-driven economy, but it certainly requires a very different financial sector. Rather than chasing the highest returns, investments would have to be made in a highly cautious and coordinated, i.e., socialist, manner.

While promoting economic change, the primacy of profits blocks the transition to more sustainable forms of consumption. As noted in Chapter 2, investors looking for profits invest billions of dollars in the development of self-driving cars, some of which are electronically powered, while public transportation is starved of money. The fact that housing has become an investment rather than a place to live has also blocked the transition to more sustainable housing. Investments in energy efficiency only make sense if homeowners plan to actually live in buildings for an extended period of time. In a situation where houses are held as financial assets or are frequently bought and sold, appearance is more important than substance. As described in Chapter 4, glass-walled condominium towers make a shiny appearance, but their energy balance is far from satisfactory. Industrialized agriculture may be more profitable than family farming, but profitability comes at the cost of the fertility of soil, with knock-on effects caused by the use of chemicals and genetically modified crops. In the same way, industrialized food is highly profitable but endangers the health of consumers. The focus on profits rather than needs also hinders the expansion of care and other social services. Rather than moving toward a care economy, production still focuses on the creation of private commodities such as automobiles, flat screens, tablets, and smartphones, along with supporting internet apps.

André Gorz (1994, chapter 9) has argued that the notion of sufficiency is incompatible with capitalist rationality. Whereas in pre-capitalist societies the goal of economic activities was to produce what is needed, in capitalism there can never be enough. There is always a need for more, even when the more does not come with additional satisfaction, except, perhaps, the gratification of owning more than others. Who, for example, needs a house with twenty rooms or a car that can drive more than two hundred miles per hour? According to Thorstein Veblen (2007, 67), differentiation is a powerful motivation, resulting in what he has described as conspicuous or wasteful consumption. Consumption needs to be wasteful precisely because its prime objective is to demonstrate the ability to pay, rather than to satisfy a need. At the same time, corporations fuel waste by designing products with limited durability, some of which are sold at extremely low prices, inducing consumers to buy stuff that they do not even need. A 2019 survey found that British consumers intended to purchase 50 million summer outfits that will only be worn once (Smithers 2019). Of course, this is only possible because of the poor quality of the garment and the extremely low wages paid to garment workers in developing countries. The lack of sufficiency, consequently, undermines efforts to improve sustainability by making production less resource-intensive. Sustainability, hence, depends on sufficiency. And sufficiency depends on democratic decision-making processes as consumers will have to decide collectively what is essential and what is not.

Solidarity

A capitalist economy is supposedly based on self-interested, utility-maximizing individuals improving their own situation with little regard for the situation of others. Jeremy Bentham argued that individual accumulation of wealth is beneficial to society because it increases overall affluence. The utilitarian theory subsequently provided a highly welcomed justification for capitalists to maximize personal wealth while a large proportion of the population, especially the newly emerging proletariat, was struggling to survive. It was only in the twentieth century, with the consolidation of the trade union movement, the formation of mass working-class parties, and the subsequent creation of the welfare state, that a large part of the population in advanced capitalist countries benefited from the expansion of economic output. And even at the height of postwar prosperity, certain social groups such as women, immigrants, and non-whites remained excluded. Four decades of neoliberalism and repeated attacks on the trade union movement have largely eliminated the postwar gains, with the result that the current level of inequality in the United States, and to a lesser extent in Europe, resembles the staggering inequality of the early twentieth century (Piketty 2014).

But self-interest is not only an expression of greed. In capitalism, competition compels capitalists, or more precisely capitalist corporations, to increase profits. Companies which fail to achieve an average profit rate risk losing investors and subsequently go out of business or are taken over by more profitable competitors. And since the average profit rate is only known ex post, i.e., after the products have been sold on the market, producers are faced with permanent pressure to increase surplus value. Some corporations may be able to escape competition through innovation—new products or services guarantee exclusive market access—but not all companies can be innovators. While most people spend little time contemplating how to maximize their utility, many are affected by competition. As discussed in Chapter 2, competition fuels commodification by forcing producers to focus on profitability rather than usefulness. However, competition does more than discipline capitalists; workers are forced to compete for jobs, and since their jobs depend on the survival of their employers, they also compete with workers in rival firms, some of which are located in other countries and continents (the resulting division of the working class ensures capital's continuous dominance over labor).

The opposite of competition is solidarity. Rather than trying to improve one's own situation at the cost of others—competition necessarily creates winners and losers—solidarity is based on mutual support. Resembling Marx's (1938, 10) description of a communist society in which each contributes according to her/his ability and expends according to his/her need, solidarity implies a mutual responsibility in which people support other people, assuming that they will be helped if needed. Contrary to the rhetoric of self-interest, there are many forms of social reciprocity within capitalist societies: family members watch out for each other, neighbors offer other neighbors help, and religions encourage their wealthier members to support those who are less fortunate. States, furthermore, promote solidarity by requiring high-income earners to pay higher taxes than those at the bottom of the income scale and by using some of the proceeds to provide welfare benefits for those in need.[11] In some cases, benefits are based on social security contributions rather than taxes. Social insurance funds promote solidarity by requiring the employed to support the unemployed and those in retirement, and the healthy those who are sick and disabled (see Chapter 4). Solidarity also exists between countries, e.g., in the form of developmental aid or by providing support in the case of natural disasters, epidemics, and famines. However, solidarity is under constant attack by racism, xenophobia, misogyny, nationalism, and other forms of exclusion.

Economic solidarity means that producers cooperate rather than compete, with the aim of promoting collective wealth rather than individual affluence. Cooperation implies that technological and other innovations are shared rather than kept secret, and that different producers work together to solve problems and improve products. In a solidarity economy there is no need to hold other producers or countries back in order to maintain privileged access to markets. On the contrary: the very fact that others are successful is beneficial because their success allows them to return assistance when needed. Solidarity, in this respect, works as a form of insurance, and the more producers that participate in a solidarity economy, the better. Many cooperatives are supportive of other nonprofit businesses, but self-management alone does not necessarily result in a solidarity economy. Worker collectives can also focus on the companies' interests and exploit exclusive access to markets at the cost of the wider society (Lebowitz 2010, 73–76). In order to make sure that particular interests do not contradict wider social needs, self-management needs to be complemented by democratic planning. Reversibly, democratic decision-making processes need solidarity in order to ensure that a majority does not simply overrule a minority.

While mutual support is essential, solidarity can mean more than helping each other out. Mutual support, especially in the form of friendly associations, played an important role in the development of the labor movement in the nineteenth century, but working-class solidarity quickly went beyond the creation of collective support systems. Workers' struggles for higher wages and the improvement of employment conditions required them to put aside individual interests in favor of the interests of the collective. It is this collective power, as Marx (1990, 412) notes, that allows labor to confront capital. Precisely because capitalists know about the power of solidarity, they typically try to divide the workforce by offering special deals to some workers in the hope that they will put short-term personal gains before long-term collective improvements. Experience has shown that it is only unions whose members reject such offers and stick to the common goal, even when it demands sacrifices, that are ultimately successful. Again, democratic participation and the fact that every member has a voice in collective decision-making processes greatly favors the generation and maintenance of solidarity. Working-class solidarity, in turn, enabled working people to win significant concessions from capital in the past two hundred years (and fading solidarity allowed capital to take back a number of these concessions in the past four decades).

Putting common goals before individual interests is not only important for winning concessions from capital; it is also crucial for tackling the ecological crisis. As mentioned before, a growing number of people buy SUVs even though they produce more emissions than regular passenger cars. According to the International Energy Agency (2019), increasing sales of SUVs in the past decade has more than offset progress in vehicle fuel efficiency and the expansion of electronically powered vehicles. Increasing taxes on gasoline and/or providing tax incentives for electric cars would make SUVs less attractive.[12] However, this would also hurt those who cannot afford a new car, let alone a comparably expensive electric automobile. Furthermore, the most sustainable solution—not only for the environment but also for communities—is to abstain from using a car altogether. Hence, if anything, there should be a monetary incentive for not buying a car at all. And this incentive should also apply to the millions of people in the developing world who do not own a car and do not pollute the environment. Hence, unless we want to pay people for walking, biking, and using public transportation, the solution to global warming is not incentivizing individual behavior, but rather promoting what some authors have called "climate solidarity" (Hampton 2015; Brecher 2017).[13] People should change their behavior not because of personal gain, but because of their collective responsibility to save the planet.

But climate solidarity also goes beyond working-class solidarity. First, climate solidarity needs to be global. While showing international solidarity is an important feature of many progressive trade unions, global warming can only be stopped if the vast majority of countries take part in the struggle against climate change. Efforts to reduce greenhouse-gas emissions by one or a few countries can be more than outdone by other countries increasing pollution. The fact that some countries have refused to accept binding goals for reducing emissions has hampered the United Nations' climate change negotiations in the past decades and has meant that outcomes have been unable to tackle global warming. Second, climate solidarity is inherently intergenerational. Welfare states promote solidarity between those who are working with those in retirement, but climate solidarity demands solidarity between current populations and future generations that are not yet born. If global warming continues at the current pace, it is these future generations who will be most affected by climate change. Hence it is not surprising that young people are the most concerned about global warming, and many have joined international protests to demand effective anti-climate-change action. At the same time, climate change also poses a series of challenges for democratic organization. Obviously, democratic decision-making processes cannot stop at national boundaries, and the interests of future generations need to be taken into account.

Use-value society

Since an alternative to commodification must be based on prioritizing use value over market/exchange value, I like to think of an alternative as being a use-value society. Prioritizing use value means focusing on human needs, rather than the needs of capital in its endless endeavor to expand profit. However, a use-value society is more than a subsistence economy; the goal is not just to satisfy basic needs, but to satisfy needs in an optimal and constantly improving manner, taking into account the ecological effects of different forms of consumption. In short, a use-value society is a collective project, driven by the development of collective capacities and open to innovation and technological progress (with technology serving human needs rather than profit maximization). This does not mean that wants must not be prioritized—but not so much because of the scarcity of resources, rather because of the avoidance of waste. As discussed earlier, a use-value society is based on sufficiency. This requires some common understanding about which needs are essential and which are dispensable, or to borrow a term from Latin American activists and scholars, a conversation and perhaps democratic decision about what constitutes a "good life" (being able to drive a car that runs more than 200 miles per hour or living in a home with more than 20 rooms are non-essential needs and people can very well enjoy life without them).

The maximization of use value also demands some form of assessment of usefulness or the ability of goods and services to satisfy needs. Here, too, decisions need to be made in a collective and democratic manner, rather than leaving them to market-mediated profit expectations. A collective decision-making process, could, for example, come to the conclusion that SUVs are a suboptimal form of transport and instead vote for the production of lighter cars, which in absence of SUVs and other heavy vehicles provide the same safety while being less destructive for the environment and other road users. Or even better, the participants could decide that expanding and improving public transportation is the best option. A use-value society, hence, is impossible without a far-reaching democratization of the economy.

Yet the focus on use value rather than market value also implies a new understanding of economic efficiency. Rather than producing the greatest possible output with the smallest possible input, the goal is to create the most favorable outcome. In the case of healthcare, for example, the goal is not to treat as many patients as possible in a day or month; the goal is to prevent illnesses, including illnesses caused by anxieties about the future and poor working conditions (which are partly responsible for the US opioid crisis). In the case of higher education, the goal is not to push as many students through the system as possible; the goal is to make sure that students actually learn something while they attend college or university. In the case of transportation, the goal is not to produce more automobiles, including electronically powered luxury cars; the goal is to move people and goods around efficiently with the least possible impact on the environment. And in the case of agriculture, the goal is not to produce as much corn, poultry, and other agricultural output as possible; the goal is to produce healthy and tasty products and to do so in a sustainable manner.

The focus on use value also includes an emphasis on the use value of labor. In a use-value society there is no place for the deskilling and disempowerment of workers. Instead, workers are encouraged to nurture their talents, develop their skills, and apply their knowledge. In order to help workers to achieve their goals, education must be inclusive and must empower students from various backgrounds, rather than producing an elite with privileged access to the labor market. The focus on use value also implies an acknowledgment of the usefulness of work, resulting in an upgrading of socially useful jobs such as nurses and a downgrading of rather useless jobs such as stock traders. This, in turn, will fundamentally reshape current labor markets, where individuals who perform socially questionable tasks, such as betting on increasing or decreasing prices, are awarded with top salaries, while others who do socially extremely useful work, such as taking care of children and the elderly, are struggling to make ends meet (for the low wages paid to home care and early childhood workers in the United States, see Thomason et al. 2018).

Nature also provides use values. There is no human life without nature. Natural products and resources are used by human beings either directly for consumption or as inputs in the production of other useful goods and services. And while some use values are lost for the foreseeable future in the consumption process, nature has the ability to renew many of its use values over time, amounting to what is described as sustainable development. Yet reproduction also involves adaptation and mutation, resulting in nature's stunning biodiversity. Biodiversity itself is an immensely important use value because it facilitates the maintenance and development of diverse natural habitats, which, again, plays a key role in the resilience of global ecosystems. As argued before, ecological sustainability is threatened by the capitalist imperative to grow, following from its need to expand profits. Precisely because the focus of a use-value society is the satisfaction of needs rather than the expansion of profit—human needs are limited, but there is no limit for the accumulation of money—a use-value society can respect natural boundaries. Sustainability is enhanced by a focus on essential needs and by the consideration of the ecological effects of different ways of satisfying them. As a result, a use-value society not only avoids waste; it also promotes a transition to more sustainable forms of living, including spatially adequate and energy-efficient homes, public transportation, local food from local farms, using sustainable forms of agriculture, as well as various social services.

A use-value society is necessarily a society structured by solidarity. Solidarity is a precondition for a use-value society, but a use-value society in turn also promotes solidarity, as there is no benefit to be gained by excluding people or holding countries back. Rather than forcing producers to compete for market shares, solidarity encourages individual producers and entire countries to support each other in a collective effort to satisfy human needs and to improve the usefulness of goods and services. Solidarity also means that collective goals, such as the fight against climate change, must take precedence over individual interests, such as driving an SUV. However, solidarity is also important to make sure that a majority does not ignore the interests of a minority, or to ensure respect for different identities, cultures, and ways of living as long as they do not contradict the overall objective of protecting the environment and providing a "good life" for all human beings.

Given the role of solidarity, it should come as no surprise that use-value societies are much more equal than capitalist social systems. However, equality is not only the result of mutual support. With the abolishment of the profit motive, all needs count, regardless of whether they are backed by money or not. In fact, those backed by a lot of money may become less important because they are non-essential and wasteful. Hence, rather than building luxury condominium towers, the construction industry focuses on the creation of affordable and sustainable forms of housing. The pharmaceutical industry develops drugs for epidemics in the Global South, rather than trying to convince people in the Global North that they need more drugs. And the auto industry builds sufficient and functional electric vehicles, including e-trucks, rather than developing luxury e-cars. Equality will also benefit from the expansion of public services, granting access to healthcare, education, water, electricity, and high-speed internet regardless of household income and location.

Contrary to other alternatives such as the one promoted by the degrowth movement, a use-value society does not imply sacrifices; instead, it implies a qualitatively different mode of living which in fact can be superior to current living conditions in the United States, where poor-quality houses can cost up to one million dollars, people are stuck in traffic in their journeys to and from work, and many eat industrialized food, cannot afford college, and have no or only limited access to healthcare.[14] Measured as GDP per capita, the United States has one of the highest living standards in the world, higher than Germany. But this does not mean that Americans live better than Germans. On average, German workers work ten weeks less per year than Americans (Hermann 2015a, 175, figure 10.1).[15] In a use-value society, people will have even more free time to pursue personal interests and to do useful things out of joy rather than coercion. In short, the mode of living will change, but for much of the population in the United States and other countries, living conditions will improve rather than deteriorate.

Because it focuses on the satisfaction of needs rather than the expansion of profits, a use-value society will at some point have to break with capitalism. As mentioned before, the main purpose of a capitalist economy is to increase profits; the satisfaction of needs is only a by-product in the endless accumulation process. Needs have no relevance in capitalism if they cannot be satisfied in a profitable manner. Profitability, in contrast, has no significance in a use-value society, where needs are evaluated according to social relevance and decisions are made in a democratic manner, taking into account the effects of different options on the environment. As such, a use-value society is a vision that reaches beyond capitalism. However, in contrast to other visions of post-capitalism, the use-value society does not depend on the invention of new technologies (Mason 2015; Albo 2020, 321–326).[16] Instead, it is rooted in a pre-capitalist priority of needs over profits, while developing and deploying the full capacities of human beings to think creatively and work collectively to provide for the universal means of existence. Hence the use-value society does not start with tech workers experimenting with peer-to-peer production (Mason 2015, 141–145). The use-value society starts wherever workers care more about products or customers than about corporate profits—including a nurse who, according to hospital management, spends too much time caring for a patient. Since the same carefulness also applies to nature, a use-value society does, furthermore, not depend on a technological fix to solve the ecological crisis. Here, too, the key to a sustainable future lies in the development of innovative collective practices. Technology is not the solution, but, of course, it can help.

The Marxist vision of post-capitalism is called socialism.[17] However, since the fall of communism in Russia and Eastern Europe, socialism has become an increasingly contested, variable, and (in a positive sense) open concept. Among other things, there is considerable disagreement about the role of markets in a future socialist economy (Rahnema 2017).[18] As mentioned before, a use-value society can include markets as long as they do not compromise the promotion of social and ecological utility. One reason for the disagreement is that Marx gave only some hints about a post-capitalist future. According to Peter Hudis (2012, conclusion), Marx's main message is that a transition to socialism requires the abandoning of exchange value and its equivalent abstract labor, resulting in the unmediated association of free producers organizing production.[19] However, the liberation from the tyranny of the commodity form, or things over people, still leaves the question, what is the goal of production in a socialist economy? In other words, socialism not only requires new forms of production, but also new forms of consumption, especially if we take into account the impact on the environment.

Some visions of a twenty-first-century socialism coming out of Latin America go beyond the system of production and address the question of social needs and ecological sustainability when they link socialism to the provision of a "good life" in harmony with nature (Houtart 2011; Boron 2010; Lebowitz 2006). As such, they have much in common with what I perceive as use-value society. However, experience in Latin America and other places also shows that a transition to socialism demands nothing short of a revolution. In contrast, the transition toward a use-value society can start with small steps—and it can begin right away. The many cooperatives, not-for-profit organizations, and small firms that produce for local markets and make little or no profit already promote use value, as do most small, family-owned farms. People who are engaged in production for self-use or the use of family members, friends, or the community also promote use value, including communal gardens, collective repair shops, public art projects, and various forms of voluntary work (arguably, capitalism would not function without them). People who reuse and repair things, rather than throwing them away, also promote use value by prolonging the usefulness of the respective goods. Public services, which in many countries have been undermined by decades of neoliberal austerity and restructuring, can be rebuilt to become examples of use-value orientation, including healthcare and education. Yet in order to do so, services need adequate funding, and students and patients must have a real say in their provision. This means real opportunities to participate—not just by taking surveys or forming committees that can voice concerns but have no power in decision-making processes. Positive experience with growing islands of use-value orientation in the sea of profit maximization can, hopefully, pave the way for systemic change, ending capitalism and commodification—and tackling the ecological crisis. In this sense, a use-value society can also be seen as a first step, or transitory phase, in the long journey to an ecologically sustainable socialism.

Notes

Chapter 1

1. *Oxford English Dictionary* (without year). Available at: https://www.oed.com/ [accessed November 1, 2020].
2. "Commodification" is not in the 1972 Supplement to the *Oxford English Dictionary* (Burchfield 1972). The 1998 edition was the next revision.
3. The French translation *marchandisation* and the German equivalent *Kommodifizierung* appeared about the same time or later. According to Wolfgang Fritz Haug (2010, 1245), *Kommodifizierung* is the German adaptation of commodification and was introduced in German academic discourses via engagement with English literature. However, at least one German author, Claus Offe, used the term *Kommodifizierung* in the early 1970s before it became popular in Anglo-American Marxism (Offe 1972). Yet Offe may be an exception, as he early on showed an interest in English debates and held visiting positions in the United States from 1969 to 1971.
4. An exception is Brennan and Jaworski (2016), who see themselves as the critics of the critics of commodification.
5. According to the *Oxford English Dictionary*, the first mention of commodification was in a review of Jürgen Habermas's book *Legitimation Crisis* in which the author mentions the increasing commodification of modern art. The author put commodification in quotation marks (Howard 1974, 277).
6. Terry Eagleton (1981, 64), in a critique of American literary theory, notes that Jameson has inherited his ruling political concepts, commodification and reification, from Lukács and the Frankfurt School and has subsequently downplayed the significance of class struggle in his cultural criticism.
7. *Society of Spectacle* was first published in French in 1967. In the French original the sentence is as follows: "Le spectacle est le moment ou la merchandise est parvenu à l'occupation totale de la vie sociale" (Debord 1967, 31).
8. Jameson does not remember when and where he encountered commodification first, but he is sure that it is not his invention. Email conversation from July 26, 2019.
9. In a 1976 article on the transition from feudalism to capitalism, Wallerstein still used Polanyi's exact terms when writing about "the proletarization of labor and the commercialization of land" (Wallerstein 1976, 273).
10. "Inevitably, my views evolved in some important respects. This did not happen unaided. I acknowledge a continuing intellectual debt to Marx, Freud, Schumpeter, and Karl Polanyi" (Wallerstein 2000, xxii). I attempted to contact Wallerstein in the early summer of 2019, but he was already too sick to respond to my email and, unfortunately, passed away a few weeks later.

11. Email communication with Claus Offe from February 27, 2018.

12. For the resurgence of Marxism in American sociology, see Burawoy (1982). As a sign of the increased significance of Marxist thought in American academia, Michael Burawoy and Theda Skocpol were invited by the editors of the prestigious *American Journal of Sociology* to edit a supplement of the journal with contributions from Marxist scholars (volume 88).

13. *Marchandisation* and *Kommodifizierung* show similar steep increases in French and German publications. For a description of Google Books' ngram viewer see: https://books.google.com/ngrams/info [accessed November 1, 2020].

14. In Europe, and especially in Germany, the fall of communism had a major impact on academic Marxism. I personally know of two (Western) Marxist scholars who were not appointed as professors even though they were ranked first by the respective search committees. As a result, all academic centers of Western German Marxist thought disappeared after the retirement of Marxist professors in the 1990s and early 2000s (more recently, two new centers emerged). In other countries the postmodern turn and the shift from class to identity politics may be more important to explain the vanishing interest in Marxist thinking. The 2008–2009 economic crisis led to renewed interest in Marxist analyses and especially in the work of Polanyi, but it seems the effect was only temporary.

15. With the exception of Deborah Satz (2012, 39–40), none of the moral critics of commodification refers to Polanyi's work. Satz mentions Polanyi's claim that markets need to be embedded in society, but leaves out his more fundamental critique of commodification, including the commodification of land, labor, and money. While largely forgotten in the previous decades, Polanyi experienced an academic revival after the 2008–2009 crisis as the deregulation of financial markets was seen as major cause of the crisis (see Chapter 5).

16. Radin's work is partly a response to the economic imperialism of the Chicago School of Economics and in particular to the writings of Gary Becker (Radin and Sunder 2005, 10–11). Becker (e.g., 1976) had suggested that we understand all human relations as exchange relations, including love, marriage, reproduction, etc. In Becker's spirit, other economists even suggested the creation of an adoption market on which babies could be bought and sold (Landes and Posner 1978).

17. Vivana Zelizer (2000) has challenged "the hostile worlds theorem of economic and intimate relations" and argued that just because something is paid for does not mean that people only value it in monetary terms, or that making money becomes the sole motive for supplying these goods or engaging in these relationships. Kieran Healy (2006) makes a similar argument with respect to the provision of blood and organs. He argues that the character of exchange depends on the institutional and cultural framework in which it occurs, more than on any money exchanged.

18. As a result, the highly educated may decide to leave the country in what is sometimes described as "brain drain."

19. See, for example, a memo by the European Commission from January 2014, available at: http://europa.eu/rapid/press-release_MEMO-14-38_en.htm [accessed November 1, 2020].

20. Ironically, Radin herself is labeled as an anti-commodification theorist by self-described critics of the critics of commodification (Brennan and Jaworski 2016, 7).

21. The German term is *ursprüngliche Akkumulation*, which is closer to "original accumulation" than "primitive accumulation."

22. Outside the Marxist literature, Fred Hirsch (1977, 93) notes that much of economic theory falsely assumes that the commercialization and related changes in the method of provision do not affect the product. Hirsch, subsequently, argues that certain needs are not fulfilled or are filled in an unsatisfactory manner when they cannot be provided in a commercialized way, but says little about how the products themselves change (90–91).

23. Horkheimer and Adorno (2002) have not only overlooked the many ways in which producers and recipients undermine the logic of commodification inhibited in the culture industry, including experimental jazz music. They have also missed the fact that cultural production, even if carried out in industrialized fashion, depends on product innovation. As such, it also depends on the persistent exploitation and commodification of alternative, non-commercial culture and ways of living—what Harvey calls accumulation by dispossession.

24. Using formula for feeding babies has since been discredited in rich countries.

25. To see the difference, one only has to look at the menus for business class and economy class passengers on transatlantic flights: While economy class passengers receive a plate full of prepacked and precooked food, business class passengers receive a slender meal with freshly prepared components. In other words, you do not receive more food when you travel business class—you receive better food.

26. GATS: General Agreement on Trade in Services; TRIPS: Agreement on Trade-Related Aspects of Intellectual Property Rights.

Chapter 2

1. Adam Reich, for example, wrote a book on *The Commodification of Hospital Care in the United States* without mentioning what commodification means (Reich 2014).

2. Karl Polanyi (1957), whom Appadurai briefly mentions without really engaging with his work, has argued that capitalism stands out because in capitalism things are commodified that are not even intended for exchange—including, most notably, labor power. Polanyi calls such items "fictitious commodities" (see Chapter 5).

3. The United Kingdom's National Health Service can, for example, be seen as a form of production for collective use. The British government as the representative of the public provides healthcare for its citizens. The question of how to make sure that what is produced for collective use is also what is needed is taken up in Chapter 7.

4. For Marx, (commodity) money has use value. But given that only a small group of artisans actually used gold and other precious metals to produce jewelry and other things, I am more inclined to follow Joseph Schumpeter (and François Quesnay), who argued that money has no use value (Nelson 2005, 75–76).

5. Unpaid household labor, for example, produces use value but no exchange value, and the fact that is has no price means that it is insignificant in economic terms (Hermann 2015a, 35–39).

6. Rather than improving their cars, GM announced plans to close several US and Canadian plants and cut up to 14,000 jobs in 2018 (Boudette 2018).

7. M = money; C = commodity.

8. Ian Steedman's critique of Marxist value theory provoked a series of defenses and counter-criticisms from Marxist scholars, resulting in what is commonly referred to as value controversy (Steedman et al. 1981).

9. Labor costs are low because assembly is carried out in China, where workers are paid extremely low wages by Western standards. But even if Apple would pay US wages, labor costs still would not explain the price of an iPhone and the fact that it is significantly more expensive than comparable smart phones. See Koen De Backer's presentation, available at: http://www.oecd.org/industry/ind/47945400.pdf [accessed November 1, 2020].

10. As Marx (1991, 278–279) notes, for exchange value to equal market value there can be "no natural or artificial monopoly to enable one of the contracting parties to sell above value or force to sell cheap, below value." And as he (1991, 281) further explains, "the pressures the various sellers exert on one another must be strong enough to put on the market the quantity of commodities that is required to fulfill the social need, i.e. the quantity for which society is able to pay the market value." Companies such as Apple succeed in branding their products as being different from and superior to those of their competitors. The ability to charge a premium over its competitors, which underlines the exclusivity of Apple products, means that Apple can make more profit by selling fewer phones for a higher price.

11. This is a point that Marxists are frequently criticized for by institutionalists (e.g., Hodgson 2015, 140). However, treating each market as a unique institution prevents institutionalists from seeing common dynamics unleashed by markets and fundamental contradictions in market societies.

12. This does not refute the labor theory of value. Apple (via its contractors) still exploits the mostly Chinese workers who assemble the iPhone and other Apple products. It only means that in addition to surplus created in the production process, Apple and others also pocket what Marx has described as commercial profits gained in sphere of circulation through market manipulations (see Marx 1991, chapter 17).

13. Marx here describes a general trend that became even more pronounced with the spread of Taylorism and Fordist mass production. However, in modern capitalism and especially in the knowledge economy, there are also a number of jobs which still offer the possibility for workers to apply skills and knowledge and, subsequently, to achieve something remarkable. For these workers the idea that they are alienated seems rather strange. Yet many knowledge workers experience a form of alienation in their daily work when they are pressured to "give their best" while at the same time being denied the necessary resources to achieve the best possible result (Hermann 2009a, 284–285).

14. Contrary to what some critics (e.g., Healy 2006, 5) think, Marx's critique of commodification is precisely not moral but material (see Chapter 1).

15. The so-called Phoebus cartel included Osram from Germany, Philips from the Netherlands, Compagnie des Lampes from France, and General Electric from the United States.

16. I recently noted that the newest model of the type of notebook that I have used for almost twenty years no longer has an external battery that can be replaced and space to add memory to allow the computer to cope with memory-consuming software updates. Of course, these changes are intended to encourage consumers to buy a new computer when the battery loses power and/or the computer slows down.

17. After mounting criticism from users, Apple has admitted that it has intentionally slowed down iPhones with older batteries, allegedly in order to keep them from shutting down suddenly. In order to appease angry customers, the company subsequently reduced the cost for battery replacements from 79 to 29 US dollars (Greenfield 2017).

18. Convenience alone may have not been such a convincing argument, especially not in urban areas with developed public transportation systems. Hence American car manufacturers, together with oil companies and tire producers, created shell companies to buy up electrified streetcar lines in the 1930s, only to terminate their services. Left without an alternative, people turned to cars to move around in cities like Los Angeles (Urry 2013, 77).

19. According to Cameron Kerry and Jack Karsten (2017), by 2016, approximately 80 billion US dollars were invested in the development of self-driving technology.

20. New York's Metropolitan Transport Authority amasses a several hundred million US dollar deficit each year and has accumulated more than 30 billion US dollars in debt (Braun 2018). In contrast, Tesla Motors Inc's stock market valuation reached 89 billion US dollars in early 2020. Ford and General Motors together were worth another 87 billion US dollars (Randewich 2020).

21. A particular infamous case is Thames Water serving about eight million customers in the southeast of England. The privatized company was losing 900 million liters of water per day in 2006, while making record profits and announcing further price increases (Millner and Brignall 2006). In spite of some improvements, the company was still losing 683 million liters a day in 2018 (Kollewe 2018).

22. The Soviet Union, in this perspective, had elements of formal commodification but clearly no real commodification. Perhaps the authoritarian imposition of quantitative output targets qualifies as fictitious commodification, but the main weakness of the Soviet economy was the lack of use value maximization (see Chapter 7).

23. What is also interesting about Stone's analysis is the author's difficulty in explaining this phenomenon without referring to use and market value.

24. The difficulties of standardizing services are also reflected in William Baumol's service sector cost disease. Because of the limits to standardization, services and in particular labor-intensive services such as healthcare show relatively low productivity gains. As a result, the prices for labor-intensive services stagnate or increase, while those for industrial output tend to fall due to mechanization and computerization (Baumol 2012).

25. Precisely because labor is a fictitious commodity, i.e., it cannot be separated from the bearer of labor power, it must not be standardized to be sold, but the codification of skills and education is certainly helpful for the functioning of labor markets.

26. In the past, such cases have also been described as market failure. However, market failures result not only from a lack of competition; market failures can also be caused by difficulties to exclude users who are not paying (Ronald Coase's famous lighthouse example) or by severe uncertainties and information asymmetries (Kenneth Arrow's critique of private healthcare).

27. This finding is confirmed by a study from the US Department of Justice (2016) who found in a comparison between public and private prisons that private prisons under-perform in a series of quality indicators such as assaults, uses of force, and lockdowns.

28. Several researchers estimate that US pharmaceutical companies spend almost twice as much on advertising and other forms of promotion than on research and development (Angell 2005, 48; Gagnon and Lexchin 2008).

29. The regulation requires (average fleet-based) carbon-dioxide emissions of new cars registered in the European Union to shrink from 145 grams per kilometer in 2000 to 95 grams per kilometer in 2021. The auto industry vehemently rejected the measure and lobbied aggressively to make sure that the targets are not too ambitious (Lütkenhorst et al. 2014, 32). President Obama also introduced mandatory fuel efficiency standards in 2012, reducing fuel consumption for most new car models to 54.5 miles per gallon in 2025.

Chapter 3

1. "Neoliberalism" is a widely used term and therefore difficult to define. Neoliberalism has at least three dimensions. First, it describes a specific school of thought that is associated with the Mont Pèlerin Society. Representatives of the "neoliberal thought collective" include Friedrich Hayek, Milton Friedman, and James Buchanan (Plehwe 2009). Second, it is used as a term for the economic and social system that replaced postwar Keynesianism in the 1980s and that lasted at least until the 2008 financial crisis (Harvey 2005). Third, neoliberalism is also used to describe major changes in economic and social policies such as the shift from demand- to supply-side economics, from import substitution to structural adjustment, or from welfare to workfare (Saad-Filho and Johnston 2005).

2. The United States, for example, experienced a slowdown in growth, high inflation, and increasing unemployment. The subsequent increase in the interest rates brought down inflation, but at the cost of even higher unemployment, at least in the short term.

3. Patenting of human DNA was a common practice in the United States and elsewhere until 2013, when the US Supreme Court ruled against an American biotech firm which held a patent on two genes linked to a higher risk of breast and ovarian cancer. The court argued that human genes are a product of nature and therefore not protected by patent law (McVeigh 2013).

4. Patenting is not only a method to privatize nature. Some authors argue that the patenting of genetic information has boosted cooperations between public universities and private biotech firms, which has subsequently led to a creeping privatization of university research (Rudy et al. 2007). In 1998, UC Berkeley signed a five-year contract with the Swiss biotech company Novartis which provided the university with funding of 25 million US dollars and, in turn, granted Novartis Agricultural Discovery Institute (and its predecessor Syngenta) exclusive access to discoveries made in the Department of Plant and Microbial Biology during the term of the agreement. Critics claimed that the deal increased corporate influence on research carried out at a major public university (Rudy et al. 2007).

5. Private contractors, including both for-profit and not-for-profit corporations, are also heavily involved in operating shelters and transporting children that have been separated from their parents at the southern US border in the summer of 2018 (Fernandez and Benner 2018).

6. Data from World Bank.

7. The emphasis on privatization reflects the Austrian economics' approach to public-sector reform in which private property rights play a key role. In contrast, for the neo-classical school the most important driver of change is competition (Sawyer 2009).

8. While some EU countries founded independent corporations that are responsible for maintaining and improving the electricity network, in others existing companies continued to own the networks but through semi-independent subsidiaries with separate accounting systems.

9. Water is also an object of re-municipalization. Among others, the city of Paris took back the provision of water into public control in 2010 (McDonald 2018).

10. Transport London, for example, puts out contracts for 675 bus routes across the British capital and sends out controllers on a daily base to check if buses arrive on time and meet other contractual obligations.

11. Adjustable means that interest rates increase over time; delayed payment means that borrowers start to pay back the loans after a certain date in the future.

12. Company-level bargaining usually means lower wage increases as employers can exert more pressure on their staff than on the sector or national level. In Greece, for example, the decentralization of collective bargaining during the crisis led to a 22 percent decrease in wages (Hermann 2014, 120).

13. California Assembly Bill 5, adopted in 2019, introduces the so-called ABC test to assess the independent nature of the status of a contractor. Accordingly, an independent contractor must be free from the control and direction of the hiring entity in connection with the performance of the work, both under the contract for the performance of the work and in fact; the worker performs work that is outside the usual course of the hiring entity's business; and the worker is customarily engaged in an independently established trade, occupation, or business of the same nature as that involved in the work performed. It is widely believed that Uber drivers and other "gig workers" must be employed as regular employees under this law.

14. A survey among more than 1,100 Uber and Lyft drivers revealed that drivers on average earn 3.37 US dollars per hour; 74 percent earn less than the minimum wage

in their state and 30 percent actually lose money once vehicle expenses are included (Zoepf et al. 2018).

15. The Kyoto protocol also allows for the purchasing of emissions rights through investments in emissions-reducing projects such as reforestation in developing countries.

16. The legal framework is based on Directive 2003/87/EC establishing a system for greenhouse gas emission allowance trading within the European Union.

17. Among these indicators were the aforementioned "average length of stay," but also "average patients per bed per year," "inpatient admission per 1,000 population," and "admission waiting list in relation to the population served."

18. The idea of creating citation indices goes back to the late 1920s, but efforts to build comprehensive cross-disciplinary data sets really took off in the 1960s. Eugene Garfield was one of the main promoters of modern citation indices. He founded the Institute for Scientific Information in Philadelphia, which developed the Science Citation Index in the 1960s. Initially, citation indices were produced to help librarians to make decisions about which journals to subscribe to (Archambault and Larivière 2009).

19. Garfield's Institute for Scientific Information and its Science Citation Index were acquired by Thomson Corporation in 1992, which became Thomson Reuters in 2008. The index and related businesses are meanwhile part of Thomson Reuters's subsidiary Clarivate Analytics.

20. The highly influential paper "Market for 'Lemons': Quality Uncertainty and the Market Mechanism," by the economist Georg Akerlof, was rejected by the renowned *American Economic Review* and published in the less prestigious *Quarterly Journal of Economics*. Akerlof later won the Nobel Prize in Economics partly based on this publication (Busch 2017, 73).

21. Some of the most influential intellectuals of recent decades, such as Michel Foucault and Pierre Bourdieu, would likely have failed in such a system because their writings would hardly adhere to the publishing style of high-ranking English-language journals. Yet, interestingly, it is these authors that continue to influence new generations of students, whereas many scholars who have published in highly ranked journals have long been forgotten.

22. From my experience, class sizes also play an important role. At UC Berkeley, smaller classes consistently receive better teaching evaluations, even though the quality of a teacher does not depend on how many students are enrolled in a course.

23. UC Berkeley, for example, uses teaching evaluations and averages scores, against the advice of its renowned statistics professor Philip B. Stark. On the overall teaching effectiveness question, adjunct faculty are expected to reach an average score of 6 or higher on a scale from 1 to 7.

24. This is not to say that students' evaluations of teaching are worthless. However, in order to assess the quality of teaching, evaluations must also be based on qualitative methods, such as, for example, in-depth interviews in which students have to argue why they think that they learned more in certain classes than in others, or focus groups in which students have to come to a collective assessment. Since such

evaluations would be time-consuming and costly, they likely will not happen in the neoliberal university.

25. Katherine Silbaugh (2011) has made a similar argument with regard to standardized testing in schools. In the United States, public primary and secondary schools carry out yearly tests to evaluate the educational progress of their students as part of the "No Child Left Behind" initiative introduced by the Bush administration in the early 2000s. For Silbaugh (2011, 311), test scores have a great deal in common with prices: in both cases a good, a service, or an achievement is measured by a unitary metric and is therefore made commensurable. Following the moral critique of commodification, Silbaugh argues that all values that are not measurable, such as creativity, insight, reasoning, and the application of skills to unrehearsed situations, are crowded out (2011, 311). Critics have subsequently contested that the focus on some skills at the expense of others amounts to an act of commodification (Healy 2011, 339). However, while the focus on some skills at the expense on others may not qualify as commodification, the "measuring" of educational performances subjugates quality to quantity and as such resembles the subjugation of use value to market/exchange value. The result is what in Chapter 2 has been described as fictitious commodification.

26. Based on historical evidence, Carmen Reinhard and Kenneth Rogoff (2011) set the threshold after which government debt negatively affects economic growth at 90 percent of GDP. However, an economic student from the University of Massachusetts found major inconsistencies in the data on which the conclusion is based (Herdon, Ash, and Pollin 2013).

27. Several European countries also introduced corporate tax cuts during the Great Recession (Hermann 2017a, 523).

28. For counter arguments, see Farnsworth and Irving (2015).

29. In contrast to the United States, British students don't have to pay back their loans if their earnings are below a certain threshold.

Chapter 4

1. In the United States, private health insurance providers include Preferred Provider Organizations (PPOs) and Health Maintenance Organizations (HMOs). PPOs cover a certain percentage of the costs charged by healthcare providers. Typically, the coverage is higher if the organization is part of the insurance's preferred provider network. In the second case, customers have no choice but to use a healthcare provider within the HMO network (except in the case of emergency care), but in turn the insurance provider covers all the costs except for a small co-payment.

2. Data from Kaiser Family Foundation Health Insurance Coverage of the Total Population. Available at: https://www.kff.org/other/state-indicator/total-population/?dataView=0&currentTimeframe=0&selectedRows=%7B%22wrapups%22:%7B%22united-states%22:%7B%7D%7D%7D&sortModel=%7B%22colId%22:%22Locat ion%22,%22sort%22:%22asc%22%7D [accessed November 1, 2020].

3. Low incomes are understood as incomes under 200 percent of the federal poverty level (22,980 US dollars for an individual and 47,100 for a family of four).

4. According to Donald Heller (2011, 22, figure 1.4), US families from the lowest income quintile had to pay 10 percent of their family income for tuition at a four-year public college in 1975. The proportion increased to more than 40 percent in 2007.

5. US student debt now accounts for more than 7 percent of GDP. Data from Federal Reserve St. Louis. Available at: https://fred.stlouisfed.org/series/SLOAS [accessed November 1, 2020].

6. The 2015 cohort includes students who started paying back loans between October 1, 2014, and September 30, 2015. Data from the US Department of Education. Available at: https://www.ed.gov/news/press-releases/national-student-loan-cohort-default-rate-falls [accessed November 1, 2020].

7. The 27.2 percent includes students who have not graduated.

8. After a series of protests, the government reacted and introduced legislation that grants a certain amount of free electricity to every South African household (Ruiters 2009).

9. Data from US Census Bureau. Available at: www.census.gov/newsroom/blogs/random-samplings/2011/09/households-doubling-up.html [accessed November 1, 2020].

10. Data from Eviction Lab. Available at: https://evictionlab.org/national-estimates/ [accessed November 1, 2020].

11. Some retailers have started to donate spare food to foodbanks which, in turn, pass it on to people who cannot afford to shop in regular stores.

12. The 1983 Orphan Drug Act introduced various incentives for pharmaceutical companies to develop drugs for diseases that affect fewer than 200,000 people. Before 1983, the pharma industry largely ignored such diseases. Whereas only ten orphan drugs had been approved by the US Food and Drug Administration in the decade before 1983, by 2010 the agency had approved more than 350 (Mikami 2017, 610). While the Orphan Drug Act, subsequently, has been celebrated as highly successful policy intervention—orphan drugs now account for about a third of all newly approved drugs and biologics—the measure channels significant public funds to an already highly profitable private-sector industry (ibid.).

13. One result of the liberalization and privatization of postal services in Europe was the systematic closure of rural post offices (Hermann 2011, 269).

14. Area Median Income is calculated and published by the US Department of Housing and Urban Development.

15. According to a data set compiled by NYU professor Aswath Damodaran, the US pharmaceutical industry had a gross margin of 70.26 percent in early 2020, compared to 36.32 percent for hospitals and other healthcare facilities. The dataset is available at: http://pages.stern.nyu.edu/~adamodar/New_Home_Page/datafile/margin.html [accessed November 1, 2020].

16. The same study also shows that for-profit hospitals are much more responsive to changes in funding than their not-for-profit peers. Reimbursement rates for home

health services in the United States changed quite a bit over the 1990s. While in the early 1990s they were relatively generous, reimbursement rates dropped after new legislation was introduced to curb expenses in 1997. As a result, the probability of for-profit urban hospitals offering home health services increased from 17.5 percent in 1988 to 60.9 percent in 1996, followed by a drop to 37.5 per cent in 2000. In contrast, not-for-profit hospitals only responded moderately to changes in reimbursement, with the effect that they continued to provide home health services at a rate of around 50 percent in 2000 (Horwitz 2005, 795–796).

17. And in order to make sure that the private partners can exploit economies of scale, the British government initially paid for a minimum number of treatments regardless of how many patients actually received surgery (Player and Leys 2008, 12).

18. India is a preferred location for medical tourists because of the availability of highly trained doctors who speak fluent English.

19. Data from UK Higher Education Statistics. Available at: https://www.hesa.ac.uk/news/12-01-2017/sfr242-student-enrolments-and-qualifications   [accessed November 1, 2020].

20. Ultra-processed food has become a major source of nutrition in the developed world. In 2000, more than half of the total purchased calories of an average household in Canada came from ultra-processed food (Monteiro et al. 2013, 23).

21. Human habits and lifestyles, including those which are unhealthy, are difficult to change, and it usually takes long periods of time before changes in behavior translate into positive health outcomes.

22. Perhaps an extreme case of such an attitude is Ian Patterson, a British surgeon who performed hundreds of unnecessary operations on women in private hospitals in order to maximize profits (Campbell and Topping 2020).

23. Kuttner (1996, 133) notes that some Health Maintenance Organizations offer members free access to fitness centers, yoga classes, and the like. Yet they do so not to promote health prevention, but to attract customers who are healthy and in good shape.

24. "Throw-Away Buildings: Toronto's Glass Condos." Available at: https://www.cbc.ca/news/canada/toronto/throw-away-buildings-toronto-s-glass-condos-1.1073319#:~:text=Many%20of%20the%20glass%20condominium,dollars%2C%20some%20industry%20experts%20say [accessed November 1, 2020].

25. Some economists argue that overfishing and other forms of environmental degradation are not the result of commodification and industrialization, but of what has been described as the tragedy of the commons, i.e., the reckless exploitation of common resources by individuals who because of a lack of ownership rights do not feel responsible. From this perspective the answer to the problem is not regulation, i.e., the imposing of fishing moratoriums and quotas; the answer is the privatization of common resources such as, for example, through the auctioning of exclusive fishing licenses (Helm 2015, 122). However, the problem is not a lack of responsibility—for centuries fishermen acted responsibly and caught less than 5 percent of the stock of Atlantic cod per year (Rose 2004, 1555). They did not become rich, but they were able to make a living. The problem is competition and production for increasingly large

and eventually global markets. These, of course, are characteristics of capitalist commodity production.

26. Still, these figures may underestimate real costs. Additional costs accrue when changes to the contract have to be made, which is not unusual given the thirty-year duration of the arrangements. The private partners charge additional fees even for minor changes. According to a newspaper report, PFI hospitals in England had to pay 242 pounds to put a padlock on a garden gate, 466 pounds to replace a light fitting, and 15,000 pounds to install a laundry door (Hope 2012).

27. The situation improved in the following years due to additional government funding. However, in 2017–2018, 44 percent of trusts still overspent their budgets. Available at: https://www.kingsfund.org.uk/projects/nhs-in-a-nutshell/trusts-deficit [accessed November 1, 2020]. At least in one case, the government let a trust go under. After accumulating 250 million pounds in debt, the South London Healthcare Trust was dissolved in 2012 (Winnet 2012).

28. According to Allyson Pollock (2004, 59), the average reduction of hospital beds in the first wave of hospitals entering PFI projects in England in the 1990s was 30 percent, while the number of clinical staffs was cut by 25 percent.

29. However, some private partners were still not satisfied with the continuous stream of income and decided to sell their stakes on secondary PPP markets. Dexter Whitfield (2010, 192–193) has analyzed 666 PPP projects in the United Kingdom in which equity was sold between 1998 and 2009. The total value of the projects amounted to 2.84 billion pounds and total profits of the sales to 257.2 million pounds (ibid.).

30. The bailout failed to revive investor confidence, and in 2002 Railtrack had to be taken into public administration and converted into Railnet, a government-owned private company (Bowman et al. 2013, 70–71).

31. Data from the Instituto Nacional de Pesquisas Espaciais. Available at: http://www.obt.inpe.br/prodes/prodes_1988_2009.htm [accessed March 1, 2019].

32. In the European Union cross-border standardization was promoted through the so-called Bologna process.

33. In 2015, the United States ranked 26th out of 35 OECD countries in terms of life expectancy and 29th in terms of infant mortality rate (United Health Foundation 2016, 23).

34. Among other changes, the shortening of patient stays has increased the proportion of admission and discharging work (Gordon 2005, 238–239).

35. Johan Diels et al. (2011) have shown that more than a few of the authors of studies that allegedly prove that genetically modified products are safe have either received funding or are otherwise connected with the industry that promotes these products.

36. Kaiser Family Foundation, "Percent of Children (Ages 10–17) Who Are Overweight or Obese." Available at: https://www.kff.org/other/state-indicator/overweightobese-children/?currentTimeframe=0&sortModel=%7B%22colId%22:%22Location%22,%22sort%22:%22asc%22%7D [accessed November 1, 2020].

37. Among the players that gamed the system was the energy giant Enron, which later collapsed amidst an accounting scandal. The traders used different code names for their "games," such as Fat Boy, Death Star, or Richochet. While Enron took most of the

blame, it was by far not the only company that made money from fake purchases and sales of electricity, by sending electricity out of and into California, and by submitting false data to the regulator.

38. While San Francisco has a homeless population of approximately 8,000 people, it is estimated that 100,000 housing units are vacant in the San Francisco metropolitan area (Graff 2019). In late 2019, a group of homeless mothers occupied a vacant home in neighboring Oakland that was owned by a real estate investment firm. The occupants were evicted in early 2020 (Swan and Cabanatuan 2020).

39. Deregulation of commodity markets also made investments more attractive (Schmidt 2016, 64–66).

40. A major factor was also the growing demand for agricultural products as the basis for biofuels. However, prices for rice also shot up, even though rice is not used for biofuels.

41. This does not, however, exclude the possibility that commodification could increase the living standard of the poor through the provision of standardized and therefore cheap goods.

42. Calculated from 2015 American Housing Survey data. Available at: https://www.census.gov/programs-surveys/ahs.html [accessed 1 November, 2019].

43. The eight Ivy League colleges, University of Chicago, Stanford, MIT, and Duke.

44. Natural gas and crude oil prices are believed to be connected because one can be substituted for the other. Some electricity is produced through gas-fired power plants.

45. While most countries have a mix of private and public pensions, Chile, with the exception of military personnel, abandoned public pensions and introduced a completely private system in the early 1980s.

46. The same mechanism also means that countries like Germany could pay out pensions right after the Second World War.

47. Thorstein Veblen (1921) has referred to the same conflict as tension between the captains of finance (who took over the large US corporations at the end of the nineteenth century from the captains of industry) and the technical experts, who keep the industrial system running. He even discussed the possibility of a "soviet of technicians" replacing a system that is primarily oriented toward profit maximization (ibid.).

48. According to a study, public school teachers in the United States earned about 21.4 percent less in 2018 than workers in other professions with comparable education and experience. In the case of male teachers, the gap was 31.5 percent (Allegretto and Mishel 2019).

49. Data from OECD. Available at: https://data.oecd.org/healthres/pharmaceutical-spending.htm [accessed November 1, 2020].

50. The main reason is higher co-payments required by US insurance companies.

51. According to the Centers for Disease Control, overdoses from prescription drugs caused approximately 35,000 deaths in the United States in 2017. Available at: https://www.cdc.gov/drugoverdose/epidemic/index.html [accessed November 1, 2020].

52. Perhaps Cuba represents the opposite model with a highly labor-intensive healthcare system (Feinsilver 1993).

53. Servicing was provided by Sallie Mae (Student Loan Marketing Association), an organization that was set up as public company in the early 1970s. Since 2004 it has been a private company and since 2014 most of its loan servicing business has been handled by a private spin-off, Navient.

54. Data from Securities Industry and Financial Market Association. Available at: https://www.sifma.org/wp-content/uploads/2017/06/sf-us-abs-sifma.xls [accessed November 1, 2020].

55. Data from Federal Student Aid, available at: https://www2.ed.gov/offices/OSFAP/defaultmanagement/cdr.html [accessed November 1, 2020].

56. The German government still holds 20 percent of the shares.

57. Data from Federal Reserve Bank St. Louis. Available at: https://fred.stlouisfed.org/series/CUSR0000SEHA [accessed November 1, 2020].

58. Data from Federal Reserve Bank St. Louis. Available at: https://fred.stlouisfed.org/series/RHORUSQ156N [accessed November 1, 2020].

59. Data from Federal Reserve Bank St. Louis. Available at: https://fred.stlouisfed.org/series/MDOAH [accessed November 1, 2020].

60. Freddie Mac and Fannie Mae had started to issue (non-government-insured) mortgage-backed securities in the early 1970s (Fabozzi and Modigliani 1992, 20–22).

61. Data from US Department of Agriculture. Available at: https://www.ers.usda.gov/webdocs/charts/83915/cornuse.jpg?v=43034 [accessed November 1, 2020]. Besides food for animals and humans, corn is also used for ethanol production.

Chapter 5

1. For institutionalists, several of whom use Polanyi's ideas, the term "dis-embedding" is not without problems. As institutionalists, they assume that economic institutions such as markets are always embedded in one way or another. Dis-embedding therefore makes no sense. But if markets are always embedded, it remains unclear how they can be self-regulated. For a discussion, see Krippner et al. (2004).

2. In contrast, in pre-capitalist societies, reciprocity and redistribution were important norms that governed economic behavior (Polanyi 1957, chapter 4).

3. On the first view, it may sound strange that money can be de-commodified. Money, after all, is the measure of exchange value/market value and as such is a precondition for commodification (see Chapter 2). However, money has different functions, including being a medium of exchange, unit of account, and a store of value. For Polanyi it is the store of value that makes money a commodity, whereas money as means of exchange and unit of account are merely technical features which could also be used in a socialist economy (as discussed in Chapter 7, note 7, Polanyi was not principally opposed to markets and money). During the period of the gold standard, which dominated international finance from the second half of the nineteenth century until the Great Depression, all other functions were subjugated to the goal of

maintaining the value of money—with devastating effects for national economies. Several authors see the gold standard as a major reason, if not the cause, for the severity and longevity of the Great Depression (e.g., Eichengreen 2008, chapters 2 and 3). In Polanyi's view, therefore, the abandoning of the gold standard amounts to an act of de-commodification.

4. Polanyi (1957, 147), for example, notes the anti-market but deeply reactionary and anti-Semitic policies of Karl Lueger, who was the major of Vienna from 1897 to 1910.

5. I think part of the problem is Polanyi's enthusiasm for anthropological studies of non-capitalist societies and economic systems that led him to underestimate the question of power and domination in traditional social settings. Marx, in contrast, was much more critical of pre-capitalist social systems.

6. The European Public Service Union (EPSU) launched the "right2water" campaign to collect signatures against the liberalization of water provision. After collecting more than one million signatures by the end of 2013, it became the first successful European citizens' initiative.

7. In order to challenge social domination, democratic decision-making processes must include some mechanisms that protect the interests of minorities.

8. Luxemburg's critique of Marx was itself criticized by contemporary and subsequent Marxists who defended the (theoretical) possibility of a pure capitalist economy (for an overview of the critique, see Albo 2016, 37–39). Perhaps Luxemburg's strongest argument is the fact that a pure capitalist economy has never existed and may never exist.

9. Luxemburg (2003, 381–385) describes how in this process largely self-sufficient agriculture is transformed into capitalist farming geared toward production for world markets.

10. The expansion of the British textile industry in the nineteenth century, for example, was partly facilitated by the destruction of domestic production in India and the subsequent sale of British textile goods to its Southeast Asian colony (Arrighi 1994, 262).

11. German authors use the German term *Landnahme*, which in the literal sense means "acquisition of land." "Internal colonization" is perhaps the most accurate English translation.

12. US automakers, for example, complain about major competitive disadvantages caused by the high costs of the largely private US healthcare system (Aaron 1991, 95).

13. Especially compared to many renewable forms of energy.

14. Data from US Energy Information Agency. Available at: https://www.eia.gov/tools/faqs/faq.php?id=33&t=6 [accessed November 1, 2020].

15. Data from US Department of Energy, Office of Energy Efficiency and Renewable Energy. Available at: www.energy.gov/eere/vehicles/articles/fact-985-july-10-2017-average-historical-annual-gasoline-pump-price-1929-2016 [accessed November 1, 2020].

16. Data from statista.com. Available at: https://www.statista.com/statistics/619788/average-smartphone-life/ [accessed November 1, 2020].

Chapter 6

1. In ancient Greek, the household economy is called *oikos*. Although it was self-sufficient, the good life of household leaders in ancient Greece greatly depended on the exploitation of slaves.

2. For Marx's appreciation but also critique of the Physiocrats, see Burkett (2006, chapter 1).

3. This is hardly a new insight by Smith. Plato (1892, 245) already noted that "only what [is] rare is valuable," and John Locke added that the "best, and most useful things are commonly the cheapest" (Locke 1824, 41).

4. One coat, for example, is worth twice as much as ten yards of linen.

5. The translation from German is somewhat misleading. Marx speaks of *Warenlehre*, which in English means something like the study of merchandise.

6. Here we are only dealing with the positive side of utility. For Bentham, utility is actually the balance of pain and pleasure. However, we can safely assume that commodities are only acquired when they are not associated with pain.

7. Bentham's concept of utility goes beyond the value of commodities. It is a way to judge all economic activities and their outcomes. Bentham's conclusion is that economic activities should not be judged on moral grounds; they should be judged with respect to their impact on utility. This suggestion played an immensely important role in modern economic thinking and provided a justification for economic agents to be egoistic and greedy as long as their activities increased the total amount of utility produced by a specific group of people, or a specific society.

8. In the 1870s, three scholars—William Jevons, Leon Walras, and Carl Menger—independently rediscovered Gossen's law of diminishing utility (Clarke 1991, chapter 6). This means it took some twenty years for the idea of marginal utility to become a dominant concept in economics.

9. As Marshall (1890: x) notes, "[t]he term 'marginal' increment I borrowed from von Thünen [nineteenth century German economist], and it is now commonly used by German economists. When Jevons' Theory appeared, I adopted his word 'final'; but I have been gradually convinced that 'marginal' is the better."

10. Not only neoclassical economists embraced the concept of marginal utility. Even economists who attempted to prove the feasibility of a socialist economy with neoclassical methods abandoned use value in favor of an individualized and quantified measure of usefulness (Lange, Taylor, and Lippincott 1938). Market socialism, accordingly, not only differs from more traditional visions of socialism by relying on markets as a key mechanism of distribution, but also by prioritizing personal utility over social utility.

11. Pierro Sraffa subsequently argued that deriving prices from marginal utility is tautological. It means explaining the price people are willing to pay by their willingness to pay (quoted in Singorino 2001, 757).

12. Neo-Ricardians also reject the concept of utility. For them, the value of a good or service follows from production costs (Rankin 1980). However, neo-Ricardians have shown little if any interest in use value.

13. Hilferding made his remarks in a response to Eugen Böhm-Bawerk's critique of Marx's labor theory of value. Therein Böhm-Bawerk (1898) had accused Marx of neglecting the role of use value when arguing that the value of a commodity is solely dependent on the (abstract) labor expended for its production. By excluding use value from the study of political economy, Hilferding hoped to render Böhm-Bawerk's critique obsolete. However, as discussed earlier, if anyone, it is the marginalists, of whom Böhm-Bawerk was a leading representative, who eliminated the concept of use value from economics.

14. Adolph Wagner published an economic textbook on political economy (*Lehrbuch der politischen Ökonomie*) in 1879.

15. For a distinction between conventional environmental economics and unconventional ecological economics see Clive Spash (1999).

16. "Deep ecology" is a term invented by Arne Naess in the early 1970s (e.g., Naess 1973). Essentially, deep ecologists reject the idea that nature is supposed to serve human beings. Human beings are part of nature and all parts are equally valuable.

17. It is ironic that marginalist economists such as Böhm-Bawerk (1923, chapter 9) use the example of Robinson Crusoe to illustrate their theories. If anything, the lesson from Daniel Defoe's novel is that humans urgently need other humans to prosper and enjoy life.

18. Even allegedly individual solutions to a social need, such as cars, need collective infrastructures such as roads to function.

19. Social utility, of course, contradicts the interpretation of utility put forward by Bentham and the marginalists.

20. In the German version, Polanyi uses the term *Gemeinnützigkeit*, which can be translated as "beneficial to the public." Johanna Bockman, Ariane Fischer, and David Woodruff have translated it as "social utility." I have decided to stick with their translation.

21. General Motors has shut down several plants in the United States in a plan to discontinue the production of regular passenger cars and focus on SUVs and other more lucrative vehicles. Ford announced similar plans (Fung 2019).

22. SUVs consume about a quarter more energy than regular mid-size cars. SUVs were responsible for an additional 3.3 million oil barrels per day used by passenger cars in 2018 compared to 2010 (International Energy Agency 2019).

23. According to the authors of a study on the climate impact of electric cars, batteries are the main negative item on the environmental balance sheet of electric vehicles (Helms et al. 2019, 58).

24. In the United States, bumper heights for passenger cars are regulated in order to make sure that they match them in case of a collision. However, SUVs are exempted from this and other regulations.

Chapter 7

1. Polanyi was rather critical of the Speenhamland System as the wage subsidies provided by the Speenhamland scheme allowed capitalist farmers to pay workers less than what would today be called a living wage.

2. The housing projects were largely financed by a special tax levied on private landlords. Under social democratic leadership, the city built 65,000 housing units between 1923 and 1934, providing space for more than 11 percent of the city's population (Krätke 2019). Vienna continued to build public housing after the Second World War, with the result that today about half a million people, or a third of the city's population, live in communal housing projects.

3. The do-it-yourself ethos and the link to squatting and other alternative living arrangements meant that part of the punk rock (sub)culture was anti-capitalist and anti-commodification in the 1970s and 1980s. While many bands and musicians have since embraced commercial success—punk has become mainstream, not only in music, but also in fashion—some are still holding out, wearing vintage clothes, and playing for fun rather than money.

4. The link between de-commodification and equality is an essential argument in the *Three Worlds of Welfare States*. Critics have rightly pointed to some simplifications in Esping-Andersen's account—actually existing welfare states rarely fit one of the three models—but if anything, Esping-Andersen underestimated the equality-enhancing effect of welfare states. Esping-Andersen focused exclusively on cash benefits and therefore did not capture the impact of government services. For the role of the public sector in reducing inequality see Hermann (2016, 8–10).

5. Offe and others saw this tension early on when they discussed the contradictions of the modern welfare state in the late 1970s and early 1980s (Offe 1984; Gough 1979).

6. Working-class families in early twentieth-century Vienna typically lived in (literally) two-room apartments, consisting of a bed/living room and a kitchen. Only the bed/living room had windows and there was no water connection and no toilet in the apartment. In contrast, public housing flats had toilets, water, windows, and many even had balconies. Furthermore, they had spacious courtyards and communal facilities such as laundry rooms. Contrary to the United States, where living in so-called projects comes with social stigma, working-class families were happy and proud to move into one of the city's cutting-edge housing projects.

7. Participants in the so-called socialist accounting debate were looking for alternatives to replace money and/or market prices as units of account in a socialist economy. One suggestion was to use labor time expended for the production of specific goods and services. Otto Neurath strongly rejected this idea on the grounds that there is no common measure for utility, usefulness, or well-being (Neurath 2004, 466–472). In a visionary statement, Neurath (ibid.) argues that no measure can possibly account for the impact of excessive exploitation of coal mines for future generations which may have to do without them. And given the impossibility of a common measurement—market prices simply ignore this problem—the only way to come to a rational decision is to compare different options in an in-kind (as opposed to monetary)

cost-benefit analysis (O'Neil 2002, 140). Neurath (2004, 345–370) assumed that such decisions could best be made by a central economic administration. Polanyi (2016) subsequently criticized Neurath and others for his belief in the feasibility of a centrally administered economy. Instead, he proposed a form of democratic socialism in which production associations negotiate with consumer organizations, while communal bodies represent the common interest. However, in Polanyi's model negotiations focus on prices, whereas the allocation of goods and services is still largely left to markets (Bockman 2016, 393). The proposed solution here is based on insights from both authors: on the one hand, negotiations and subsequent decisions should not be limited to prices since markets do not reflect real costs, including, most notable, ecological costs; on the other hand, decisions should be made in a democratic manner, including the participation of producer and consumer representatives, rather than leaving them to a central authority.

8. Because of the problem of measuring public-sector output without market prices, output is usually equated with inputs in national statistics, meaning that public-sector productivity is per definition stagnant. More recently, national statistical offices have tried to solve the problem by counting public-sector activities such as pupil attendance or health procedures and multiplying them by a certain cost factor (Hermann 2016, 16). Of course, this is just another attempt to quantify something that is inherently unquantifiable, or an example of what in Chapter 2 has been described as fictitious commodification.

9. This is different from a market socialism that seeks the allocation of goods and services by competitive markets while producers are publicly or commonly owned. In theory there could be some overlap when market socialists intend to limit the scope of markets and the intensity of competition.

10. The idea of a stationary-state economy goes back to the nineteenth-century British economist John Stuart Mill (O'Connor 1997).

11. The flat tax is so popular among neoliberal academics and politicians precisely because it undermines a widely accepted form of solidarity.

12. The US government offers tax credits for up to 7,500 US dollars for the purchase of a new electric car as long the manufacturer of the vehicle has sold less than 200,000 electric cars. As a result, Tesla has been subsidized with public funds in the range of 1.5 billion US dollars—assuming that the new owners have claimed and received the tax credit. 2019 prices for Tesla models range from 32,815 to 97,815 US dollars. Total credit for electric cars is estimated to amount to several billion US dollars. Perhaps the money would be put to better use with the modernization and expansion of public transportation.

13. This does not mean that free public transportation is not a valid demand. But in order to present an alternative to a car, it not only has to be free, but also efficient and reliable. A bus that only comes every half hour and sometimes doesn't turn up at all (as it is frequently the case in the Bay Area) is not attractive, even if it is free.

14. In the Bay Area (where I live), family homes can easily cost one million US dollars and still lack proper insulation. And during rush hour it can take an hour to cross the Bay Bridge from Oakland to San Francisco. The Bay Area Rapid Transit system

operates a subway below the Bay, but the infrastructure is from the 1970s, with little improvement since then, and with hopelessly overcrowded cars during peak hours in the morning and in the afternoon.

15. This does not mean that all Germans work less. The German average includes a comparably high female part-time employment rate, which implies the existence of ongoing discrimination against women on the labor market. But it shows that it is possible to attain a similar living standard with significantly fewer work hours.

16. In Paul Mason's (2015) vision of post-capitalism, new technology plays a key role in promoting peer-to-peer production, substituting networks for markets, reducing the advantage of economies of scale, and minimizing work through automation. Mason, even though not a Marxist, stands in a long tradition of Marxists who assume that socialism will come about by productive forces outliving relations of production.

17. While there are important differences between communist and socialist parties, there is no difference between communism and socialism as a post-capitalist system. However, given the association of communism with the political systems that existed in Russia and Eastern Europe for much of the twentieth century, I prefer the label "socialism."

18. Saeed Rahnema (2017) interviewed a number of eminent Marxist scholars about their views on a possible future and possible ways to get there.

19. Marx distinguishes abstract labor from concrete labor. While concrete labor refers to the hours and minutes used for the production of a certain product, abstract labor is the monetary equivalent of average work time expended for the production of a specific category of goods. According to Hudis (2012, 148–152), Marx not only distinguishes between use value and exchange value, but also between exchange value and *value*—the latter reflecting abstract labor. Accordingly, socialism demands an abolishment of not only exchange value but also value. I'm not clear about the practical consequences of this statement. Hudis (ibid.) argues that it implies that it is not enough to alter exchange relations; a socialist system must include a radical transformation of the system of production. In my view, a system that aims for the maximization of use value rather than exchange value also requires a profound change of the mode of production.

Bibliography

Aaron, Henry J. 1991. *Serious and Unstable Condition: Financing America's Health Care.* Washington, DC: Brookings Institution.

Agency for Healthcare Research and Quality. 2017. *2016 National Healthcare Quality and Disparities Report. Chartbook on Access to Healthcare.* Rockville, MD: AHRQ.

Aiken, Linda H., Douglas Sloane, Peter Griffiths, Anne Marie Rafferty, Luk Bruyneel, Matthew McHugh, Claudia B. Maier, Teresa Moreno-Casbas, Jane E. Ball, Dietmar Ausserhofer, and Walter Sermeus. 2017. "Nursing Skill Mix in European Hospitals: Cross-Sectional Study of the Association with Mortality, Patient Ratings, and Quality of Care." *BMJ Quality and Safety* 26 (7): 559–568.

Albert, Michael. 2003. *Parecon: Life after Capitalism.* London: Verso.

Albo, Gregory. 2007. "Neoliberalism and the Discontented." In *Socialist Register 2008*, edited by Leo Panitch and Colin Leys, 354–362. London: Merlin Press.

Albo, Gregory. 2016. "Rosa Luxemburg and Contemporary Capitalism." In *Rosa Luxemburg: A Permanent Challenge for Political Economy*, edited by Judith Dellheim and Frieder Otto Wolff, 25–54. Houndmills, UK: Palgrave Macmillan.

Albo, Gregory. 2020. "Postcapitalism: Alternatives or Detours?" In *Socialist Register 2021*, edited by Leo Panitch and Gregory Albo, 310–330. London: Merlin Press.

Albritton, Robert. 2007. *Economics Transformed: Discovering the Brilliance of Marx.* London: Pluto Press.

Albritton, Robert. 2009. *Let Them Eat Junk: How Capitalism Creates Hunger and Obesity.* London: Pluto.

Alford, John. 2009. *Engaging Public Sector Clients: From Service-Delivery to Co-Production.* Houndmills: Palgrave Macmillan.

Algretto, Sylvia, and Lawrence Mishel. 2019. *The Teacher Weekly Wage Penalty Hit 21.4 Percent in 2018, A Record High: Trends in the Teacher Wage and Compensation Penalties Through 2018.* Washington, DC: Economic Policy Institute.

Altieri, Miguel A. 1998. "Ecological Impacts of Industrial Agriculture and the Possibilities for Truly Sustainable Farming." *Monthly Review* 50 (3): 60–71.

Altvater, Elmar. 1990. "The Foundations of Life (Nature) and the Maintenance of Life (Work)." *International Journal of Political Economy* 20 (1): 10–34.

Altvater, Elmar. 2004. "What Happens When Public Goods Are Privatized?" *Studies in Political Economy* 74: 45–77.

Altvater, Elmar. 2005. *Das Ende des Kapitalismus wie wir ihn kennen: Eine radikale Kapitalismuskritik.* Münster: Westfälisches Dampfboot.

Altvater, Elmar. 2006. "The Natural and Social Environment of Fossil Fuel Capitalism." In *Socialist Register 2007*, edited by Leo Panitch and Colin Leys, 37–59. London: Merlin Press.

Altvater, Elmar. 2007. "Der kurze Sommer des akademischen Marxismus." *Prokla* 146: 9–24.

Anderson, Elizabeth. 1993. *Value in Ethics and Economics*. Cambridge, MA: Harvard University Press.

Anderson, Michael L., and Maximiliam Auffhammmer. 2014. "Pounds That Kill: The External Costs of Vehicle Weight." *Review of Economic Studies* 81 (2): 535–571.

Anderson, Perry. 1983. *In the Tracks of Historical Materialism*. London: Verso.

Angell, Marcia. 2005. *The Truth about the Drug Companies*. New York: Random House.

Appadurai, Arjun. 1986. "Introduction." In *The Social Life of Things: Commodities in Cultural Perspective*, edited by Arjun Appadurai, 3–63. Cambridge: Cambridge University Press.

Applbaum, Kalman. 2009. "Marketing Global Health Care. The Practices of Big Pharma." In *Socialist Register 2010*, edited by Leo Panitch and Colin Leys, 84–102. London: Merlin Press.

Applegate, Jamie. 2012. "UC Turns to Nonresident Enrollment to Cope with Funding Shortfalls." *The Daily Californian*, December 9, 2012. Available at: https://www.dailycal. org/2012/12/09/uc-looks-to-nonresidents [accessed March 20, 2021].

Archambault, Éric, and Vincent Larivière. 2009. "History of the Journal Impact Factor: Contingencies and Consequences." *Scientometrics* 79 (30): 639–653.

Archer, David, Michael Eby, Victor Brovkin, Andy Ridgwell, Long Cao, Uwe Mikolajewicz, Ken Caldeira, Katsumi Matsumoto, Guy Munhoven, Alvaro Montenegro, and Kathy Tokos. 2009. "Atmospheric Lifetime of Fossil Fuel Carbon Dioxide." *Annual Review of Earth and Planetary Sciences* 37: 117–134.

Aristotle. 1988. *The Politics*. Cambridge: Cambridge University Press.

Arrighi, Giovanni. 1994. *The Long Twentieth Century: Money, Power and the Origins of Our Time*. London: Verso.

Ash, Amin, ed. 1994. *Post-Fordism: A Reader*. Oxford: Blackwell.

Asthana, Anushka, and Adam Vaughan. 2017. "Theresa May to Promise Price Cap on Energy Bills in Tory Manifesto." *Guardian*, May 9, 2017. Available at: https://www. theguardian.com/money/2017/may/08/theresa-may-to-promise-price-cap-on-energy-bills-in-tory-manifesto [accessed March 20, 2021].

Baker, David R. 2017. "Huge Wildfires Can Wipe Out California's Greenhouse Gas Gains." *San Francisco Chronicle*, November 22, 2017. Available at: https://www.sfchronicle. com/bayarea/article/Huge-wildfires-can-wipe-out-California-s-12376324. php#:~:text=The%20huge%20scale%20of%20the,emissions%2040%20percent%20 by%202030. [accessed March 20, 2021].

Bakker, Karren. 2004. *An Uncooperative Commodity: Privatizing Water in England and Wales*. Oxford: Oxford University Press.

Bakker, Karen. 2007. "Neoliberalizing Nature? Market Enviornmentalism in Water Supply in England and Wales." In *Neoliberal Environments*, edited by Nick Heynen, 101–113. New York: Routledge.

Bambra, Clare. 2005. "Cash versus Services: 'Worlds of Welfare' and the Decommodification of Cash Benefits and Health Care Services." *Journal of Social Policy* 34 (2): 195–213.

Barbon, Nicolas. 1905. *A Discourse of Trade*. Baltimore, MD: Lord Baltimore Press.

Barrett, Ron, and George J. Armelagos. 2013. *An Unnatural History of Emerging Infections*. Oxford: Oxford University Press.

Bauman, Dan, Tyler Davis, and Brian O'Leary. 2020. "Executive Compensation at Public and Private Colleges." *Chronicle of Higher Education*, July 17, 2020. Available at: https:// www.chronicle.com/article/executive-compensation-at-public-and-private-colleges/ #id=table_public_2019 [accessed March 20, 2021].

Baumol, William. 1977. "On the Proper Cost Tests for Natural Monopoly in a Multiproduct Industry." *American Economic Review* 67 (5): 809–822.

Baumol, William. 2012. *The Cost Disease: Why Computers Get Cheaper and Health Care Doesn't*. New Haven, CT: Yale University Press.

Becker, Gary. 1976. *The Economic Approach to Human Behavior*. Chicago: University of Chicago Press.

Belfield, Chris, Claire Crawford, and Luke Sibieta. 2017. *Long-Run Comparisons of Spending per Pupil across Different Stages of Education*. London: Institute for Fiscal Studies.

Bentham, Jeremey. 1907. *An Introduction to the Principles of Morals and Legislation*. Oxford: Clarendon Press.

Bentham, Jeremey.1954. "True Alarm." In *Jeremey Bentham's Economic Writings, Volume Three*, edited by Werner Stark, 61–216. London: Allen and Unwin.

Block, Fred. 1990. *Postindustrial Possibilities*. Berkeley: University of California Press.

Block, Fred, and Margaret Sommers. 2014. *The Power of Market Fundamentalism*. Cambridge, MA: Harvard University Press.

Blumstein, Carl, Lee S. Friedman, and Richard Green. 2002. "The History of Electricity Restructuring in California." *The Journal of Industry, Competition and Trade* 2 (1): 9–38.

Blyth, Mark. 2013. *Austerity: History of a Dangerous Idea*. Oxford: Oxford University Press.

Bockman, Johanna. 2016. "Socialism and the Embedded Economy." *Theory and Society* 45 (5): 386–397.

Böhm-Bawerk, Eugen v. 1898. *Karl Marx and the Close of His System: A Criticism*. London: T. Fisher Unwin.

Böhm-Bawerk, Eugen v. 1923. *The Positive Theory of Capital*. New York: G. E. Stechert.

Bolton, Paul. 2016. *Tuition Fee Statistics: House of Commons Library*. Briefing Paper No. 917, December 2, 2016.

Bolton, Paul. 2018. *Student Loan Statistics*. House of Commons Library. Briefing Paper 1079, July 18, 2018.

Bond Darwin, Graham, and Tim Redmond. 2015. "Condo Ownership Worsens San Francisco's Housing Crisis." *Race, Poverty and the Environment* 20 (1): 98–100.

Booth, William James. 1993. *Households: On the Moral Architecture of the Economy*. Ithaca, NY: Cornell University Press.

Boron, Atilio. 2010. *Den Sozialismus neu denken: Gibt es ein Leben nach dem Neoliberalismus*. Hamburg: VSA Verlag.

Borras, Saturnino M., and Jennifer C. Franco. 2012. "Global Land Grabbing and Trajectories of Agrarian Change: A Preliminary Analysis." *Journal of Agrarian Change* 12 (1): 34–59.

Bosch, Gerhard. 2004. "Towards a New Standard Employment Relationship in Western Europe." *British Journal of Industrial Relations* 42 (4): 617–636.

Boudette, Neal E. 2018. "GM to Idle Plants and Cut Thousands of Jobs as Sales Slow." *New York Times*, November 26, 2018. Available at: https://www.nytimes.com/2018/11/26/business/general-motors-cutbacks.html#:~:text=General%20Motors%20announced%20Monday%20that,consumer%20tastes%20and%20sluggish%20sales. [accessed March 20, 2021].

Bowman, Andrew, Peter Folkman, Julie Froud, Sukhdev Johal, John Law, Adam Leaver, Michael Moran, and Karel Williams. 2013. *The Great Train Robbery: Rail Privatization and After*. Centre for Research on Socio-Cultural Change. Manchester: University of Manchester.

Bowman, Shanthy A., Steven L. Gortmaker, Cara B. Ebbeling, Mark A. Pereira, and David S. Ludwig. 2014. "Effects of Fast-Food Consumption on Energy Intake and Diet Quality among Children in a National Household Survey." *Pediatrics* 113 (1): 112–118.

Boyd, William, Scott Prudham, and Rachel Schurman. 2001. "Industrial Dynamics and the Problem of Nature." *Society and Natural Resources* 14 (7): 555–570.

Brand, Ulrich. 2005. *Gegen-Hegemonie: Perspektiven globalisierungskritischer Strategien.* Hamburg: VSA Verlag.

Brand, Ulrich, and Markus Wissen. 2014. "The Financialization of Nature as Crisis Strategy." *Journal für Entwicklungspolitik* 30 (2): 16–45.

Brand, Ulrich, and Markus Wissen. 2017. *Imperiale Lebensweise: Zur Ausbeutung von Mensch und Natur im globalen Kapitalismus.* München: Oekom.

Braun, Martin Z. 2018. "MTA's Rising Debt and Payroll Cost Take Toll on Bond Rating." *Bloomberg News*, March 12, 2018. Available at: https://www.bloomberg.com/news/articles/2018-03-12/mta-s-rising-debt-and-payroll-costs-take-toll-on-credit-rating (accessed April 15, 2021).

Braverman, Harry. 1974. *Labor and Monopoly Capitalism: The Degradation of Work in the Twentieth Century.* New York: Monthly Review.

Brecher, Jeremy. 2017. *Climate Solidarity: Workers vs. Warming.* Takoma Park, MD: Labor Network for Sustainability.

Brennan, Jason, and Peter M. Jaworski. 2016. *Markets without Limits: Moral Virtues and Commercial Interests.* New York: Routledge.

Brie, Michael. 2015. *Polanyi neu entdecken.* Hamburg: VSA Verlag.

Brown, Wendy. 2006. "American Nightmare: Neoliberalism, Neoconservatism, and De-Democratization." *Political Theory* 34 (6): 690–714.

Burawoy, Michael. 1982. "Introduction: The Resurgence of Marxism in American Sociology." *American Journal of Sociology* 88 (Supplement): 1–30.

Burawoy, Michael. 2010. "From Polanyi to Pollyanna: The False Optimism of Global Labor Studies." *Global Labor Journal* 1 (2): 301–313.

Burchfield, R. W., ed. 1972. *Supplement to the Oxford English Dictionary* (Vol. 1, A–G). Oxford: Oxford University Press.

Bureau of Justice Statistics. 2001. *Prisoners in 2000.* Washington, DC: US Department of Justice.

Bureau of Justice Statistics. 2018. *Prisoners in 2015.* Washington, DC: US Department of Justice.

Burkett, Paul. 1999. *Marx and Nature: A Red Green Perspective.* New York: St. Martin's Press.

Burkett, Paul. 2006. *Marxism and Ecological Economics: Toward a Red and Green Political Economy.* Leiden: Brill.

Busch, Klaus, Christoph Hermann, Klaus Hinrichs, and Thorsten Schulten. 2013. *Euro Crisis, Austerity Policy and the European Social Model.* Berlin: Friedrich Ebert Stiftung.

Bush, Lawrence. 2017. *Knowledge for Sale: The Neoliberal Takeover of Higher Education.* Cambridge, MA: MIT Press.

Buzby, Jean C., Hodan F. Wells, and Jeffrey Hyman. 2014. *The Estimated Amount, Value, and Calories of Postharvest Food Losses at the Retail and Consumer Levels in the United States.* Economic Information Bulletin Number 121. Washington, DC: US Department of Agriculture.

Campbell, Denis. 2013. "Mid Staffs Hospital Scandal: The Essential Guide." *Guardian*, February 6, 2013. Available at: https://www.theguardian.com/society/2013/feb/06/mid-staffs-hospital-scandal-guide [accessed March 20, 2021].

Campbell, Denis, and Alexandra Topping. 2020. "Ian Paterson Inquiry: More Than 1,000 Patients Had Needless Operations." *Guardian,* February 4, 2020. Available at: https://www.theguardian.com/society/2020/feb/04/ian-paterson-inquiry-culture-of-denial-allowed-rogue-breast-surgery [accessed March 20, 2021].

Carnevale, Anthony P., and Martin Van Der Werf. 2017. *The Twenty Percent Solution: Selective Colleges Can Afford to Admit More Pell Grant Recipients.* Washington, DC: Georgetown University Center on Education and the Workforce.

Castree, Noel. 2003. "Commodifying What Nature?" *Progress in Human Geography* 27 (3): 273–297.

Centers for Disease Control. 2013. *Antibiotic Resistance Threats in the United States.* Atlanta, GA: CDC.

Centre for Health and the Public Interest. 2017. *PFI: Profiting from Infirmaries.* August 2017. London: CHPI.

Chandler, Alfred. 1990. *Scale and Scope: The Dynamics of Industrial Capitalism.* Cambridge, MA: Belknap Press.

Chetty, Raj, John N. Friedman, Emmanuel Saez, Nicholas Turner, and Danny Yagan. 2017. *Mobility Report Cards: The Role of Colleges in Intergenerational Mobility.* Opportunity Insights Project. Available at: http://www.equality-of-opportunity.org/papers/coll_mrc_paper.pdf [accessed November 1, 2020].

Clarke, John, Janet Newman, Nick Smith, Elizabeth Vidler, and Louise Westmarland. 2007. *Creating Citizen-Consumers: Changing Publics and Changing Public Services.* London: Sage.

Clarke, Simon. 1991. *Marx, Marginalism and Modern Sociology: From Adam Smith to Max Weber.* Houndmills: Palgrave Macmillan.

Coase, Ronald H. 1974. "The Lighthouse in Economics." *Journal of Law and Economics* 17 (2): 357–376.

Coleman-Jensen, Alisha, Matthew P. Rabbitt, Christian A. Gregory, and Anita Singh. 2016. *Household Food Security in the United States in 2015.* Economic Research Report Number 215. Washington, DC: US Department of Agriculture.

Collins, Sara R., Petra W. Rasmussen, Sophie Beutel, and Michelle M. Doty. 2015. *The Problem of Underinsurance and How Rising Deductibles Will Make It Worse: Findings from the Commonwealth Fund Biennial Health Insurance Survey 2014.* New York: Commonwealth Fund.

Commonwealth Fund. 2015. *Average Number of Prescription Drugs Taken Regularly, Age 18 or Older, 2013.* Available at: https://www.commonwealthfund.org/chart/2015/average-number-prescription-drugs-taken-regularly-age-18-or-older-2013 [accessed November 1, 2020].

Conrad, Peter. 2007. *The Medicalization of Society: On the Transformation of Human Conditions into Treatable Disorders.* Baltimore, MD: Johns Hopkins Press.

Cooper, Melinda. 2017. *Family Values: Between Neoliberalism and the New Social Conservatism.* Cambridge, MA: MIT Press.

Cotterill, Ronald W. 1999. "High Cereal Prices and the Prospects for Relief by Expansion of Private Label and Antitrust Enforcement." *Agribusiness* 15 (2): 229–245.

Cronon, William. 1991. *Nature's Great Metropolis: Chicago and the Great West.* New York: W. W. Norton.

Crotty, James. 2019. *Keynes against Capitalism: His Economic Case for Liberal Socialism*. New York: Routledge.

Dahlmann, Simone. 2008. "The End of the Road, No More Walking in Dead Men Shoes: IT Professionals' Experiences of Being Outsourced to the Private Sector." *Work Organisation Labour and Globalisation* 2 (2): 148–161.

Dale, Gareth. 2010. "Social Democracy, Embeddedness and Decommodification: On the Conceptual Innovations and Intellectual Affiliations of Karl Polanyi." *New Political Economy* 15 (3): 369–393.

Dale, Gareth. 2016. *Karl Polanyi: A Life on the Left*. New York: Columbia University Press.

Daly, Hermann. 1977. *Steady-State Economics: The Economics of Biophysical Equilibrium and Moral Growth*. San Francisco: W. H. Freeman.

Davies, Steve. 2010. "Fragmented Management, Hospital Contract Cleaning and Infection Control." *Policy and Politics* 38 (3): 445–463.

Davis, Donald R. 2009. "Declining Fruit and Vegetable Nutrient Composition: What Is the Evidence?" *Hortscience* 44 (1): 15–19.

Davis, Richard. 1983. *Encyclopedia of Forest History*, Vol. I. New York: Macmillan.

De Schutter, Olivier. 2010. *Food Commodities Speculation and Food Price Crises*. United Nations Special Rapporteur on the Right to Food. Briefing Note 2, September 2010.

Debord, Guy. 1967. *La Société du spectacle*. Paris: Editions Buchet-Chastel.

Debord, Guy. 1977. *Society of Spectacle*. Detroit: Black and Red.

Debord, Guy. 1983. *Society of Spectacle*. Translated by Ken Knapp. London: Rebel Press.

Deininger, Klaus, Derek Byerlee, Jonathan Lindsay, Andrew Norton, Harris Selod, and Mercedes Stickler. 2011. *The Rising Global Interest in Farmland: Can It Yield Sustainable and Equitable Benefits?* Washington, DC: World Bank.

Deming, David J., Claudia Goldin, and Lawrence F. Katz. 2012. "The For-Profit Postsecondary School Sector: Nimble Critters or Agile Predators?" *Journal of Economic Perspectives* 26 (1): 139–164.

Department for Business, Energy and Industrial Strategy. 2018. *Annual Fuel Poverty Statistics Report*. June 2018. London.

Desai, Kamal R., Carol Van Deusen Lukas, and Gary J. Young. 2000. "Public Hospitals: Privatization and Uncompensated Care." *Health Affairs* 19 (2): 167–172.

Deutsche Post. 2017. *Annual Report 2016*. Bonn.

Devine, Pat J. 1988. *Democracy and Economic Planning: The Political Economy of a Self-Governing Society*. Cambridge: Polity Press.

Diederen, André. 2009. "Metal Minerals Scarcity: A Call for Managed Austerity and the Elements of Hope." *The Oil Drum*, available at: http://europe.theoildrum.com/node/5239 [accessed November 1, 2020].

Diefenbach, Thomas. 2009. "New Public Management in Public Sector Organizations: The Dark Side of Managerialistic 'Enlightenment.'" *Public Administration* 87 (4): 892–909.

Diels, Johan, Mario Cunha, Célia Manaia, Bernardo Sabugosa-Madeira, and Margarida Silva. 2011. "Association of Financial or Professional Conflict of Interest to Research Outcomes on Health Risks or Nutritional Assessment Studies of Genetically Modified Products." *Food Policy* 36 (2): 197–203.

Dörre, Klaus. 2013. "Landnahme and Grenzen sozialer Reproduktion. In *Rosa Luxemburgs Akkumulation des Kapitals*, edited by Ingo Schmidt, 82–116. Hamburg: VSA Verlag.

Dörre, Klaus. 2015a. "The New Landnahme: Dynamics and Limits of Financial Market Capitalism." In *Sociology, Capitalism, Critique*, edited by Klaus Dörre, Stephan Lessenich, and Harmut Rosa, 11–66. London: Verso.

Dörre, Klaus. 2015b. "Social Capitalism and Crisis: From Internal to External Landnahme." In *Sociology, Capitalism, Critique*, edited by Klaus Dörre, Stephan Lessenich, and Harmut Rosa, 247–279. London: Verso.

Dörre, Klaus. 2016. "Limits to Landnahme: Growth Dilemma as Challenge." In *Rosa Luxemburg: A Permanent Challenge for Political Economy*, edited by Judith Dellheim and Frieder Otto Wolff, 219–260. Houndmills: Palgrave Macmillan.

Domingo, José L. 2007. "Toxicity Studies of Genetically Modified Plants: A Review of the Published Literature." *Critical Reviews in Food Science and Nutrition* 47 (8): 721–733.

Drewnowski, Adam. 2004. "Obesity and the Food Environment: Dietary Energy Density and Diet Costs." *American Journal of Preventive Medicine* 27 (3 Supplement): 154–162.

Duménil, Gérard, and Dominique Levy. 2005. "The Neoliberal (Counter-)Revolution." In *Neoliberalism: A Critical Reader*, edited by Alfredo Saad-Filho and Debroah Johnston, 9–19. London: Pluto Press.

Dutra Aguiar, Ana Paula, Ima Celia Guimaraes Vieira, Talita Oliveira Assis, Eloi L Dalla-Nora, Peter Mann Toledo, Roberto Araujo Oliveir Asantos-Junior, Mateus Batistella, Andrea Santos Coelho, Elza Kawakami Savaget, Luiz Eduarado Olivereia Cruz Argos, Carlos Alfonso Nobre, and Jean Pierre H. Ometto. 2016. "Land Use Change Emission Scenarios: Anticipating a Forest Transition Process in the Brazilian Amazon." *Global Change Biology* 22 (5): 1821–1840.

Eagleton, Terry. 1981. "The Idealism of American Criticism." *New Left Review* 127: 52–65.

Eaton, Charlie, Jacob Habinek, Adam Goldstein, Cyrus Dioun, Daniela García Santibáñez Godoy, and Robert Osley-Thomas. 2016. "The Financialization of US Higher Education." *Socio-Economic Review* 14 (3): 507–535.

Ebbinghaus, Bernhard. 2015. "The Privatization and Marketization of Pensions in Europe: A Double Transformation Facing the Crisis." *European Policy Analysis* 1 (1): 56–73.

Ebbinghaus, Bernhard, and Mareike Gronwald. 2011. "The Changing Public-Private Pension Mix in Europe: From Path-Dependence to Path-Departure." In *The Varieties of Pension Governance: Pension Privatization in Europe*, edited by Bernhard Ebbinghaus, 23–56. Oxford: Oxford University Press.

Edelman, Benjamin, and Damien Geradin. 2016. "Spontaneous Deregulation: How to Compete with Platforms That Ignore the Rules." *Harvard Business Review* 94 (4): 80–87.

Eichengreen, Barry. 2008. *Globalizing Capital: A History of the International Monetary System*. Princeton, NJ: Princeton University Press.

Ellerman, Denny A., Frank J Convery, and Christian de Perthuis. 2010. *Pricing Carbon: The European Union Emissions Trading Scheme*. Cambridge: Cambridge University Press.

Ellerman, Denny A., Claudio Marcantonini, and Aleksandar Zaklanz. 2015. "The European Union Emissions Trading System: Ten Years and Counting." *Review of Environmental Economics and Policy* 10 (1): 89–107.

Ellis, Charles D., Alicia H. Munnel, and Andrew D. Eschtruth. 2014. *Falling Short: The Coming Retirement Crisis and What to Do about It*. Oxford: Oxford University Press.

Engels, Friedrich. 1937. *Engels on Capital: Synopsis, Reviews, Letters and Supplementary Material*. New York: International.

Epstein, Gerard, ed. 2005. *Financialization and the World Economy*. Cheltenham: Edward Elgar.

Ertman, Martha M., and Joan C. Williams. 2005. "Preface." In *Rethinking Commodification. Cases and Readings in Law and Culture*, edited by Martha M. Ertman and Joan C. Williams, 1–7. New York: New York University Press.

Esping-Andersen, Gøsta. 1987. "Citizenship and Socialism: Decommodification and Solidarity in the Welfare State." In *Stagnation and Renewal in Social Policy: The Rise and Fall of Policy Regimes*, edited by Martin Rein, Gøsta Esping-Andersen, and Lee Rainwater, 78–104. Armonk: M. E. Sharpe.

Esping-Andersen, Gøsta. 1990. *Three Worlds of Welfare Capitalism*. Cambridge: Polity Press.

Estache, Antonio. 2006. *Infrastructure: A Survey of Recent and Upcoming Issues*. World Bank Paper. Washington, DC: World Bank.

Etxezarreta, Miren, and Mejra Festić. 2009. "Privatization of Pensions." In *Privatization against the European Social Model: A Critique of European Policies and Proposals for Alternatives*, edited by Marica Frangakis, Christoph Hermann, Jörg Huffschmid, and Károly Lóránt, 164–186. Houndmills: Palgrave Macmillan.

Evans, Peter. 2005. "Counter-Hegemonic Globalization: Transnational Social Movements in the Contemporary Global Political Economy." In *Handbook of Political Sociology*, edited by Thomas Janoski, Robert R. Alford, Alexander M. Hicks, and Mildred A. Schwartz, 655–670. Cambridge: Cambridge University Press.

Fabozzi, Frank J., and Franco Modigliani. 1992. *Mortgage and Mortgage-Backed Securities Market*. Boston: Harvard Business School Press.

Fairbarn, Madeleine. 2020. *Fields of Gold: Financing the Global Land Rush*. Ithaca, NY: Cornell University Press.

Farnsworth, Kevin, and Zoë Irving, eds. 2011. *Social Policy in Challenging Times: Economic Crisis and Welfare Systems*. Bristol: Policy Press.

Farnsworth, Kevin, and Zoë Irving. 2015. "Austerity: More than the Sum of Its Parts." In *Social Policy in Times of Austerity: Global Economic Crisis and the New Politics of Welfare*, edited by Kevin Farnsworth and Zoë Irving, 9–42. Bristol: Policy Press.

Fearnside, Philip M. 2005. "Deforestation in Brazilian Amazonia: History, Rates, and Consequences." *Conservation Biology* 19 (3): 680–688.

Featherstone, Mike. 1991. *Consumer Culture and Postmodernism*. London: Sage.

Federal Communications Commission. 2020. *2020 Broadband Progress Report*. April 24, 2020. Washington, DC: FCC.

Feinsilver Julie M. 1993. *Healing the Masses: Cuban Health Politics at Home and Abroad*. Berkeley: University of California Press.

Fernandez-Cornejo, Jorge, Richard Nehring, Craig Osteen, Seth Wechsler, Andrew Martin, and Alex Vialou. 2014. *Pesticide Use in US Agriculture: 21 Selected Crops, 1960–2008*. Economic Research Service. Washington, DC: US Department of Agriculture.

Fernandez-Cornejo, Jorge, Seth Wechsler, Mike Livingston, and Lorraine Mitchell. 2014. *Genetically Engineered Crops in the United States*. Economic Research Service. Washington, DC: US Department of Agriculture.

Fernandez, Manny, and Katie Benner. "The Billion-Dollar Business of Operating Shelters for Migrant Children." *New York Times*, June 21, 2018. Available at: https://www.nytimes.com/2018/06/21/us/migrant-shelters-border-crossing.html [accessed March 20, 2021].

Flassbeck, Rainer, David Bicchetti, Jörg Mayer, and Katja Rietzler. 2011. *Price Formation and Financialized Commodity Markets: The Role of Information*. Geneva: United Nations Conference on Trade and Development.

Flecker, Jörg, and Christoph Hermann. 2012. "Company Responses to Liberalization and Privatization and Consequences for Employment and Working Conditions." In *Privatization of Public Services: Impacts for Employment, Working Conditions, and*

Service Quality in Europe, edited by Christoph Hermann and Jörg Flecker, 109–123. New York: Routledge.

Florio, Massimo. 2006. *The Great Divestiture: Evaluation the Welfare Impact of the British Privatizations 1979–1997.* Cambridge, MA: MIT Press.

Florio, Massimo. 2013. *Network Industries and Social Welfare: The Experiment That Reshuffled European Utilities.* Oxford: Oxford University Press.

Forgacs, David. 2000. *The Gramsci Reader: Selected Writings 1916–1935.* New York: New York University Press.

Foster, John Bellamy, Brett Clark, and Richard York. 2010. *The Ecological Rift: Capitalism's War on the Earth.* New York: Monthly Review Press.

Frangakis, Marica, and Jörg Huffschmid. 2009. "Privatization in Western Europe." In *Privatization against the European Social Model*, edited by Marica Frangakis, Christoph Hermann, Jörg Huffschmid, and Károly Lóránt, 20–29. Houndmills: Palgrave Macmillan.

Frank, T. Kenneth, Brian Petrie, Jae S. Choi, and William C. Leggett. 2005. "Trophic Cascades in a Formerly Cod-Dominated Ecosystem." *Science* 308 (5728): 1621–1623.

Fraser, Nancy. 2014. "Can Societies Be Commodities All the Way Down?" *Economy and Society* 43 (4): 541–558.

Frey, Bruno S., Felix Oberholzer-Gee, and Reiner Eichenberger. 1996. "The Old Lady Visits Your Backyard: A Tale of Morals and Markets." *Journal of Political Economy* 104 (6): 1297–1313.

Fryar, Cheryl D., and R. Bethene Ervin. 2013. *Caloric Intake from Fast Food among Adults: United States, 2007–2010.* Data Brief No. 114. Hyattsville, MD: National Center for Health Statistics.

Fung, Brian. 2019. "'Steamrolled by Trump': How the White House Has Made Life Harder for US Automakers." *Washington Post*, January 14, 2019. Available at: https://www.washingtonpost.com/business/2019/01/14/automakers-are-grappling-with-changing-market-trump-administration-hasnt-made-it-easier/ [accessed March 20, 2021].

Funnel, Warwick, Robert Jupe, and Jane Andrew. 2009. *In Government We Trust: Market Failure and the Delusions of Privatization.* London: Pluto Press.

Gagnon, Marc André, and Joel Lexchin. 2008. "The Cost of Pushing Pills: A New Estimate for Pharmaceutical Promotion Expenditures in the United States." *PLOS Medicine* 5 (1): 29–33.

Gallbraith, John Kenneth. 1958. *The Affluent Society.* New York: Houghton Mifflin.

Gibbs, Paul. 2013. "The Commodidization and Standardization of Higher Education." In *Globalization and Internationalization in Higher Education: Theoretical, Strategic and Management Perspectives*, edited by Felix Maringe and Nick Foskett, 241–254. London: Continuum.

Giddens, Anthony. 1985. *The Nation State and Violence: Volume Two of a Contemporary Critique of Historical Materialism.* Cambridge: Polity Press.

Gindin, Sam. 2018. "Socialism for Realists." *Catalyst* 2 (3): 6–45.

Ginsburg, Norman. 2005. "The Privatization of Council Flats." *Critical Social Policy* 25 (1): 115–135.

Girth, Amanda M., Amir Hefetz, Jocelyn M. Johnston, and Mildred E. Warner. 2012. "Outsourcing Public Service Delivery: Management Responses in Noncompetitive Markets." *Public Administration Review* 72 (6): 887–900.

Goddard, Maria, Russell Mannion, and Brian Ferguson. 1997. *Contracting in the UK NHS: Purpose, Process and Policy.* Centre For Health Economic Discussion Paper 156. York: University of York.

Gordon, Suzanne. 2005. *Nursing against the Odds*. Ithaca, NY: Cornell University Press.

Gordon, Suzanne, John Buchanan, and Tanya Bretherton. 2009. *Safety in Numbers: Nurse-to-Patient Ratios and the Future of Health Care*. Ithaca, NY: IRL Press.

Gorz, André. 1994. *Capitalism, Socialism, Ecology*. London: Verso.

Gossen, Heinrich. 1854. *Entwicklung der Gesetze des menschlichen Verkehrs und der daraus fließenden Regeln für Menschliches Handeln*. Braunschweig: Friedrich Vieweg.

Gough, Ian. 1979. *The Political Economy of the Welfare State*. London: Macmillan.

Graff, Amy. 2019. "An Estimated 100,000 Homes Are Sitting Empty in the San Francisco Metro Area." Sfgate, March 17, 2019. Available at: https://www.sfgate.com/realestate/article/An-estimated-100-000-homes-are-sitting-empty-in-13692007.php [accessed March 20, 2021].

Greene, Jay P., Brian Kisida, and Jonathan Mills. 2010. *Administrative Bloat at American Universities: The Real Reason for High Costs in Higher Education*. Policy Report No. 2391. Phoenix: Goldwater Institute.

Greene, Jeremy. 2007. *Prescribing by Number: Drugs and the Definition of Disease*. Baltimore, MD: Johns Hopkins University Press.

Greenfield, Patrick. 2017. "Apple Apologizes for Slowing Down Older iPhones with Ageing Batteries." *Guardian*, December 29, 2017. Available at: https://www.theguardian.com/technology/2017/dec/29/apple-apologises-for-slowing-older-iphones-battery-performance [accessed March 20, 2021].

Grossman, Henryk. 1977. "Marx, Classical Political Economy and the Problem of Dynamics Part I." *Capital and Class* 1 (2): 32–55.

Gunters, Dana, Joanne Berkenkamp, Darby Hoover, and Andrea Spacht Collins. 2017. *Wasted: How America Is Losing Up to 40 Percent of Its Food from Farm to Fork to Landfill*. New York: Natural Resources Defense Council.

Gupta, Indrani, and Mrigesh Bhatia. n.d. *The Indian Healthcare System: The Commonwealth International Healthcare Profiles*. New York: Commonwealth Fund.

Hahnel, Robin. 2020. "Democratic Socialist Planning: Back to the Future." In *Socialist Register 2021*, edited by Leo Panitch and Gregory Albo, 291–309. London: Merlin Press.

Hampton, Paul. 2005. *Workers and Trade Unions for Climate Solidarity. Tackling Climate Change in a Neoliberal World*. New York: Routledge.

Handelsblatt. 2016. "9000 Jobs in neuen Paketgesellschaften." *Handelsblatt*, February 13, 2016. Available at: https://www.handelsblatt.com/unternehmen/dienstleister/deutsche-post-9000-jobs-in-neuen-paketgesellschaften/12958840.html?ticket=ST-5701596-TBKTFocQlPVxh5ddpcRr-ap5 [accessed March 20, 2021].

Harrington, Charlene, Steffie Woolhandler, Joseph Mullan, Helen Carrillo, and David U. Himmelstein. 2001. "Does Investor Ownership of Nursing Homes Compromise the Quality of Care?" *American Journal of Public Health* 91 (9): 1452–1455.

Harvey, David. 1990. *The Condition of Postmodernity*. Oxford: Blackwell.

Harvey, David. 2003. *The New Imperialism*. Oxford: Oxford University Press.

Harvey, David. 2005. *A Brief History of Neoliberalism*. Oxford: Oxford University Press.

Harvey, David. 2008. "The Right to the City." *New Left Review* 53: 23–40.

Harvey, David. 2014. *Seventeen Contradictions of Capitalism*. London: Profile Books.

Haug, Wolfgang Fritz. 2010. "Kommodifizierung." In *Historisch-Kritisches Wörterbuch des Marxismus* 7/II, edited by Wolfgang Fritz Haug, Frigga Haug, and Peter Jehle, 1243–1255. Hamburg: Argument Verlag.

Healy, Kieran. 2006. *Last Best Gifts: Altruism and the Market for Human Blood and Organs*. Chicago: University of Chicago Press.

Healy, Kieran. 2011. "Counting as Commodifying?" *Washington University Journal of Law and Policy* 35: 337–347.

Heller, Donald E. 2011. "Trends in the Affordability of Public Colleges and Universities: The Contradiction of Increasing Prices and Increasing Enrollment." In *The States and Public Higher Education Policy. Affordability, Access, and Accountability*, edited by Donald E. Heller, 11–38. Baltimore, MD: Johns Hopkins Press.

Heller, Henry. 2016. *The Capitalist University: The Transformation of Higher Education in the United States since 1945*. London: Pluto Press.

Helm, Dieter. 2015. *Natural Capital: Valuing the Planet*. New Haven, CT: Yale University Press.

Helm, Dieter, and David Pearce. 1991. "Economic Policy towards the Environment: An Overview." In *Economic Policy towards the Environment*, edited by Dieter Helm, 1–24. Oxford: Blackwell.

Helms, Hinrich, Claudia Kämper, Kirsten Biemann, Udo Lambrecht, Julius Jöhrens, and Kerstin Meyer. 2019. *Klimabilanz von Elektroautos. Einflussfaktoren und Verbesserungspotenzial*. Berlin: Agora Verkehrswende.

Herdon, Thomas, Michael Ash, and Robert Pollin. 2013. *Does Public Debt Consistently Stifles Economic Growth? A Critique of Reinhard and Rogoff*. Political Economy Research Institute Working Paper 332. Amherst: University of Massachusetts.

Hermann, Christoph. 2009a. "Value and Knowledge: Insights from Marxist Value Theory for the Transformation of Work in the Digital Economy." *Rethinking Marxism* 21 (2): 275–289.

Hermann, Christoph. 2009b. "The Marketisation of Healthcare in Europe." In *Socialist Register 2010*, edited by Leo Panitch and Colin Leys, 125–144. London: Merlin Press.

Hermann, Christoph. 2011. "The Liberalization of European Postal Markets: The Response of Firms and Impacts on Employment and Services." *Competition and Change* 15 (4): 253–273.

Hermann, Christoph. 2013. *Crisis, Structural Adjustment and the Dismantling of the European Social Model(s)*. Institute for International Political Economy Working Paper 26. Berlin: Berlin School of Economics and Law.

Hermann, Christoph. 2014. "Structural Adjustment and Neoliberal Convergence in Labor Markets and Welfare." *Competition and Change* 18 (2): 111–130.

Hermann, Christoph. 2015a. *Capitalism and the Political Economy of Work Time*. New York: Routledge.

Hermann, Christoph. 2015b. *Green New Deal and the Question of Environmental and Social Justice*. Global Labor University Working Paper 31. Berlin: Berlin School of Economics and Law.

Hermann, Christoph. 2016. "The Public Sector and Equality." *Global Social Policy* 16 (1): 4–21.

Hermann, Christoph. 2017a. "Another 'Lost Decade'? Crisis and Structural Adjustment in Europe and Latin America." *Globalizations* 14 (4): 519–534.

Hermann, Christoph. 2017b. "Crisis, Structural Reform and the Dismantling of the European Social Model(s)." *Economic and Industrial Democracy* 38 (1): 51–68.

Hermann, Christoph, and Jörg Flecker, eds. 2012a. *Privatization of Public Services: Impacts for Employment, Working Conditions and Service Quality in Europe*. New York: Routledge.

Hermann, Christoph, and Jörg Flecker. 2012b. "Conclusion: Impacts of Public Service Liberalization and Privatization." In *Privatization of Public Services: Impacts for*

Employment, Working Conditions, and Service Quality in Europe, edited by Christoph Hermann and Jörg Flecker, 192–206. New York: Routledge.

Hermann, Christoph, Julia Kubisa, and Thorsten Schulten. 2012. "The Struggle for Public Services." In *Privatization of Public Services: Impacts for Employment, Working Conditions, and Service Quality in Europe*, edited by Christoph Hermann and Jörg Flecker, 153–168. New York: Routledge.

Hermann, Christoph, and Richard Pond. 2012. "Concentration and Disintegration: Company Responses in the Electricity Sector and Consequences for Employment." In *Privatization of Public Services: Impacts for Employment, Working Conditions, and Service Quality in Europe*, edited by Christoph Hermann and Jörg Flecker, 33–54. New York: Routledge.

Hermann, Christoph, and Koen Verhoest. 2012. "The Process of Liberalization, Privatization, and Marketization." In *Privatization of Public Services: Impacts for Employment, Working Conditions, and Service Quality in Europe*, edited by Christoph Hermann and Jörg Flecker, 6–34. New York: Routledge.

Hilferding, Rudolf. 1919. *Böhm-Bawerk's Cricitism of Marx*. Glasgow: Socialist Labour Press.

Himmelstein, David U., Miraya Jun, Reinhard Busse, Karine Chevreul, Alexander Geissler, Patrick Jeurissen, Sarah Thomson, Marie-Amelie Vinet, and Steffie Woolhandler. 2014. "A Comparison of Hospital Administrative Costs in Eight Nations: US Costs Exceed All Others by Far." *Health Affairs* 33 (9): 1586–1594.

Hirsch, Fred. 1977. *Social Limits to Growth*. London: Routledge and Kegan Paul.

Hirsch, Joachim, and Roland Roth.1986. *Das neue Gesicht des Kapitalismus: Vom Fordismus zum Post-Fordismus*. Hamburg: VSA-Verlag.

HM Government. 2013. *International Education, Global Growth and Prosperity*. London: Department for Business, Innovation and Skills.

Hochschild, Arlie Russel. 2003. *The Commercialization of Intimate Life: Notes from Home and Work*. Berkeley: University of California Press.

Hodgson, Geoffrey M. 2015. *Conceptualizing Capitalism*. Chicago: University of Chicago Press.

Holst, Hajo, and Ingo Singe. 2011. *Precariousness and Informality: Work and Employment in the German Parcel and Delivery Industry*. Research Report. Vienna: Working Life Research Centre, Vienna.

Holt-Gimenez, Eric. 2017. *A Foodie's Guide to Capitalism*. New York: Monthly Review Press.

Hood, Chris. 1991. "A Public Management for All Seasons?" *Public Administration* 69 (1): 3–19.

Hope, Christopher. 2012. "PFI Contracts Costing Departments Twelve Times More than They Raise." *Telegraph*, May 16, 2012. Available at: https://www.telegraph.co.uk/news/politics/9270816/PFI-contracts-costing-departments-12-times-more-than-they-raise.html [accessed March 20, 2021].

Hopkins, Laura, Ronald Labonté, Vivien Runnels, and Corinne Packer. 2010. "Medical Tourism Today: What Is the State of Existing Knowledge?" *Journal of Public Health Policy* 31 (2): 185–198.

Hopkins, Terence K., and Immanuel Wallerstein. 1977. "Patterns of Development of the Modern World-System." *Review* 1 (2): 111–145.

Horkheimer, Max, and Theodor Adorno. 2002. *Dialectic of Enlightenment*. Stanford, CA: Stanford University Press.

Horwitz, Jill R. 2005. "Making Profits and Providing Care: Comparing Nonprofit, For-Profit, and Government Hospitals." *Health Affairs* 24 (3): 790–801.

House of Commons. 2011. *Private Finance Initiative: Seventeenth Report of Session 2010–12.* July 18, 2011. London.

Houtart, François. 2011. "From 'Common Goods' to the 'Common Good of Humanity.'" *Historia Actuel Online* 26: 87–102. Available at: https://citeseerx.ist.psu.edu/viewdoc/download?doi=10.1.1.691.3816&rep=rep1&type=pdf [accessed November 1, 2020].

Howard, Dick. 1974. "A Politics in Search of the Political." *Theory and Society* 1 (3): 271–306.

Howey, Richard. 1972. "The Origins of Marginalism." *History of Political Economy* 4 (2): 281–302.

Hubbert, M. King. 1962. *Energy Resources.* Washington DC: National Academy of Sciences—National Research Council.

Huber, Evelyne, and John D. Stephens. 2000. *The Political Economy of Pension Reform: Latin America in Comparative Perspective.* Occasional Paper No. 7. Geneva: United Nations Research Institute for Social Development.

Huber, Evelyne, and John D. Stephens. 2001. *Development and Crisis of the Welfare State.* Chicago: University of Chicago Press.

Hudis, Peter. 2012. *Marx's Concept of the Alternative to Capitalism.* Leiden: Brill.

Hunter, Duncan, Meika Foster, Jennifer O. McArthur, Rachel Ojha, Peter Petocz, and Samir Samman. 2011. "Evaluation of the Micronutrient Composition of Plant Foods Produced by Organic and Conventional Agricultural Methods." *Critical Reviews in Food Science and Nutrition* 51 (6): 571–582.

Huws, Ursula. 1985. "Challenging Commodidisation: Producing Usefulness Outside the Factory." In *Very Nice Work if You Can Get It: The Society Useful Production Debate*, edited by Collective Design/Project, 149–167. London: Spokesman.

Huws, Ursula. 2011. "Crisis as Capitalist Opportunity: New Accumulation through Public Service Commodification." In *Socialist Register 2012*, edited by Leo Panitch, Gregory Albo, and Vivek Chibber, 64–84. London: Merlin Press.

Huws, Ursula. 2014. *Labor in the Global Digital Economy: The Cybertariat Comes of Age.* New York: Monthly Review Press.

Hyman, Richard. 2007. "Labor, Markets, and the Future of 'Decommodification.'" In *Social Embedding and the Integration of Markets: An Opportunity for Transnational Trade Union Action or an Impossible Task?*, edited by Otto Jacobi, Maria Jepsen, Berndt Keller, and Manfred Weiss, 11–30. Düsseldorf: Hans-Böckler-Stiftung.

Indart, Gustavo. 1987. "Marx's Law of Market Value." *Science and Society* 51 (4): 458–467.

International Energy Agency. 2019. *Growing Preference for SUVs Challenges Emissions Reductions in Passenger Car Market.* Available at: https://www.iea.org/commentaries/growing-preference-for-suvs-challenges-emissions-reductions-in-passenger-car-market [accessed November 1, 2020].

Itoh, Makoto, and Nobuharu Yokokawa. 1979. "Marx's Theory of Market Value." In *Value: The Representation of Labour in Capitalism*, edited by Diane Elson, 102–114. London: CSE Books.

Jackson, Jeremy B. C. 2008. "Ecological Extinction and Evolution in the Brave New Ocean." *Proceedings of the National Academy of Science* 105 (Supplement 1): 11458–11465.

Jackson, Peter. 1999. "Commodity Cultures: The Traffic in Things." *Transactions of the Institute of British Geographers* 24 (1): 95–108.

Jackson, Tim. 2009. *Prosperity without Growth: Economics for a Finite Planet.* London: Earthscan.

Jacobs, Michael. 1991. *The Green Economy: Environment, Sustainable Development and the Politics of the Future.* London: Pluto Press.

Jameson, Frederic. 1979. "Reification and Utopia in Mass Culture." *Social Text* 1: 130–148.

Jameson, Frederic. 1984. "Postmodernism, or, the Cultural Logic of Late Capitalism." *New Left Review* 146: 52–92.

Jameson, Frederic. 1991. *Postmodernism, or, the Cultural Logic of Late Capitalism.* Durham, NC: Duke University Press.

Jevons, William. 1879. *The Theory of Political Economy.* London: Macmillan.

Jowett, Paul, and Margaret Rothwell. 1988. *Performance Indicators in the Public Sector.* London: Macmillan.

Julius, DeAnne. 2008. *Public Services Industry Review Understanding the Public Services Industry: How Big, How Good, Where Next?* London: Department of Business, Enterprises and Regulatory Reform.

Kaiser Family Foundation. 2020. *Key Facts about the Uninsured Population. Supplemental Tables.* Available at: http://files.kff.org/attachment/Key-Facts-about-the-Uninsured-Population-Supplemental-Tables.pdf [accessed November 1, 2020].

Kalman, Applbaum. 2009. "Marketing Global Health Care: The Practices of Big Pharma." In *Socialist Register 2010*, edited by Leo Panitch and Colin Leys, 84–102. London: Merlin Press.

Kelly, Ronna, Susan Burns, and Mathis Wackernagel. 2015. *State of the States: A New Perspective on the Wealth of Our Nation.* Oakland, CA: Ecological Footprint Network.

Kerry, Cameron F. ,and Jack Karsten. 2017. *Gaugin Investment in Self-Driving Cars.* Available at: https://www.brookings.edu/research/gauging-investment-in-self-driving-cars/ [accessed November 1, 2020].

Kershaw, Peter, Saido Katsuhiko, Sangjin Lee, Jon Samseth, and Dour Woodring. 2011. "Plastic Debris in the Ocean." In *UNEP Year Book 2011: Emerging Issues in Our Global Environment*, edited by the United Nations Environment Program, 21–33. Nairobi: United Nations Environment Program.

Kesselheim, Aaron S., Jerry Avorn, and Ameet Sarpatwari. 2016. "The High Cost of Prescription Drugs in the United States: Origins and Prospects for Reform." *JAMA* 316 (8): 858–871.

Keynes, John M. 2007. *The General Theory of Employment, Interest, and Money.* Houndmills: Palgrave Macmillan.

Khomami, Nadia. 2017. "University Vice-Chancellors' Average Pay Now Exceeds 275,000 Pounds." *Guardian*, February 23, 2017. Available at: https://www.theguardian.com/education/2017/feb/23/university-vice-chancellors-average-pay-now-exceeds-275000 [accessed March 20, 2021].

Kings Fund. 2017. *Is the NHS Being Privatized?* Available at: https://www.kingsfund.org.uk/publications/articles/big-election-questions-nhs-privatised [accessed November 1, 2020].

Kings Fund. 2018. *Trusts in Deficit.* Available at: https://www.kingsfund.org.uk/projects/nhs-in-a-nutshell/trusts-deficit [accessed November 1, 2020].

Kirsch, Irving. 2010. *The Emperor's New Drugs: Exploding the Antidepressant Myth.* New York: Basic Books.

Kloppenburg, Jack Ralph. 2004. *First the Seed: The Political Economy of Plant Biotechnology.* Madison: University of Wisconsin Press.

Kollewe, Julia. 2018. "Hot and Cold. Thames Water Blames Problem Leaks on Weather." *Guardian*, December 6, 2018. Available at: https://www.theguardian.com/business/2018/dec/06/thames-water-blames-leak-repair-delays-on-weather#:~:text=Hot%20and%20cold%3A%20Thames%20Water%20blames%20problem%20leaks%20on%20the%20weather,-This%20article%20is&text=The%20firm%20blamed%20the%20increase,led%20to%20more%20burst%20pipes. [accessed March 20, 2021].

Kovner, Christine T., Carol S. Brewer, Farida Fatehi, and Jin Jun. 2014. "What Does Nurse Turnover Rate Mean and What Is the Rate?" *Policy, Politics, and Nursing Practice* 15 (3–4): 64–71.

Krajewski, Markus. 2003. "Public Services and Trade Liberalization: Mapping the Legal Framework." *Journal of International Economic Law* 6 (2): 341–367.

Krajewski, Markus. 2011. "Vom Krieg des Lichtes zur Geschichte von Glühlampenkartellen." In *Das Glühbirnenbuch*, edited by Peter Berz, Helmut Höge, and Markus Krajewski, 173–193. Wien: Braunmüller.

Krätke, Michael. 2019. "Das Rote Wien: Eine sozialdemokratische Utopie." *SPW— Zeitschrift für sozialistische Politik und Wirtschaft* 232: 89–92.

Kreiss, Christian. 2014. *Geplanter Verschleiß*. Berlin: Europa Verlag.

Krippner, Greta, Mark Granovetter, Fred Block, Nicole Biggart, Tom Beamish, Youtien Hsing, Gillian Hart, Giovanni Arrighi, Margie Mendell, Johan Hall, Michael Burawoy, Steve Vogel, and Sean O'Rian. 2004. "Polanyi Symposium: A Conversation on Embeddedness." *Socio-Economic Review* 2 (1): 109–135.

Krippner, Greta. 2011. *Capitalizing on Crisis: The Political Origins of the Rise of Finance*. Cambridge, MA: Harvard University Press.

Krogstad, Jens Manuel, and Richard Fry. 2014. *More Hispanics, Blacks Enrolling in College, but Lag in Bachelor's Degrees*. Pew Research Center. Available at: https://www.pewresearch.org/fact-tank/2014/04/24/more-hispanics-blacks-enrolling-in-college-but-lag-in-bachelors-degrees/ [accessed November 1, 2020].

Krugman, Paul. 2001. "Reckonings: The Price of Power." *New York Times*, March 25, 2001. Available at: https://www.nytimes.com/2001/03/25/opinion/reckonings-the-price-of-power.html [accessed March 20, 2021].

Kutney-Lee, Ann, Matthew D. McHugh, Douglas M. Sloane, Jeannie P. Cimiotti, Linda Flynn, Donna Felber Neff, and Linda H. Aiken. 2009. "Nursing: A Key to Patient Satisfaction." *Health Affairs* 28 (40): 669–677.

Kuttner, Robert. 1996. *Everything for Sale: The Virtues and Limits of Markets*. Chicago: University of Chicago Press.

Kymlicka, Will. 1989. *Liberalism, Community, and Culture*. Oxford: Clarendon Press.

Landes, Elisabeth M., and Richard A. Posner. 1978. "The Economics of the Baby Shortage." *The Journal of Legal Studies* 7 (2): 323–348.

Lange, Oskar, Fred M. Taylor, and Benjamin E. Lippincott. 1938. *On the Economic Theory of Socialism*. Minneapolis: University of Minnesota Press.

Laxer, Gordon. 2006. "Cosmopolitan Elites versus Nationally-focused Citizens: Cycles of Decommodification Struggles." In *Not for Sale: Decommodifying Public Life*, edited by Gordon Laxer and Dennis Soron, 61–91. Peterborough: Garamond Press.

Le Grand, Julian. 2007. *The Other Visible Hand: Delivering Public Services through Choice and Competition*. Princeton, NJ: Princeton University Press.

Lebowitz, Michael A. 2006. *Build it Now: Socialism for the 21st Century*. New York: Monthly Review Press.

Lebowitz, Michael A. 2010. *The Socialist Alternative*. New York: Monthly Review Press.

Lehrer, Ute, and Thorben Widietz. 2009. "Condominium Development and Gentrification: The Relationship between Policies, Building Activities and Socio-economic Development in Toronto." *Canadian Journal of Urban Research* 18 (1): 140–161.

Levien, Michael. 2018. *Dispossession without Development: Land Grabs in Neoliberal India.* Oxford: Oxford University Press.

Levine Coley, Rebekah, Tama Leventhal, Alicia Doyle Lynch, and Melissa Kull. 2013. "Relations between Housing Characteristics and the Well-Being of Low-Income Children and Adolescents." *Developmental Psychology* 49 (9): 1775–1789.

Lewis, Jenny M. 2016. "The Paradox of Health Care Performance Measurement and Management." In *The Oxford Handbook of Health Care Management*, edited by Ewan Ferlie, Kathleen Montgomery, and Anne Reff Pedersen, 375–392. Oxford: Oxford University Press.

Leys, Colin. 2001. *Market-Driven Politics: Neoliberal Democracy and the Public Interest.* London: Verso.

Leys, Colin. 2017. "The English NHS: From Market Failure to Trust, Professsionalism, and Democracy." *Soundings* 64: 11–40.

Lie, John. 1991. "Embedding Polanyi's Market Society." *Sociological Perspectives* 34 (2): 219–235.

Lister, John. 2008. *The NHS after 60: For Patients or Profits?* London: Middlesex University Press.

Lobina, Emanuele. 2000. *Cochabamba Water War.* Public Services International Research Unit. London: University of Greenwich.

Locke, John. 1824. *The Works of John Locke.* Vol. 4. London: Printed for C. and J. Rivington.

Lora, Eduardo. 2012. *Structural Reform in Latin America: What Has Been Reformed and How It Can Be Quantified (Updated Version).* Working Paper No. 346. Washington, DC: Inter-American Development Bank.

Lóránt, Károly. 2009. "Privatization in Central and East European Countries." In *Privatization against the European Social Model*, edited by Marica Frangakis, Christoph Hermann, Jörg Huffschmid, and Károly Lóránt, 30–38. Houndmills: Palgrave Macmillan.

Lunn, Emma. 2013. "Energy Bills: Prepay Meters Can Cost Poorer Households Hundreds." *Guardian*, April 20, 2013. Available at: https://www.theguardian.com/money/2013/apr/20/energy-bills-prepay-meters-cost-poorer-households [accessed March 20, 2021].

Lütkenhorst, Wilfried, Tilman Altenburg, Anna Pegels, and Georgeta Vidican. 2014. *Green Industrial Policy. Managing Transformation under Uncertainty.* Discussion Paper 28. Bonn: Deutsches Institut für Entwicklungspolitik.

Lutz, Burkart. 1984. *Der kurze Traum immerwährender Prosperität.* Frankfurt: Campus.

Luxemburg, Rosa. 2003. *The Accumulation of Capital.* New York: Routledge.

Macdonald, David A. 2009. "Electrical Capitalism: Conceptualizing Electricity and Capital Accumulation in South Africa." In *Electrical Capitalism: Recolonizing Africa on the Power Grid*, edited by David A. Macdonald, 1–50. Cape Town: HSRC Press.

Madden, David, and Peter Marcuse. 2016. *In Defense of Housing: The Politics of Crisis.* London: Verso.

Mahnkopf, Birgit. 2013. *Peak Everything?—Peak Capitalism?* Working Paper 02/2013, DFG-KollegforscherInnengruppe Postwachstumsgesellschaften. Jena: Friedrich-Schiller-Universität.

Malhi, Yadvinder, J. Timmons Roberts, Richard A. Betts, Timothy J. Killeen, Wenhong Li, and Carlos A. Nobre. 2008. "Climate Change, Deforestation, and the Fate of the Amazon." *Science* 319: 169–172.

Marquand, David. 2004. *The Decline of the Public: The Hollowing Out of Citizenship*. Cambridge: Polity Press.

Marshall, Alfred. 1890. *Principles of Economics*. London: Macmillan.

Martinez-Alier, Joan, Unai Pascual, Franck-Dominique Vivien, and Edwin Zaccai. 2010. "Sustainable De-Growth: Mapping the Context, Criticisms and Future Prospects of an Emergent Paradigm." *Ecological Economics* 69 (9): 1741–1747.

Marx, Karl. 1938. *Critique of the Gotha Program*. New York: International.

Marx, Karl. 1964. *Economic and Philosophical Manuscript of 1844*. New York: International.

Marx, Karl. 1969. *Theories of Surplus Value, Part I*. London: Lawrence and Wishart.

Marx, Karl. 1970. *A Contribution to the Critique of Political Economy*. New York: International.

Marx, Karl. 1975. "Notes on Adolph Wagner (1879–80)." In *Karl Marx Texts on Method*, edited by Terrel Carver, 179–219. Oxford: Basil Blackwell.

Marx, Karl. 1990. *Capital: A Critique of Political Economy*, Vol. I. London: Penguin Books.

Marx, Karl. 1991. *A Critique of Political Economy*, Vol. III. London: Penguin Books.

Marx, Karl. 1993. *Grundrisse: Foundation of the Critique of Political Economy (Rough Draft)*. London: Penguin Books.

Mason, Paul. 2015. *Postcapitalism: A Guide to Our Future*. New York: Farrar, Strauss and Giroux.

May, Peter H., and Ronaldo Seroa da Motta, eds. *Pricing the Planet: Economic Analysis for Sustainable Development*. New York: Columbia University Press.

Mayes, Rick. 2007. "The Origins, Development, and Passage of Medicare's Revolutionary Prospective Payment System." *Journal of the History of Medicine and Allied Sciences* 62 (1): 21–55.

Mayosi, Bongani M., and Solomon R. Benatar. 2014. "Health and Health Care in South Africa 20 Years after Mandela." *New England Journal of Medicine* 371 (14): 1344–1352.

Mazoyer, Marcel, and Laurence Roudart. 2006. *A History of World Agriculture*. New York: Monthly Review Press.

Mazucatto, Marianna. 2013. *The Entrepreneurial State*. New York: Anthem Press.

McAfee, Kathleen. 2003. "Neoliberalism on the Molecular Scale: Economic and Genetic Reductionism in Biotechnology Battles." *Geoforum* 34 (2): 203–219.

McAfee, Kathleen. 2012. "The Contradictory Logic of Global Ecosystem Services Markets." *Development and Change* 43 (1): 105–131.

McBrunie, Grant, and Christopher Ziguras. 2006. *Transnational Education: Trends and Issues in Offshore Higher Education*. New York: Routledge.

McCarthy, Niall. 2013. *One in Five Americans Eat Fast Food Several Times a Week*. Available at: https://www.statista.com/chart/1349/one-in-five-americans-eat-fast-food-several-times-a-week/ [accessed November 1, 2020].

McConnell, John J., and Stephen A. Buser. 2011. "The Origins and Evolution of the Market for Mortgage-Backed Securities." *Annual Review of Financial Economic* 3: 173–192.

McDonald, David A. 2018. "Remunicipalization: The Future of Water Services?" *Geoforum* 91: 47–56.

McFate, Sean. 2014. *The Modern Mercenary: Private Armies and What They Mean for World Order*. Oxford: Oxford University Press.

McGettigan, Andrew. 2013. *The Great University Gamble: Money, Markets and the Future of Higher Education*. London: Pluto Press.

Mcintyre, Di, Lucy Gilson, Haroon Wadee, Michael Thiede, and Oktore Okarafori. 2006. "Commercalisation and Extreme Inequality in Health: The Policy Challenges in South Africa." *Journal for International Development* 18 (3): 435–446.

McLean, Bethany, and Peter Elkind. 2004. *The Smartest Guys in the Room: The Amazing Rise and Scandalous Fall of Enron*. London: Penguin.

McVeigh, Karen. 2013. "US Supreme Court Rules Human Genes Cannot Be Patented." *Guardian*, June 13, 2013. Available at: https://www.theguardian.com/law/2013/jun/13/supreme-court-genes-patent-dna [accessed March 20, 2021].

Meek, James. 2015. *Private Island: Why Britain Now Belongs to Somebody Else*. London: Verso.

Meiksins-Wood, Ellen. 1986. *The Retreat from Class: A New True Socialism*. London: Verso.

Mészáros, István. 1994. *Beyond Capital: A Theory of Transition*. New York: Monthly Review Press.

Mettler, Suzanne. 2014. *Degrees of Inequality: How Politics of Higher Education Sabotaged the American Dream*. New York: Basic Books.

Mid Staffordshire NHS Foundation Trust Public Inquiry. 2013. *Report on the Mid Staffordshire NHS Foundation Trust Public Inquiry* (Francis Report). Executive Summary. London: Stationery Office.

Mies, Maria. 1986. *Patriarchy and Accumulation on a World Scale: Women in the International Division of Labour*. London: Zed Books.

Mikami, Koichi. 2017. "Orphans in the Market: The History of Orphan Drug Policy." *Social History of Medicine* 32 (3): 609–630.

Millner, Mark, and Miles Brignall. 2006. "Profits Up, Prices Up—And So Are Excuses as Thames Water Fails to Plug the Leaks." *Guardian*, June 22, 2006. Available at: https://www.theguardian.com/business/2006/jun/22/utilities.water [accessed March 20, 2021].

Milonakis, Dimitris, and Ben Fine. 2009. *From Political Economy to Economics*. New York: Routledge.

Mitchell, Michael, and Michael Leachman. 2015. *Years of Cuts Threaten to Put College Out of Reach for More Students*. Washington, DC: Center on Budget and Policy Priorities.

Moerman, Lee C., and S. L. van der Laan. 2006. "TRIPS and the Pharmaceutical Industry: Prescription for Profit?" *Critical Perspectives on Accounting* 17 (8): 1089–1106.

Mojtabai, Ramin, and Mark Olfson. 2011. "Proportion of Antidepressants Prescribed Without a Psychiatric Diagnosis Is Growing." *Health Affairs* 30 (8): 1434–1442.

Monteiro, Carlos A., Jean-Claude Moubaracl, Geoffrey Cannon, Shu Wen Ng, and Barry M. Popkin. 2013. "Ultra-Processed Products Are Becoming Dominant in the Global Food System." *Obesity Reviews* 14 (Supplement 2): 21–28.

Moore, Jason W. 2015. *Capitalism in the Web of Life*. London: Verso.

Moynihan, Ray, and Alan Cassels. 2005. *Selling Sickness*. New York: Nation Books.

Moynihan, Ray, Iona Heath, and David Henry. 2002. "Selling Sickness: The Pharmaceutical Industry and Disease Mongering." *British Medical Journal* 324: 886–891.

Munnel, Alicia H., and Matthew S. Rutledge. 2013. "The Effects of the Great Recession on the Retirement Security of Older Workers." *Annals* 650: 124–142.

Naess, Arne. 1973. "The Shallow and the Deep, Long-Range Ecology Movement: A Summary." *Inquiry* 16 (1): 95–100.

National Agricultural Statistics Service. 2016. *Crop Production 2015 Summary*. Washington, DC: US Department of Agriculture.

National Audit Office. 2009. *The Failure of Metronet*. Report by the Comptroller and Auditor General. June 4, 2009. London: Stationery Office.

National Audit Office. 2015. *Financial Sustainability of NHS Bodies*. Report by the Comptroller and Auditor General. January 19, 2015. London: Stationery Office.

National Audit Office. 2018. *PFI and PF2*. Report by the Comptroller and Auditor General. January 12, 2018. London: Stationery Office.

National Center for Health Statistics. 2017. *Health, United States, 2016*. Hyattsville, MD: NCHS.

National Low-Income Housing Coalition. 2017. *The Gap: A Shortage of Affordable Homes*. March 2017. Washington, DC: National Low-Income Housing Coalition.

National Oceanic and Atmospheric Administration. 2017. *Gulf of Mexico 'Dead Zone' Is the Largest Ever Measured*. Available at: https://www.noaa.gov/media-release/gulf-of-mexico-dead-zone-is-largest-ever-measured [accessed November 1, 2020].

Needham, Catherine. 2007. *The Reform of Public Services under New Labour: Narratives of Consumerism*. Houndmills: Palgrave Macmillan.

Nellis, John. 2006. *Privatization: A Summary Assessment*. Working Paper 87. Washington, DC: Center for Global Development.

Nelson, Anita. 2005. "Marx's Objections to Credit Theories of Money." *In Marx's Theory of Money: Modern Appraisals*, edited by Fred Mosely, 65–77. Houndmills: Palgrave Macmillan.

Nestle, Marion. 2007. *Food Politics: How the Food Industry Influences Food and Health*. Berkeley: University of California Press.

Neurath, Otto. 2004. *Economic Writings: Selections 1904–1945*. Edited by Thomas E. Uebel and Robert S. Cohen. Dordrecht: Kluwer Academic.

Newfield, Christopher. 2016. *The Great Mistake: How We Wrecked Public Universities and How We Can Fix It*. Baltimore, MD: Johns Hopkins University Press.

Ngwane, Trevor. 2011. *Ideology and Agency in Protest Politics: Service Delivery Struggles in Post-Apartheid South Africa*. Thesis, University of KwaZulu-Natal.

Noble, Davis F. 2001. *Digital Diploma Mills: The Automation of Higher Education*. New York: Monthly Review Press.

Nordhaus, William. 2013. *The Climate Casino: Risk, Uncertainty, and Economics for a Warming World*. New Haven, CT: Yale University Press.

Nuffield Trust. 2010. *The Coalition Government's NHS Reforms: An Assessment of the White Paper*. Briefing. London.

O'Connor, Martin. 1997. "John Stuart Mill's Utilitarianism and the Social Ethics of Sustainable Development." *Journal of the History of Economic Thought* 4(3): 478–506.

O'Neil, Kate. 2019. *Waste*. Cambridge: Polity Press.

O'Neil, John. 2002. "Socialist Calculation and Environmental Valuation: Money, Markets and Ecology." *Science and Society* 66 (1): 137–151.

OECD. 2017. *Main Science and Technology Indicators*. Volume 2017/1. Paris: OECD.

Offe, Claus. 1972. *Strukturprobleme des kapitalistischen Staates: Aufsätze zur politischen Soziologie*. Frankfurt: Suhrkamp.

Offe, Claus. 1976. "Crisis of Crisis Management: Elements of a Political Crisis Theory." *International Journal of Politics* 6 (3): 29–67.

Offe, Claus. 1984. *Contradictions of the Modern Welfare State*. London: Hutchinson.

Offe, Claus, and Volker Ronge. 1975. "Theses on the Theory of the State." *New German Critique* 6: 137–147.

Office of National Statistics. 2017. *People in Employment on a Zero-Hours Contract*. Available at: https://www.ons.gov.uk/employmentandlabourmarket/peopleinwork/ earningsandworkinghours/articles/contractsthatdonotguaranteeaminimumnumbero fhours/mar2017 [accessed November 1, 2020].

Ollman, Bertell. 1971. *Alienation: Marx's Concept of Man in Capitalist Society*. Cambridge: Cambridge University Press.

Osborne, David, and Ted Gaebler. 1993. *Reinventing Government*. New York: Plume.

Oxford English Dictionary. n.d. Available at: https://www.oed.com/ [accessed November 1, 2020].

Paeratakul, Sahasporn, Daphne P. Ferdinand, Catherine M. Champagne, Donah H. Ryan, and George A. Bray. 2003. "Fast-Food Consumption among US Adults and Children: Dietary and Nutrient Intake Profile." *Journal of the American Dietic Association* 103 (10): 1332–1338.

Palast, Greg, Jerrold Oppenheim, and Theo MacGregor. 2003. *Democracy and Regulation: How the Public Can Govern Essential Services*. London: Pluto Press.

Peck, Jamie. 2001. *Workfare States*. New York: Guilford Press.

Pedrique, Belen, Nathalie Strub-Wourgaft, Claudette Some, Piero Olliaro, Patrice Trouiller, Nathan Ford, Bernard Pécoul, and Jean-Hervé Bradol. 2013. "The Drug and Vaccine Landscape for Neglected Diseases (2000–11): A Systematic Assessment." *The Lancet Global Health* 1 (6): e371–e379.

Pell Institute for the Study of Opportunity in Higher Education. 2015. *Indicators of Higher Education Equity in the United States: 45 Years Trend Report*. Washington, DC: Pell Institute for the Study of Opportunity in Higher Education.

Pereira, Mark A., Alex I. Kartashov, Cara B. Ebbeling, Linda Van Horn, Martha L. Slattery, David R. Jacobs Jr., and David S. Ludwig. 2005. "Fast-Food Habits, Weight Gain, and Insulin Resistance (the CARDIA Study): 15-Year Prospective Analysis." *Lancet* 365: 36–42.

Perelman, Michael. 2006. *Railroading Economics: The Creation of a Free Market Mythology*. New York: Monthly Review Press.

Pew Commission on Industrial Farm Animal Production. 2008. *Putting Meat on the Table: Industrial Farm Animal Production in America*. Philadelphia and Baltimore: Pew Charitable Trust and Johns Hopkins Bloomberg School of Public Health.

Pierson, Christopher, and Francis G. Castells, eds. 2006. *The Welfare State Reader*. Cambridge: Polity Press.

Pierson, Paul. 1994. *Dismantling the Welfare State? Reagan, Thatcher, and the Politics of Retrenchment*. Cambridge: Cambridge University Press.

Pierson, Paul, ed. 2001. *The New Politics of the Welfare State*. Oxford: Oxford University Press.

Piketty, Thomas. 2014. *Capital in the 21st Century*. Cambridge, MA: Belknap Press.

Plato. 1892. *The Dialogues of Plato*. Translated by Benjamin Jowett. Vol. 1. Oxford: Oxford University Press.

Player, Stewart, and Colin Leys. 2008. *Confuse and Conceal: The NHS and Independent Sector Treatment Centre*. London: Merlin Press.

Plehwe, Dieter. 2009. "Introduction." In *The Road from Mont Pèlerin*, edited by Dieter Plehwe and Philip Mirovski, 1–42. Cambridge, MA: Harvard University Press.

Plimmer, Gill. 2018. "Amazon and Delivery Companies Face Bogus Self-Employment Complaint." *Financial Times*, June 3, 2018. Available at: https://www.ft.com/content/837c1e50-6722-11e8-8cf3-0c230fa67aec [accessed March 20, 2021].

Polanyi, Karl. 1957. *The Great Transformation*. Boston: Beacon Press.

Polanyi, Karl. 2016. "Socialist Accounting." *Theory and Society* 45 (5): 398–424.

Pollan, Michael. 2006. *The Omnivore's Dilemma: A Natural History of Four Meals*. London: Penguin Press.

Pollan, Michael. 2008. *In Defense of Food*. London: Penguin Press.

Pollock, Allyson. 2004. *NHS Plc.: The Privatization of Our Health Care*. London: Verso.

Probst, Janice, Jan Marie Eberth, and Elizabeth Crouch. 2019. "Structural Urbanism Contributes to Poorer Health Outcomes for Rural America." *Health Affairs* 38 (12): 1976–1984.

Prudham, Scott. 2008. "The Fiction of Autonomous Invention: Accumulation by Dispossession, Commodification, and Life Patents in Canada." In *Privatization. Property and the Remaking of Nature-Society Relations*, edited by Becky Mansfield, 14–37. Malden, MA: Willey-Blackwell.

Prudham, Scott. 2009. "Commodification." In *A Companion to Environmental Geography*, edited by Noel Castree, David Demeritt, Diana Liverman, and Bruce Rhoads, 88–101. Malden, MA: Willey-Blackwell.

Quesnay, François. 1963. "Extracts from 'Men.'" In *The Economics of Physiocracy*, edited by Ronald Meek, 88–101. Cambridge, MA: Harvard University Press.

Radin, Margaret. 1987. "Market-Inalienability." *Harvard Law Review* 100 (8): 1849–1937.

Radin, Margaret. 1996. *Contested Commodities*. Cambridge, MA: Harvard University Press.

Radin, Margaret, and Madhavi Sunder. 2005. "Introduction: The Subject and Object of Commodification." In *Rethinking Commodification: Cases and Readings in Law and Culture*, edited by Martha M. Ertman and Joan C. Williams, 8–29. New York: New York University Press.

Rahnema, Saeed, ed. 2017. *The Transition from Capitalism: Marxist Perspectives*. Houndmills: Palgrave.

Randewich, Noel. 2020. "Tesla's Market Value Zooms Past That of GM and Ford—Combined." *Reuters*, January 8, 2020. Available at: https://www.reuters.com/article/us-usa-stocks-tesla/teslas-market-value-zooms-past-that-of-gm-and-ford-combined-idUSKBN1Z72MU [accessed March 20, 2021].

Rankin, S. C. 1980. "Supply and Demand in Ricardian Price Theory: A Re-Interpretation." *Oxford Economic Papers* New Series (32) 2: 241–262.

Rattner, Michael, and Carol Glover. 2014. *US Energy: Overview and Key Statistics*. Congressional Research Service 7-5700. Washington, DC: Congressional Research Service.

Raza, Werner. 2016. "Politics of Scale and Strategic Selectivity in the Liberalisation of Public Services: The Role of Trade in Services." *New Political Economy* 21 (2): 204–219.

Reeves, Aaron, Martin McKee, Sanjay Basu, and David Stuckler. 2014. "The Political Economy of Austerity and Healthcare: Cross-National Analysis of Expenditure Changes in 27 European Nations 1995–2011." *Health Policy* 115 (1): 1–8.

Reich, Adam D. 2014. *Selling Our Souls: The Commodification of Hospital Care in the United States*. Princeton, NJ: Princeton University Press.

Reinhard, Carmen M., and Kenneth S. Rogoff. 2011. *Growth in Times of Debt*. NBER Working Paper No. 15639. Cambridge, MA: National Bureau of Economic Research.

Rice, Thomas, Pauline Rosenau, Lynn Y. Unruh, and Andrew J. Barnes. 2013. *United States: Health Systems in Transition*, Vol. 15, No. 3. European Observatory on Health System Policies. Copenhagen: World Health Organization Europe.

Ritzer, Georg. 2013. *The McDonaldization of Society, 20th Anniversary Edition*. London: Sage.

Robbins, Paul, and April Luginbuhl .2005. "The Last Enclosure: Resisting Privatization of Wildlife in the Western United States." *Capitalism, Nature, Socialism* 16 (1): 45–61.

Roberts, Callum. 2007. *The Unnatural History of the Sea*. Washington, DC: Island Press.

Roberts, Helen. 1990. "Performance and Outcome Measures in the Health Service." In *Output and Performance Measurement in Government: The State of the Art*, edited by Martin Cave, Maurice Kogan, and Robert Smith, 86–105. London: Jessica Kingsley.

Robertson, Morgan M. 2004. "The Neoliberalization of Ecosystem Services: Wetland Mitigation Banking and Problems in Environmental Governance." *Geoforum* 35 (3): 361–373.

Robertson, Morgan M. 2006. "The Nature That Capital Can See: Science, State, and Market in the Commodification of Ecosystem Services." *Environment and Planning D: Society and Space* 24 (3): 367–387.

Rodolsky, Roman. 1977. *The Making of Marx's Capital*, Vol. I. London: Pluto Press.

Rose, George A. 2004. "Reconciling Overfishing and Climate Change with Stock Dynamics of Atlantic Cod (Gadus Morhua) over 500 Years." *Canadian Journal of Fisheries and Aquatic Sciences* 61 (9): 1553–1557.

Rosenthal, Elisabeth. 2014. "Medicine's Top Earner Are Not the M.D.s." *New York Times*, May 17, 2014. Available at: https://www.nytimes.com/2014/05/18/sunday-review/doctors-salaries-are-not-the-big-cost.html [accessed March 20, 2021].

Rothstein, Richard. 2013. "Why Children from Lower Socioeconomic Classes, on Average, Have Lower Academic Achievement than Middle-Class Children." In *Closing the Opportunity Gap: What America Must Do to Give Every Child an Even Chance*, edited by Prudence L. Carter and Kevin G. Weber, 62–67. Oxford: Oxford University Press.

Rubery, Jill, and Damian Grimshaw. 2006. "Precarious Work and the Commodification of the Employment Relationship: The Case of Zero Hours in the UK and Mini-Jobs in Germany." In *Den Arbeitsmarkt verstehen, um ihn zu gestalten*, edited by Gerhard Bäcker, Seffen Lehndorff, and Claudia Weiskopf, 239–254. Wiesbaden: Springer.

Rudy, Alan P., Lawrence Busch, Dawn Coppin, Toby Ten Eyck, Craig Harris, Jason Konefal, and Bradley T. Shaw. 2007. *Universities in the Age of Corporate Science: The UC Berkeley-Novartis Controversy*. Philadelphia: Temple University Press.

Ruggie, John G. 1982. "International Regimes, Transactions, and Change: Embedded Liberalism in the Postwar Economic Order." *International Organization* 36 (2): 379–415.

Ruiters, Greg. 2009. "Free Basic Electricity in South Africa: A Strategy for Helping or Containing the Poor?" In *Electrical Capitalism: Recolonising Africa on the Power Grid*, edited by David A. Macdonald, 249–263. Cape Town, South Africa: HSRC Press.

Ryan, Camille L., and Kurt Bauman. 2016. *Educational Attainment in the United States: 2015. Current Population Reports*. September 2016. Suitland, MD: United States Census Bureau.

Saad-Filho, Alfredo, and Deborah Johnston, eds. 2005. *Neoliberalism: A Critical Reader*. London: Pluto Press.

Sachs, Wolfgang. 1999. *Planet Dialectics. Explorations in Environment and Development*. London: Zed Books.

San Francisco Declaration. 2012. *San Francisco Declaration on Research Assessment.* Available at: https://sfdora.org/read/ [accessed November 1, 2020].

Sandel, Michael. 2012. *What Money Can't Buy: The Moral Limits of Markets.* London: Allen Lane.

Sarnak, Dana O., David Squires, Greg Kuzmak, and Shawn Bishop. 2017. *Paying for Prescription Drugs around the World: Why Is the US an Outlier?* Issue Brief October 2017. New York: Commonwealth Fund.

Satz, Debra. 2012. *Why Some Things Should Not Be for Sale.* Oxford: Oxford University Press.

Saunders, Peter. 1994. *Welfare and Inequality: National and International Perspectives on the Australian Welfare State.* Cambridge: Cambridge University Press.

Sawyer, Malcolm. 2009. "Theoretical Approaches to Explaining and Understanding Privatization." In *Privatization against the European Social Model,* edited by Marica Frangakis, Christoph Hermann, Jörg Huffschmid, and Károly Lóránt, 61–76. Houndmills: Palgrave Macmillan.

Sayer, Andrew. 2003. "(De)commodification, Consumer Culture, and Moral Economy." *Environment and Planning D: Society and Space* 21 (3): 341–357.

Sayer, Andrew, and Richard Walker. 1992. *The New Social Economy: Reworking the Division of Labour.* Oxford: Blackwell.

Schindler, David W., and John R. Vallentyne. 2008. *The Alga Bowl: Overfertilization of the World's Freshwaters and Estuaries.* Edmonton: University of Alberta Press.

Schmidt, Ingo. 2013. "Geschichte und politische Ökonomie." In *Rosa Luxemburgs Akkumulation des Kapitals,* edited by Ingo Schmidt, 13–36. Hamburg: VSA Verlag.

Schmidt, Ted B. 2016. *The Political Economy of Food and Finance.* New York: Routledge.

Schor, Juliet. 2010. *Plentitude: The Economics of True Wealth.* London: Penguin.

Schumpeter, Joseph. 1954. *Economic Doctrine and Method: An Historical Sketch.* Oxford: Oxford University Press.

Scott-Clayton, Judith. 2018. *The Looming Student Default Crisis Is Worse than We Thought.* Evidence Speaks Report, Vol. 2, No. 34. Washington, DC: Brookings Institution.

Sengupta, Amit, and Samiran Nundy. 2005. "The Private Health Sector in India Is Burgeoning, but at the Cost of Public Health Care." *British Medical Journal* 331 (7526): 1157–1158.

Sennet, Richard. 2009. *The Craftsman.* New Haven, CT: Yale University Press.

Sheldrake, John. 1989. *Municipal Socialism.* Farnham: Gower.

Shelter. 2018. *Homeless in Britain: The Number behind the Story.* London: Shelter.

Sherman, Matthew. 2009. *A Short History of Financial Deregulation in the United States.* Washington, DC: Center for Economic and Policy Research.

Shultz, Jim. 2003. "Bolivia: The Water War Widens." *NACLA Report on the Americas* 36 (4): 34–37.

Signorino, Rudolfo. 2001. "Piero Sraffa on Utility and the 'Subjective Method' in the 1920s: A Tentative Appraisal of Sraffa's Unpublished Manuscripts." *Cambridge Journal of Economics* 25 (6): 749–763.

Silbaugh, Katharine B. 2011. "Testing as Commodification." *Washington University Journal of Law and Policy* 35: 309–337.

Silver, Beverly. 2003. *Forces of Labor: Workers' Movements and Globalization since 1870.* Cambridge: Cambridge University Press.

Simmel, Georg. 2004. *The Philosophy of Money.* New York: Routledge.

Simmonds, Charlotte, Gloria Dickie, and Jen Byers. 2018. "Lost Lands? The American Wilderness at Risk in the Trump Era." *Guardian*, December 5, 2018 Available at: https://www.theguardian.com/environment/2018/dec/05/american-wilderness-trump-energy-threat#:~:text=The%20American%20wilderness%20at%20risk%20in%20the%20Trump%20era,-Exclusive%3A%20a%20new&text=This%20would%20only%20be%20possible,a%20quarter%20of%20the%20country. [accessed March 20, 2021].

Skinner, Brett J. 2013. "Medical Devices and Healthcare Costs in Canada and 65 Other Countries, 2006 to 2011." *Canadian Health Policy*, May 9, 2013. Toronto: Canadian Health Policy Institute.

Slade, Giles. 2006. *Made to Break: Technology and Obsolescence in America*. Cambridge, MA: Harvard University Press.

Smith, Adam. 1896. *Lectures on Justice, Police, Revenue and Arms: Delivered in the University of Glasgow*. Oxford: Clarendon Press.

Smith, Adam. 1900. *An Inquiry into the Nature and Causes of the Wealth of Nations*. London: Routledge.

Smith, Andrew F. 2016. *Fast Food: The Good, the Bad and the Hungry*. London: Reaktion Books.

Smith, Neil. 2006. "Nature as Accumulation Strategy." In *Socialist Register 2007*, edited by Leo Panitch and Colin Leys, 16–36. London: Merlin Press.

Smithers, Rebecca. 2019. "Fast Fashion: Britons to Buy 50 Million 'Throwaway Outfits' This Summer." *Guardian*, July 11, 2019. Available at: https://www.theguardian.com/fashion/2019/jul/11/fast-fashion-britons-to-buy-50m-throwaway-outfits-this-summer#:~:text=Britons%20will%20spend%20%C2%A32.7,only%20once%2C%20a%20poll%20reveals. [accessed March, 2021].

Soederberg, Susanne. 2014. "Student Loans, Debtfare and the Commodification of Debt: The Politics of Securitization and the Displacement of Risk." *Critical Sociology* 40 (5): 689–709.

Spash, Clive L. 1999. "The Development of Environmental Thinking in Economics." *Environmental Values* 8 (4): 413–435.

Spooren, Pieter, Bert Brockx, and Dimitri Mortelmans. 2013. "On the Validity of Student Evaluation of Teaching: The State of the Art." *Review of Educational Research* 83 (4): 598–642.

Squires, David, and Chloe Anderson. 2015. *US Health Care from a Global Perspective: Spending, Use of Services, Prices, and Health in 13 Countries*. Issues in International Health Policy. New York: Commonwealth Fund.

Sraffa, Piero. 1975. *Production of Commodities by Means of Commodities: Prelude to a Critique of Economic Theory*. Cambridge: Cambridge University Press.

Standing, Guy. 2011. *Precariat: The New Dangerous Class*. London: Bloomsbury.

Stark, Philip B., and Richard Freistaht. 2014. "An Evaluation of Course Evaluations." *Science Open Research and Publishing Network*, September 29, 2014. Available at: https://www.scienceopen.com/hosted-document?doi=10.14293/S2199-1006.1.SOR-EDU.AOFRQA.v1 [accessed November 1, 2020].

Starke, Peter. 2006. "The Politics of Welfare State Retrenchment: A Literature Review." *Social Policy and Administration* 40 (1): 104–120.

Starr, Paul. 1998. "The Meaning of Privatization." *Yale Law and Policy Review* 6 (1): 6–41.

Statistisches Bundesamt. 2016. *Gesundheit: Grunddaten der Krankenhäuser*. Statistisches Bundesamt, Fachserie 12, Reihe 6.1.1. Wiesbaden.

Steedman, Ian. 1977. *Marx after Sraffa*. London: NLB.

Steedman, Ian, Paul Sweezy, Simon Mohun, Anwar Shaik, Sue Himmelweit, Geoff Hodgson, Erik Olin Wright, Pradeep Bandyopadhyay, Michel De Vroey, Makoto Itoh, and G. A. Cohen. 1981. *The Value Controversy*. London: NLB.

Stockhammer, Engelbert. 2004. "Financialization and the Slowdown of Accumulation." *Cambridge Journal of Economics* 28 (5): 719–741.

Stone, Deborah. 2005. "For Love Nor Money: The Commodification of Care." In *Rethinking Commodification*, edited by Martha Ertman and Joan Williams, 271–290. New York: New York University Press.

Stroebe, Wolfgang. 2016. "Why Good Teaching Evaluations May Reward Bad Teaching: On Grade Inflation and Other Unintended Consequences of Student Evaluations." *Perspectives on Psychological Science* 11 (6): 800–816.

Stuckler, David, and Sanjay Basu. 2013. *The Body Economic: Why Austerity Kills*. London: Allen Lane.

Sundararajan, Arun. 2016. *The Sharing Economy: The End of Employment and the Rise of Crowd-Based Capitalism*. Cambridge, MA: MIT Press.

Swan, Rachel, and Michael Cabanatuan. 2020. "Homeless Mothers Evicted before Dawn from Oakland House, Highlighting Crisis." *San Francisco Chronicle*, January 14, 2020. Available at: https://www.sfchronicle.com/crime/article/Homeless-mothers-evicted-from-Oakland-home-in-14973659.php [accessed March 20, 2021].

Sweezy, Paul. 1946. *Theory of Capitalist Development*. London: Dennis Dobson.

Swyngedouw, Eric. 2006. "Water, Money, Power." In *Socialist Register 2007*, edited by Leo Panitch and Colin Leys, 195–212. London: Merlin Press.

Talbot-Smith, Alison, and Allyson Pollock. 2016. *The New NHS: A Guide*. New York: Routledge.

Taylor, Laurie, and Simeon Underwood. 2015. "Academics versus Administrators." *Times Higher Education*, May 28, 2015. Available at: https://www.timeshighereducation.com/content/laurie-taylor-on-academics-v-administrators [accessed March 20, 2021].

Teeple, Gary. 2017. "Austerity Policies: From the Keynesian to the Corporate Welfare State." In *The Austerity State*, edited by Stephen McBride and Bryan M. Evans, 25–43. Toronto: University of Toronto Press.

Ther, Philip. 2016. *Europe since 1989*. Princeton, NJ: Princeton University Press.

Thomason, Sarah, Lea J. E. Austin, Annette Bernhardt, Laura Dresser, Ken Jacobs, and Marcy Whitebook. 2018. *At the Wage Floor: Covering Home Care and Early Education Workers in the New Generation of Minimum Wage Laws*. Center for the Study of Child Care Employment. Berkeley: University of California.

Thompson, Don. 2001. "Report Says Power Wholesalers Overcharged State Six Billion Dollars." *San Diego Union Tribune*, March 22, 2001. Available at: http://www.sandiegouniontribune.com/sdut-report-says-power-wholesalers-overcharged-state-6-2001mar22-story.html (accessed April 15, 2021).

Titmuss, Richard. 1970. *The Gift Relationship: From Human Blood to Social Policy*. London: Allen and Unwin.

Toffolutti, Veronica, Aaron Reeves, Martin McKee, and David Stuckler. 2017. "Outsourcing Cleaning Services Increases MRSA Incidence: Evidence from 126 English Acute Trusts." *Social Science and Medicine* 174: 64–69.

Tornaghi, Chiara, and Chiara Certoma, eds. 2019. *Urban Gardening as Politics*. New York: Routledge.

Trouiller, Patrice, Piero Olliaro, Els Torreele, James Orbinski, Richard Laing, and Nathan Ford. 2002. "Drug Development for Neglected Diseases: A Deficient Market and a Public-Health Policy Failure." *Lancet* 359: 2188–2194.

Turner, Simon, Pauline Allen, Will Bartlett, and Virgine Pérotin. 2011. "Innovation and the English National Health Service: A Qualitative Study of the Independent Sector Treatment Centre Programme." *Social Science and Medicine* 73 (4): 522–529.

Tzannatos, Zafiris, and Yannis Monogious. 2013. "Public Sector Adjustment Amidst Structural Adjustment in Greece: Subordinate, Spasmodic and Sporadic." In *Public Sector Shock: The Impact of Policy Retrenchment in Europe*, edited by Daniel Vaughan-Whitehead, 259. Cheltenham: Edward Elgar.

Union of Concerned Scientists. 2008. *CAFOs Uncovered: The Untold Costs of Confined Animal Feeding Operations*. Cambridge, MA: UCS.

United Health Foundation. 2016. *United States Health Rankings: Annual Report*. Minneapolis: UHF.

Urry, John. 2013. *Societies beyond Oil*. London: Zed Books.

US Department of Housing and Urban Development. 2018. *The 2018 Annual Homeless Assessment Report to Congress*. Washington, DC.

US Department of Justice. 2016. *Review of the Federal Bureau of Prisons' Monitoring Contract Prisons*. Washington, DC.

US Senate Committee on Health Education Labor and Pensions. 2012. *For Profit Higher Education: The Failure to Safeguard the Federal Investment and Ensure Student Success*. Executive Summary. Washington, DC.

Vanclay, Jerome K. 2012. "Impact Factor: Outdated Artefact or Stepping-Stone to Journal Certification?" *Scientometrics* 92 (2): 211–238.

Vaughan-Whitehead, Daniel, ed. 2013. *Public Sector Shock: The Impact of Policy Retrenchment in Europe*. Cheltenham: Edward Elgar.

Veblen, Thorstein. 1921. *The Engineers and the Price System*. New York: Viking Press.

Veblen, Thorstein. 2007. *The Theory of the Leisure Class*. Oxford: Oxford University Press.

Villa, Stefano, and Nancy Kane. 2013. "Assessing the Impact of Privatizing Public Hospitals in Three American States: Implications for Universal Health Coverage." *Value in Health* 16 (1 Supplement): 524–533.

Waddams Price, Catherine, and Alison Young. 2003. "UK Utility Reform: Distributional Implications and Government Response." In *Utility Privatization and Regulation: A Fair Deal for Consumers?*, edited by Cecilia Ugaz and Catherine Waddams Price, 101–124. Cheltenham: Edward Elgar.

Wahl, Peter. 2009. *Food Speculation as the Main Factor of the Price Bubble in 2008*. Briefing Paper. Berlin: World Economy, Ecology and Development.

Waldfogel, Joel. 2007. *The Tyranny of the Market: Why You Can't Always Get What You Want*. Cambridge, MA: Harvard University Press.

Walks, Alan R., and Richard Maaranen. 2008. "Gentrification, Social Mix, and Social Polarization: Testing the Linkages in Large Canadian Cities." *Urban Geography* 29 (4): 293–326.

Wallerstein, Immanuel. 1976. "From Feudalism to Capitalism: Transition or Transitions?" *Social Forces* 55 (2): 273–283.

Wallerstein, Immanuel. 1983. *Historical Capitalism*. London: Verso.

Wallerstein, Immanuel. 2000. *The Essential Wallerstein*. New York: New Press.

Walzer, Michael. 1983. *Spheres of Justice*. New York: Basic Books.

Wang, Youfa, and May A. Beydoun. 2007. "The Obesity Epidemic in the United States—Gender, Age, Socioeconomic, Racial/Ethnic, and Geographic Characteristics: A Systematic Review and Meta-Regression Analysis." *Epidemiologic Reviews* 29 (1): 6–28.

Warrel, Helen, and Thomas Hale. 2017. "UK To Sell Record £4bn of Student Loans to Investors." *Financial Times*, February 6, 2017. Available at: https://www.ft.com/content/2b66bfaa-ec7a-11e6-930f-061b01e23655 [accessed March 20, 2021].

Waters, Tony. 2007. *The Persistence of Subsistence Agriculture: Life Beneath the Level of the Market Place*. Lanham, MD: Lexington Books.

Watt, Nicholas, Denis Campbell, and Randeep Ramesh. 2015. "Circle Pulls Plug on Hospital Deal and Sparks Storm over Private Firms in NHS." *Guardian*, January 9, 2015. Available at: https://www.theguardian.com/society/2015/jan/09/circle-hospital-private-firms-nhs-report-poor-care-hinchingbrooke [accessed March 20, 2021].

Weare, Christopher. 2003. *The California Electricity Crisis: Causes and Option*. San Francisco: Public Policy Institute of California.

Weeks, John. 1981. *Capital and Exploitation*. Princeton, NJ: Princeton University Press.

Weinstein, Lisa. 2013. "Demolition and Dispossession: Toward an Understanding of State Violence in Millennial Mumbai." *Studies in Comparative International Development* 48 (3): 285–307.

Whiteside, Heather. 2015. *Purchase for Profit: Public-Private Partnerships and Canada's Public Healthcare System*. Toronto: University of Toronto Press.

Whitfield, Dexter. 2010. *Global Auction of Public Assets: Public Sector Alternatives to the Infrastructure Market and Public Private Partnerships*. Nottingham: Spokesman.

Winnet, Robert. 2012. "Ministers Take over 'Bankrupt' Hospitals." *Telegraph*, June 25, 2012. Available at: https://www.telegraph.co.uk/news/health/news/9355452/Ministers-take-over-bankrupt-hospitals.html [accessed March 20, 2021].

Woo, Jennie H., Alexander H. Bentz, Stephen Lew, Erin Dunlop, and Velez Nichole Smith. 2017. *Repayment of Student Loans as of 2015 among 1995–96 and 2003–04 First-Time Beginning Students*. Washington, DC: Institute of Education Science.

Woolhandler, Steffie, Terry Campbell, and David U. Himmelstein. 2003. "Costs of Health Care Administration in the United States and Canada." *New England Journal of Medicine* 349: 768–775.

World Bank. 2016. *Reducing Inequalities in Water Supply, Sanitation, and Hygiene in the Era of the Sustainable Development Goals*. Washington, DC: World Bank.

World Commission on Environment and Development. 1987. *Our Common Future* (Brundtland Report). Oxford: Oxford University Press.

Zelizer, Viviana A. 2000. "The Purchase of Intimacy." *Law and Social Inquiry* 25 (3): 817–848.

Zoepf, Stephen, Stella Chen, Paa Adu, and Gonzalo Pozo. 2018. *The Economic of Ride Hailing: Driver Revenue, Expenses, and Taxes*. MIT Center for Energy and Environmental Policy Research Working Paper 2018-005. Cambridge: Massachusetts Institute of Technology.

Index